Blood Ties

Other Books by Joseph Kolb

Teen Violence in America: How Do We Save Our Children?

Blood Ties

How a Texas Prison Gang Became a Mexican Cartel Proxy

Joseph J. Kolb

FORT WORTH, TEXAS

Copyright © 2021 by Joseph Kolb

Library of Congress Cataloging-in-Publication Data
Names: Kolb, Joseph, author.
Title: Blood ties : the transformation of a Texas prison gang into a transnational criminal organization / Joseph Kolb.
Description: Fort Worth : TCU Press, [2021] | Includes bibliographical references and index. | Summary: "In the late 1980s and 1990s, street gang members from the impoverished Segundo Barrio in El Paso, Texas, united in the Texas prison system to create the Barrio Aztecas gang. They quickly rose to power in the Texas prison system and ultimately became a powerful transnational criminal organization. Kolb describes the prison dynamic of predator and prey and the need for the prey to unify for protection against gangs such as the Texas Syndicate and Texas Mexican Mafia, also known as the Mexikanemi. The protective cocoon formed by this group soon morphed into a criminal enterprise that would be headquartered in the Coffield Unit of the Texas Department of Criminal Justice, where the gang would engage in drug sales and violent crimes while behind bars. The skill sets they acquired served members well as they were released from custody and went on to exploit US immigration policies as well as friends and familial ties in Ciudad Juárez, Mexico. There they established alliances with regional drug trafficking organizations such as Vicente Carrillo Fuentes (Juarez cartel), to whom they would serve as foot soldiers in the proxy war that would consume Ciudad Juárez and turn it into the "Murder Capital of the World." Blood Ties describes the Azteca's organizational structure and ranks, identifying characteristics such as tattoos and code words, and how the organization appropriated Aztec culture to form the basis for their identity. Some of the gang's most horrific crimes are revealed here, and the author explores how Azteca's leadership was eroded through the violation of the very tenets that served as the gang's foundation"—Provided by publisher.
Identifiers: LCCN 2021036918 (print) | LCCN 2021036919 (ebook) |
 ISBN 9780875657882 (paperback) | ISBN 9780875657967 (ebook)
Subjects: LCSH: Barrio Aztecas (Gang)—History. | Prison gangs—Texas—El Paso—History—20th century. | Mexican American gangs—History. | Mexican American criminals—Mexico—Ciudad Juárez. | Drug traffic—Mexican-American Border Region. | Violent crimes—Mexican-American Border Region. | BISAC: HISTORY / United States / State & Local / Southwest (AZ, NM, OK, TX)
Classification: LCC HV6439.U7 K65 2021 (print) | LCC HV6439.U7 (ebook) |
 DDC 364.106/60976496—dc23
LC record available at https://lccn.loc.gov/2021036918
LC ebook record available at https://lccn.loc.gov/2021036919

TCU Box 298300
Fort Worth, Texas 76129
To order books: 1.800.826.8911

Design by Julie Rushing

Dedication

Anyone who naïvely believes recreational drug use is a victimless crime need only look at the tens of thousands that have died in Mexico at the hands of the criminal gangs and drug trafficking organizations and the plague of overdoses and destroyed lives that have occurred from drug use in the US. This book describes a major contributor to this scourge. Read of their pernicious behavior. This book is dedicated to law enforcement on both sides of the border who fight the good fight daily. Many have paid the ultimate sacrifice to keep the criminals at bay. May God bless you and watch over you.

Goodness prevails over evil.

CONTENTS

Preface ix

INTRODUCTION 1

CHAPTER 1 **MI BARRIO** 9

CHAPTER 2 **COFFIELD** 23

CHAPTER 3 **STAKING THEIR CLAIM** 43

CHAPTER 4 **CERESO PRISON** 48

CHAPTER 5 **CROSSING THE LINE** 55

CHAPTER 6 **DEADLY MARRIAGE** 75

CHAPTER 7 **WAR FOOTING** 89

CHAPTER 8 **DEATH OF A CITY** 97

CHAPTER 9 **MATANZA** 108

CHAPTER 10 **AMERICANS IN THE CROSSHAIRS** 116

CHAPTER 11 **INSURGENCY** 133

CHAPTER 12 **TRANSITIONS** 140

EPILOGUE 159

Acknowledgments 161

References 163

Index 177

About the Author 189

PREFACE

Getting to the heart of the Barrio Azteca gang is a daunting process. The sources cited in this project include a search of published articles and open-source intelligence reports. I have interviewed both gang members and law enforcement officials who, because of the very tenuous nature of the issue, were reluctant to provide their names. I have respected these wishes. The lion's share of the material for this manuscript is testimony from the pivotal 2014 trial in El Paso, Texas, of Arturo Gallegos Castrellón, at the time the highest-ranking gang member to be prosecuted. I have taken other testimonies from law enforcement and gang members.

Introduction

Street gangs in the United States are not new. They have existed for more than two hundred years, dating back to colonial times. Their numbers increased significantly in the mid-nineteenth century, with the influx of Irish immigrants. It was then that native-born Americans took notice of "others" infringing on their society (Howell and Moore 2010). Subsequent waves of immigrants faced similar persecution from the increasing number of dominant cultures and were ultimately forced to create their own gangs for protection. Eventually, these groups saw opportunities within their own communities and quickly turned their criminal attention to extortion, loan sharking, bootlegging, and drug trafficking.

The FBI has identified some thirty-three thousand gangs across the US (FBI, n.d.). This staggering number is further divided into street gangs, prison gangs, and outlaw motorcycle gangs. The emergence of prison gangs such as the Mexican Mafia, Aryan Brotherhood, and others rapidly changed the dynamic of inmate control, and a black market economy behind the walls of supposedly secure facilities would extend its reach beyond the concrete and barbed wire. This development not only impacted the streets of the US but also had an international impact due to immigration policies that allowed American street gangs such as MS-13, Barrio Azteca, and 18th Street to become transnational criminal organizations disrupting public safety in Latin America.

Organized prison gangs are a relatively recent criminal phenomenon, with the first recognized group not appearing until the mid-1950s. Fleisher and Decker (2001) identify the Washington state-based Gypsy Jokers as the first organized prison gang. This was soon followed in 1956 by the Mexican Mafia, which spread across the country and effectively defined the prison gang model.

Part of the story behind the Barrio Azteca is the unique relationship between El Paso and its sister city, Ciudad Juárez. Despite being separated by a physical barrier, the organic relationship remains strong, based on contiguous family bloodlines, commercial and educational ties.

El Paso, Texas, saw a large influx of Mexican nationals fleeing the revolution against the regime of Porfirio Díaz between 1910 and 1920. Most of this diaspora settled in the Segundo Barrio and nearby Chihuahuita—the Primer Barrio, which lie adjacent to today's border and between the Stanton Street and International Bridges.

The earliest signs of a "gang" culture emerged around the 1920s with the rise of the *pachucos*. On the streets of El Paso, which is affectionately referred to as "Chuco Town," this subculture was defined by a distinct slang and form of dress. Durán (2018) attributes to the pachucos the earliest form of Mexican American gang culture, which proliferated across other parts of the country as employment opportunities expanded during World War II.

It's remarkable to note the impact one square mile of an impoverished barrio in south El Paso had on the genealogy of Mexican American gangs. Sureños, Norteños, Mexican Mafia, Texas Syndicate, Tangos, and countless more can look back on the migration of the pachuco culture from this region as their genesis, evolving with variations based upon geographic settlement and inter- and intra-racial confrontation. These groups showed a proud commitment to ancient Aztec culture with distinguishing tattoos and other practices.

The BA remain an enigma to most of the United States. Despite their violent exploits in the El Paso-Cuidad Juárez corridor for nearly three decades, very few in the media, law enforcement, or government outside of the region have ever heard of them. From my personal observations, this is the result of a subliminal policy of ignorance to regional border issues as well as the distraction of events occurring a world away in Iraq and Afghanistan. I would even go so far as to say a sense of institutional racism toward Mexico has existed in the US—including US media—for more than one hundred years.

It is puzzling that in 2012 a gang like MS-13, while violent and spread across the United States, would be designated a transnational criminal organization with accompanying sanctions against specific members by the US Department of the Treasury, while the BA were not. Both were equally adept at vicious acts of violence, but it would be hard to dispute that the BA had a much more lucrative and functional drug trafficking model than did the MS-13, and had direct ties to Mexican drug trafficking organizations as well.

According to a US Department of the Treasury press release at the time, "MS-13 is being targeted for its involvement in serious transnational criminal activities, including drug trafficking, kidnapping, human smuggling, sex trafficking, murder, assassinations, racketeering, blackmail, extortion, and immigration offenses" (2012).

My hypothesis is that many MS-13 crimes were spotlighted because they were committed in the backyard of Washington, DC, Long Island, and the region around Houston, Texas, whereas the BA were mostly isolated in El Paso, which garners very little national attention. I would also argue the BA operated on a higher scale of the aforementioned characteristics identified with MS-13 that would include a body count well into the thousands in a smaller geographic area that would also include US citizens and officials.

To understand the Barrio Azteca's growth and unique transnational proliferation is to understand gang paradigms and immigration policy. How did a relatively benign group of El Paso-bred inmates at a maximum security prison in Texas grow to be a provocative force in border violence that would essentially define a major border city as the "Murder Capital of the World"?

As I will discuss later, this dynamic played out on the streets of the Segundo Barrio in three specific incidents: the El Paso Race Riot, the Bath Riots, and the Chamizal Dispute. All three are little-known events that were locally significant and that impacted the residents' sense of isolation.

There are other elements that foment gang membership: social disenfranchisement, low income and lack of employment opportunities, and absentee parents—whether the parents have to work or are simply irresponsible—all of which are rampant in the Segundo Barrio. As I have seen so often in gang culture, gang association spans multiple generations, giving a child the impression that gang membership is the natural course to follow through adolescence and into adulthood.

Deported gang members try to exploit vulnerabilities in border security in order to return to their American home bases and lucrative criminal activities. According to US Border Patrol data (U.S. Customs and Border Protection 2019c), between 2015 and the middle of fiscal year 2019 only thirteen BA members were apprehended attempting to cross the border illegally. This is in contrast to 1,640 MS-13 members apprehended during the same period. A BA member often has little need to attempt an illegal crossing, since family members often live both in Ciudad Juárez and El Paso, Texas. If their names are not on a criminal watch list at the port of entry, all the Azteca needs to do is present the appropriate identification and be waved in.

I consider El Paso my second home. Residents here, especially in the El Segundo Barrio, are among the humblest and most hardworking I have come across in my national and international travels. Despite the rampant poverty, the barrio is relatively well kept. There is both a sense of pride and a sense of place. Surprisingly, despite the long-standing presence of gangs in the barrio, taggings, or gang-defined graffiti, are relatively sparse. A plethora of murals dot the barrio depicting its rich cultural history and prominent residents. Among the more prominent is the Sacred Heart mural on Sacred Heart Tortilleria, which includes the iconic image of Father Harold Joseph Rahm, the "Bicycle Priest" who attempted to quell gang violence and juvenile delinquency in the 1950s.

Blood Ties depicts the emergence of one of the most, if not the most, violent gangs in the United States. It also examines the sociological dynamic that contributes to the development and proliferation of prison gangs and shows how their influence is projected beyond the walls of their correctional facilities. Much of the text describes the gang's exploits in the words of the gang members themselves, taken under oath in pivotal federal trials of their leaders.

On the academic level there has been exemplary work done by my friend and colleague Mike Tapia, PhD, who has studied the *Barrio Gangs of San Antonio, 1915-2015* (2017) and *Gangs of the El Paso-Juárez Borderland* (2019). Also looking at this fragile borderland is Robert J. Durán in *The Gang Paradox: Inequalities and Miracles on the U.S.-Mexico Border* (2018). Both Tapia and Durán spell out the complex relationships between culture, socioeconomic disparities, and financial opportunities from illicit gains. These books discuss the organic cross-border relationships that are merely impeded, but not eliminated, by physical and policy obstacles. These cannot resist the combined forces of familial ties, financial need, opportunity, desperation, and simple desire that fuel gang membership. It is this dynamic that has allowed the BA to take root and proliferate in the border region.

Other than work by R. V. Gundur (2019a, 2019b, 2020) the academic literature on the BA is scant, despite the fact they are responsible for death tolls in Mexico that rank in the thousands rather than the dozens caused by other gang subsets (Knox, pers. comm. 2019). Information gleaned by such competent news outlets as the *El Paso Times* and *El Diario,* which have been at ground zero of the narco crisis since it began in 2006, have benefited academic research.

The breadth of the psychopathy of BA members is revealed in statements by Arturo Gallegos Castrellón, an Azteca lieutenant, who admitted to being involved in 80 percent of the homicides in Ciudad Juárez in a fifteen-month span between 2009 and 2010 (Malkin 2010). During this period the city was known as the "Murder Capital of the World," with 2,643 killed in 2009 and 3,111 in 2010 (InSight Crime 2011). Another prolific *sicario*-killer, Jesús Ernesto Chávez Castillo, reported that he stopped counting how many people he had murdered at eight hundred (Fox News 2014). I would question the accuracy of these numbers, since killers typically inflate them. There is little doubt, however, that during this period these two were among the most prolific purveyors of death and mayhem in Ciudad Juárez.

One example of a lack of media coverage and analysis involving the BA occurred in early October 2019 at a safe house in southern Ciudad Juárez, when a *National Geographic* reporter was shot in the leg while interviewing a BA member, who died in the fusillade. The majority of coverage referred to the gang merely as drug dealers, and the *El Paso Times*, the main English-written newspaper in the region, along with a local television station, neglected to reference the gang by name (Associated Press 2019; Gaytan, 2019; Ramirez 2019; Chávez 2019). Outlets that did refer to the BA by name were the BorderReport (Resendiz 2019) and *El Diario* (2019), the major newspaper in Ciudad Juárez that reports on the BA and other criminal organizations at the reporters' great peril. Two of their staff members have been killed for their work.

When analyzing the murder rates between the BA and MS-13, the former far outweighs the latter in terms of an impact on public safety. In terms of perception based on publicity, however, the danger posed by MS-13 far outweighs that posed by the BA. This data should be cause for concern in the debate on border security and immigration policy. One cannot look at either of these two gangs and ignore border issues. When Ciudad Juárez was considered the "Murder Capital of the World," the murder rate was 191/100,000 in 2009 (Borderland Beat 2010g) and 229/100,000 in 2010 (Figueroa 2017), just in the city of 1.5 million people. On the other hand, during the same period the entire country of El Salvador experienced murder rates of 71.4/100,000 in 2009 and 64/100,000 in 2010 (Macrotrends 2019). Homicides in El Savaldor didn't reach a twenty-five-year peak until 2015, when the murder rate spiked to 105.44/100,000 (Macrotrends 2019)—still less than half of that in Ciudad Juárez during their worst era. These rates were the entire homicide rates and are not attributed to any single gang.

Considering that Gallegos and his crew were responsible for 80 percent of the homicides (Malkin 2010), which could be considered a conservative estimate, that would mean the BA accounted for some 168/100,000 homicides between 2009 and 2010. Even if that number was pared down to a more conservative 40 percent, they would still have accounted for 84/100,000 between 2009 and 2010 in just one city, as opposed to an entire nation, as is the case of MS-13 in El Salvador. Even at the peak homicide year of 2015 in El Salvador, the BA would likely have exceeded that country's rate alone.

The fundamental goal of this project is to shed light on a large transnational criminal organization that needs to be recognized officially as such. I hope the reader will also gain a better understanding of the street gang-to-prison gang dynamic and how they essentially contrast in organization, recruitment, and criminal model. We also need to understand the socioeconomic dynamics in prison populations that attract individuals to this subculture. The last element to consider is the unintended consequences of US immigration policy intended to rid the country of criminal illegal aliens. This has resulted in deportation of Northern Triangle criminals, which allowed MS-13 to flourish and return again. A similar dynamic also occurred with the Azteca.

The BA phenomenon is exemplified by exploiting space. Gundur (2019b) describes how the convergence of settings impacted the protection dynamic of the illicit drug trade in the El Paso-Ciudad Juárez corridor, and how this presented unique opportunities to the gang through their binational influences, based on Marcus Felson's (2006) theory of illicit enterprise protection in regard to settings, events, and sequences.

This book addresses the prison gang dynamic and the unique circumstances surrounding the genesis of the BA gang. Although it is one of the most violent organizations in the region, few people outside of it have ever heard of the gang. The book will progress to the cross-border proliferation of the gang to alliances with two powerful Mexican drug trafficking organizations that would go to war with each other and turn a vibrant cosmopolitan city into a virtual ghost town.

Circumstances surrounding the development of the gang and its alliances deserve more study to develop efficient prevention and suppression strategies. I hope this book will serve as a jumping-off point for further research by academics as well as a tool for law enforcement, who do not deal with the abstract behavioral nature of gangs but with the bloody violence and human misery they create.

CHAPTER 1

Mi Barrio

Gang creation is the result of socioeconomic drivers such as poverty, domestic and social dysfunction, alienation, and marginalization. These create what I call the secondary drivers of substance abuse, group unity, and social control through violence. Well before the Barrio Azteca were created, the stepping stones toward covert meetings at the Coffield Unit of the Texas prison system in the mid-1980s for the need to create the gang were in place.

The Paseo del Norte Bridge, also known to locals as the Santa Fe Bridge, is one of three main thoroughfares connecting Ciudad Juárez, Mexico, to El Paso, Texas. Each day some twelve thousand pedestrians and more than five thousand vehicles (U.S. Customs and Border Protection 2019b) cross into this vibrant shopping area composed of discount stores along what used to be the Golden Horseshoe, whose name was changed by the Downtown Management District to the more culturally marketable El Centro District (Sanchez 2017). This area is a key shopping and employment destination for Juarenses (residents of Ciudad Juárez). Not so much for most El Pasoans, especially Caucasian residents, who typically avoid the economically depressed and predominately Mexican area, which contributes to the perception of a subtle segregation most avoid discussing. To most non-Hispanic El Pasoans, the neighborhoods south of Paisano Drive, euphemistically called the "Tortilla Curtain," may as well be on the Mexican side of the border. Whether a sense of subliminal racism or fear of the "other," this phenomenon has existed for generations, an indelible blemish on the perceived unity of the city.

This shopping district is in the heart of the Chihuahuita Barrio, the Primer Barrio—essentially the birthplace of modern-day El Paso but the longtime home of *campesinos*, illegal immigrants, and low-income working-class Mexican and Mexican American families. Despite the rich cultural and historical relevance, Chihuahuita and its neighboring barrio, El Segundo, are endangered historic gems. In 2016 the National Trust for Historic Preservation put the two barrios on its list of the 11 Most Endangered Historic Places (Sanchez 2016).

On the map of south El Paso, El Segundo and Chihuahuita create a distinct bulge extending into Mexico, almost as if longing to maintain a close connection to their roots. Chihuahuita is the oldest neighborhood in El Paso and is defined by Paisano Drive to the north, Franklin Canal to the south, Kansas Street to the east, and the Burlington Northern and Santa Fe Railyards to the west. This First Ward saw Mexican settlers escape poverty and political upheaval for more than a century. The Mexican Revolution of 1910-1920 was a significant contributor to Mexican migration into the area.

Faith runs deep in El Paso's El Segundo Barrio. Author collection.

Adjacent to Chihuahuita is the more sublime but more populated El Segundo Barrio, which has less shopping and pedestrian traffic but no less proud cultural roots. El Segundo—the *Second Ward*—is defined by Paisano Drive to the north, Cotton Street to the east, Border West Expressway to the south, and Stanton Street to the west.

In 2019 these two barrios were named as among the friendliest neighborhoods in the United States (Barger 2019). Referred to as the "Ellis Island of the Border," these neighborhoods defined a burgeoning culture that would eventually proliferate throughout the United States.

This recognition is remarkable, considering both barrios are among the poorest communities in the United States. Poverty has long been predominant in these barrios, and there is no indication economic relief is on the horizon. Two decades into the new millennium prospects remain bleak. The median household income in the Segundo Barrio is $14,684, with an average household size of 16.3 people, and 18.2 percent of residents are single mother households (City-data.com n.d., "Segundo Barrio neighborhood"). The much smaller Chihuahuita enclave does not fare much better, with a median household income of $17,949 and with 14.5 percent of residents single mothers (City-data.com n.d., "Chihuahuita neighborhood").

Life is gritty in Chihuahuita, more so in the much more densely populated El Segundo Barrio. Modest homes and dilapidated tenements remain the norm, with sporadic apartment developments emerging. These factors all contribute to a sense of alienation and disenfranchisement. Remarkably, there is also a strong sense of pride—almost a unity bred from struggle. It is a badge of honor to say you are from El Segundo: so much that a local screen print shop started a line of El Segundo apparel.

Some might construe El Segundo Barrio as quaint. Exquisite murals depicting the barrio's history dot the community. The Bowie bakery has served a multitude of fresh baked goods for three generations, and rising above the modest single-family homes and duplexes surrounding it is the Sacred Heart Roman Catholic Church, which opened on South Oregon Street in 1893 and serves as a religious and social anchor.

The murals, in particular, tell a story of pride and struggle. One mural which profoundly depicts the reality of life in the barrio is found on Sixth Street between Ochoa and Virginia Streets. Prominently displayed in the middle of the cinderblock canvas is the image of a young man with a makeshift tourniquet around his left arm as he prepares to inject a syringe

The mural of a heroin addict depicts the darker side of life in El Segundo Barrio. Author collection.

of heroin. The image depicts a reality that has been part of the barrio for nearly a century, a legacy that leaves a trail of multigenerational addiction, sorrow, and crime.

There has always existed an "Us versus Them" attitude in El Segundo and Chihuahuita, adding to its strength but also its isolation. This attitude took a violent turn more than a century ago, during the height of the Mexican Revolution, which forced thousands of refugees into the area.

A history of struggle and isolation lies beneath the proud veneer that is depicted in multiple murals painted on walls throughout the barrio. Two of the pivotal incidents occurred during the rise of migration from the south that reflected the racism that greeted this new wave of immigrants. One occurred in each of the barrios nearly exactly a year apart, in 1916 and

1917. A more contemporary incident created extensive social disruption in 1963 and likely had a greater and more distinct impact on our subject population.

Tapia (2019) refers to the cultural value system of *La Raza* as a provocative reference to the struggles against discrimination, poverty, and unequal justice faced by Chicanas/Chicanos in the US. However, the effort itself can become corrupted as a perception of dominance evolves and criminal opportunities are exploited, in most cases involving others in the same demographic.

By 1916 tensions were running high between the US and Mexico. Mexico's internal conflict that began with the overthrow of President Porfirio Díaz in 1910 resulted in a string of presidents who were either killed or exiled. Behind the scenes was Pancho Villa, seen by some as a recalcitrant murderer, while others in the northern provinces, especially in Chihuahua state, saw him as salvation against the repressive fiefdom-like *hacendado* structure that plunged thousands into a perpetual state of poverty and uncertainty. This instability caused not only thousands to flee into Texas, especially into El Paso, but also prompted opposition factions of the Carranza government to establish liaison, recruiting, and fundraising sites in the city.

Villa maintained a stringent anti-American posture after he saw President Woodrow Wilson provide support to President Venustiano Carranza. On the night of January 12, 1916, some one hundred of Villa's troops led by Colonel Pablo Lopez attacked a stalled train in central Chihuahua that contained American employees of the Cusi mining company. Eighteen Americans were murdered in the attack and later brought to El Paso funeral homes for processing.

A vigilante group, with the urging of Carranza, was mobilized to go into Mexico to avenge the murdered Americans. As the bodies were transported across the Santa Fe Bridge into Chihuahuita, crowds began to gather, looking to project their anger on any Mexican they saw. Given the neighborhood, the targets were readily available. Troops from nearby Fort Bliss, under the command of John "Black Jack" Pershing, were rushed to Chihuahuita to "contain" the crisis, but the soldiers quickly found opportunities to engage in altercations with residents as well.

Residents from the nearby El Segundo Barrio armed with bats and sticks quickly came to the aid of their compatriots. Martial law was established. The Santa Fe Bridge was closed down, and soldiers made a concerted effort to separate the Mexicans from the Caucasian residents.

This "Dead Line" or "Pershing Line," as it was locally called, resulted in a quarantine of Mexican residents in Chihuahuita. Even a century later, remnants of the attitudes engendered by the quarantine remain among the population of southern El Paso—including a more defiant attitude among residents of the twin barrios that contributes to the alienation prompting gang involvement among its youth (Levario n.d.).

Only three months later, on March 9, 1916, Villa arrogantly crossed into the United States and attacked the small New Mexico village of Columbus, some eighty miles west of El Paso. In this surprise dawn attack eleven civilians and nine soldiers were killed. Once again, troops from Fort Bliss were deployed to the scene, and eventually the Punitive Expedition—the Pershing-led incursion into Chihuahua state in search of Villa. Rather than being punitive, the expedition was futile. A byproduct of the raid, however, was the rise of Villa's reputation to mythical proportions in Mexico for having the audacity to attack the United States but then evade capture and certain death. This too must have had an impact on the rebellious attitude of Mexican youth, as images of Villa continue to be sold in shops or appear on murals along the border.

The next act of defiance, the Bath Riots, occurred once again in Chihuahuita, but this time at the Santa Fe Bridge. It involved an unlikely protagonist, but one who had had enough of what she perceived to be a racist and degrading policy (Perez Jr. n.d.).

Almost exactly a year after the "Race Riot," very little had changed in regard to interracial relationships in El Paso. While the physical circling of the barrios had evaporated, the lingering taint of repression remained. So pervasive was this anti-Mexican sentiment that El Paso Mayor Tom Lea Jr. implemented a policy whereby any Mexican crossing into the US over the Santa Fe Bridge would have to undergo a dehumanizing delousing process. Lea was not reticent about expressing his disdain for his cross-border neighbors.

He would write, "Hundreds (of) dirty lousey destitute Mexicans arriving at El Paso daily will undoubtedly . . . bring and spread Typhus unless quarantine is placed at once" (Perez Jr. n.d.).

The establishment of a requisite "bath" facility was installed at the Santa Fe Bridge on January 27, 1917. The insulting process required every northbound border crosser to have their clothing cleaned at the facility, undergo a physical examination, then be deloused in a caustic mixture of gasoline, insecticide, and other dangerous chemicals.

The day after the policy was imposed seventeen-year-old Carmelita Torres was planning to cross the bridge to her job as a maid in El Paso. When approached by bridge officials to undergo the process, she vehemently refused. Words were exchanged, and before long rocks, bottles, and epithets were thrown at the station. By the next day more than five hundred other mostly domestic workers joined in the revolt. The disturbance would ultimately close the border for two days. The disturbance was quelled, but the policy, in a more modest form, continued well into the 1950s, with certificate-issuing stations now placed on the Mexican side (Perez Jr. n.d.).

Such incidents doubtless shaped the mindset of the Mexican American population in south El Paso. It is not unreasonable to assume that the parents and grandparents of future gang members had endured these indignities and expressed their anger at the racist Anglos who perpetrated these acts. The message was received by the younger generation that they would have to stand on their own.

A more contemporary incident that impacted the residents of El Segundo Barrio, and most likely some of the future members of the Barrio Azteca, occurred in 1963, although the situation had been festering for more than a century. The Chamizal Convention of 1963 resulted in more than five thousand people being relocated from El Segundo Barrio when a stretch of long-disputed land was returned to Mexico. This resulted in a massive relocation of residents and the demolition of their houses.

Border tensions between the US and Mexico had festered for nearly a century. Based on the Treaty of Guadalupe Hidalgo at the end of the Mexican-American War in 1848, the newly established border between the two countries would be defined by the deepest channels down the middle of the Rio Grande River, called the Rio Bravo south of the border. But erosion, weather, and changing currents typically cause changes in a river's course.

In 1864 a massive flood caused a significant shift in the perceived boundary that nine years later eliminated 630 acres from the Mexican side. This was a source of great contention to Mexican landowners who wanted to maintain their ownership (Utley 1996). Also in the disputed area was a peninsula that jutted into the river from the El Paso side called Cordova Island. During and since Prohibition this had become a hotbed of alcohol and narcotics smuggling. Decades of arbitration did little to assuage these border tensions. By the 1950s the socialist revolutionary movement was gaining momentum in Latin America, and the United States wanted to avoid losing their southern neighbor, which would ultimately bring Soviet influence directly to our border (Payan 2016).

By 1960 there were 5,600 American residents living on the disputed tract assuming it belonged to the United States. At the time there was little evidence suggesting otherwise. It wouldn't be until 1963 that both countries finally agreed on the stipulations made in a 1911 agreement whereby the contested land was returned to Mexico and the residents bought out of their homes and businesses and relocated. This caused significant trauma to most of the residents, who had lived in this part of the barrio for decades.

The introduction of narcotics into this area has had a multigenerational impact on the barrios for more than a century and can be traced to two dynamics. The first is the influx of Chinese, who arrived in the area to work on the railroads in the mid- to late nineteenth century. They opened opium dens up and down Oregon Street in the shadow of the prominent cathedral. The impact of the Chinese on El Paso was profound. In 1889 the *El Paso Daily Herald* pronounced the city the "Chinese Mecca of the Southwest." Monopolies on certain businesses such as laundries arose in the barrios, causing animosity as prices rose.

There was also a heavy Chinese presence in Ciudad Juárez. Once the US began cracking down on opium in El Paso, it would be smuggled across the border to satisfy an already established taste for the euphoric high. The Chinese exploited this into the 1930s before their market was effectively crushed by an enigmatic couple few knew about and even fewer talked about.

Ignacia *"La Nacha"* Jasso Gonzales and her husband Pablo, known as *El Pablote*, established what would become the genesis of the border narcos. Specializing in heroin trafficking into El Paso, which incidentally coincided with Prohibition, the couple quickly and violently dispatched their Chinese competitors. The trafficking of Mexican heroin through the porous border, with well-established smuggling routes that exist to this day, began well before the sophisticated and deadly machinations of contemporary drug trafficking organizations.

La Nacha, a squat dark-haired woman, was born in Durango, Mexico, around 1892. She and El Pablote worked for the most prominent gangster in the region at the time, Enrique Fernandez. The couple hired runners to bring heroin into the United States starting in the 1920s and effectively vaporized the Chinese market through the violent overthrow of their competitors, a modus operandi that exists a century later (Campbell 2009).

The turning point in their takeover likely occurred with the killing of eleven Chinese competitors in Ciudad Juárez (Fregoso 2018). When El Pablote was killed in a Ciudad Juárez bar in 1930, La Nacha did not slow down. In fact, her peak years were during World War II, when she often enticed soldiers from Fort Bliss to Ciudad Juárez to sample her products, which included both drugs and prostitutes. This garnered the attention of US federal officials, who sought her extradition but failed. Some sixty years later, the likes of *El Chapo* and Arturo Gallegos Castrellón would follow in her footsteps.

La Nacha involved her children and grandchildren in the family business, which maintained the flow of heroin across the border. There, local gangs such as the precursors of the BA would help distribute. Outside distributors helped insulate the family from direct culpability. Although it was reported that she lived in Chihuahuita briefly in the late 1920s, her primary residence was in a modest neighborhood in Ciudad Juárez, where she evaded American law enforcement and facilitated local corruption. This is not to say she didn't spend jail time in Mexico, where she was often the victim of violent assaults. But La Nacha and her dynasty would endure well into the 1970s. La Nacha died of natural causes in 1977, no small feat in her industry, at the age of eighty-five.

Her legacy opened the door for future female narcos such as María *Lola la Chata* Dolores Estévez Zuleta, Sandra Ávila Beltrán, and Enedina Arellano Félix in the wake of their husbands' deaths (Carey and Cisneros Guzmán 2011). La Nacha's fifty-year legacy of infusing heroin into the streets and veins of south El Paso would have profound implications for the next generation of street life in the barrio.

What La Nacha and El Pablote created was the foundation for the mega cartels that would arise in the 1970s and reach new heights in the new millennium. The Juarez Plaza was relegated to Amado Carrillo Fuentes by Miguel Ángel Félix Gallardo of Guadalajara, who believed it would be more advantageous to break up the central organization into more regional operations in Tijuana, Sinaloa—the epicenter of marijuana and heroin production—Ciudad Juárez, and the Gulf of Mexico.

To expand and protect their products, each of the organizations would require foot soldiers. These would typically be in the form of well-organized gangs who could mete out acts of aggression while at the same time insulating the organization's hierarchy.

BARRIO GANG CULTURE

There are between three hundred to five hundred gangs thought to be operating in El Paso. This number can fluctuate based on myriad factors, including crackdowns by law enforcement. Arrests are made as a result of validation practices based on self-admission, tattoos, and multiple confirmed sources, among other means.

In 2009 El Paso officials reported the existence of 539 gangs with approximately 5,665 members (Borderland Beat 2009c). In 2014 the *El Paso Times* reported the presence of 307 gangs with 5,664 members (Borunda 2014). These numbers suggest that gang data needs to be questioned. What explanation could there be for having 232 fewer gangs but essentially the same number of gang members? I've made a career of studying gangs, and one thing I've noticed is that they are extremely fluid in terms of changing names, consolidating with other gangs, evaporating because members have aged out, or realizing the gang life is a waste of their formative years. So while the number of gangs may have decreased, the number of gang members hasn't, producing a net zero difference in terms of potential criminal activity. There are also ebbs and flows perhaps based on population migration and criminal opportunities, such as what occurred in the 1980s with the introduction of crack into impoverished communities. This created a new wave of gang violence for control of lucrative marketplaces.

An institutional methodology is utilized by law enforcement to identify gangs. There are uniform identifiers, but as law enforcement becomes aware of these the gangs will change their idiosyncracies to stay a step ahead. Then there is the political willpower to accept the fact that a school district or community has criminal street gangs. These entities are often reluctant to admit this scourge. In their eyes, acceptance indicates policy failure or the devaluation of their institutions.

The fact is, gangs will always exist. El Paso garnered recent attention from authors Tapia and Durán. It is hard to ignore that this border city has been an incubator for these organizations. The previously mentioned socioeconomic circumstances are main drivers, but the proximity to Mexico affords a unique nexus many other gangs across the United States lack. Familial and criminal networks crisscrossing the border have been established and maintained over generations, so that these gang members can routinely cross back and forth to evade their respective law enforcement agencies or to market their products.

Durán notes the paradox in the existence of El Paso gangs and the relatively low incidence of violent crime. El Paso has ranked as one of the top ten safest cities in the United States (Madrid 2019). Durán contends that the mere presence of gangs is not necessarily synonymous with violence and that they serve mainly as social anchors for their members. This is an oversimplification and apologetic.

But why the low level of violence? For starters, there is gang violence in El Paso—just not on the scale of Chicago. One possible explanation is that El Paso gangs have accepted a social order. Turf wars in El Paso are essentially a thing of the past, although there are still a few conflicts. One local law enforcement official says many of the gangs actually work together with the common goal of making money through narcotic sales. Another possible explanation is that the more dominant gangs such as the BA and Chuco Tangos maintain order among their members in an attempt to avoid attention by law enforcement.

Gang proliferation in barrios across the country is indicative of marginalization, alienation, poverty, and opportunity. This is contrary to Durán's (2018) argument that the region's underlying conflict in reconciling generations of colonization, dating back some four hundred years, served as a subliminal catalyst for gang membership. I submit that contemporary issues are likely more relevant to gang attraction among youth because these are much more tangible than the impact of four-hundred-year-old historical events. Did double colonization of Mexico by Spain and France, and then the economic influence of the United States, which Durán described, have an impact on Mexico when they occurred? Likely so, but over the ensuing four hundred years these have evaporated as influences (Durán 2018).

I believe contemporary incidents such as the El Paso Race and Bath Riots and the Chamizal Agreement had a more profound societal impact through the oral histories passed down by those who experienced them. But I still believe the greater impact on these youths comes from the traditional drivers of living in poverty and lack of supervision from parents working long hours, resulting in a need for the emotional comfort and stability a surrogate family such as a gang can provide. Criminality does not always serve as the primary driver, but is a byproduct of gang association.

The first signs of organized street gangs emerged shortly after World War I, as the wave of immigrants flooded across the border to escape the Mexican Revolution. By 1942 the issue was profound enough that law enforcement declared anti-gang initiatives. Making matters worse, by 1970 the city all but gave up on the barrio, calling it a seventy-year-old slum beyond conventional redevelopment methods, and even calling it potentially "explosive" (City of El Paso 1970). The proverbial deck was stacked against the residents in south El Paso.

The sense of isolation and alienation within the barrio causes individuals to unite within their own communities. This has been a strength of barrios across the United States, allowing the residents to create a "safe place" where they could launch into what they considered to be mainstream society and thrive. The barrio culture is Mexican, where close-knit family ties and oral histories are traditionally passed down through generations, and historic tales are recounted in folk songs called *corridos*. These can mold both conscious and subconscious attitudes. Given the dynamic of the two border barrios, the desire for a sense of unity, especially among vulnerable youth, emerged into an entirely new identity known as *Pachuco*.

To say you are from Chuco (short for Pachuco) Town is a badge of honor. It indicates pride and resilience in the face of adversity. At the heart of this phenomenon is Lincoln Park, affectionately referred to as Chicano Park, a small patch of grass located a block off of Interstate 10 and Patriot Parkway heading south to Ciudad Juárez. There on overpass pillars are a series of murals depicting the styles of Pachuco.

To understand what Pachuco is is to understand a movement toward identity in the face of adversity. Through this identity the seeds of street gangs were sown. While not all Pachucos subscribed to criminal activity, there were many who asserted this identity through less than idealistic means. The origins of the Pachuco style is nebulous, but most agree it emerged in the 1930s in the El Paso-Ciudad Juárez corridor. It was a style adopted by young people of Mexican descent as a step toward a personal identity outside the norms. The style was defined by specific clothing such as the Zoot suit, by music, tattoos, and even their own slang, *Calo*. Because of racial discrimination this overt expression of unity and uniqueness launched perceptions that anyone who was a Pachuco was a gangster. This wasn't the case, just as not all of the Swing Kids of the same era were mobsters. There were Pachucos, however, who used their unified strength as an opportunity for criminal behavior.

Haldeen Braddy (1960) had a more cynical impression of the Pachucos and saw very little socially cohesive or constructive self-identifying benefit other than the commission of crime. He directly correlates the Pachucos to juvenile delinquents engrossed in smoking and selling marijuana. He found that initiation took on a religious fervor since the majority, if not all, of its members were Catholic.

"They would swear by the cross or take an oath in a cemetery above the graves of their mothers," he says (Braddy 1960).

Once initiated, members were required to wear a crucifix and believe in God. This practice was appropriated in succeeding Mexican American gangs that were notorious for wearing Rosary beads or having Our Lady of Guadalupe or St. Jude tattoos.

The criminal enterprises the Pachucos engaged in were crimes of easy opportunity in their neighborhoods. Braddy said this would involve "Energetically push(ing) dope, procur(ing) girls, or smuggl(ing) contraband" (1960). Researchers have found that in the 1940s "Chihuahuita was being run by savage Pachuco gangs considered to be the meanest and cruelest in the city" (Morales 1991). The barrio took on the moniker of *La Mancha Roja,* Blood Stained Barrio, because of its history of violence.

A 1954 *Police Gazette* article by George McGrath (1954) said the gang's behavior could be traced to the origin of the name. He said the town of Pachuco in Hidalgo state was known for bandit gangs, rapists, thieves, and murderers.

Chuco would come to identify a clique of a dominant Texas prison gang. The Tangos came to dominate the Texas prison system in the new millennium and took to the streets of Austin, Dallas, San Antonio, and El Paso. Each clique took on a name and iconography related to their genesis as they returned home. The El Paso element named themselves the Chuco Tangos in homage to the city's cultural impact on the first Americanized Mexican subculture.

Both Durán and Tapia identified dozens of street gangs that permeate the El Paso street scene. Among these are the X14 Gang that would ultimately spawn the BA, the Thunderbirds, Los Fatherless, and myriad others that would become feeder gangs once behind prison walls.

A significant confrontation occurred in 1972 between the Thunderbirds, a self-proclaimed sports club but a designated gang by the El Paso Police Department, and a group of former convicts and heroin addicts called *Tecatos* who were allegedly shooting drugs behind the popular Marcos B.

Armijo Community Center on Seventh Street. Words were exchanged and tensions rose, eventually leading to the shooting death of Vietnam veteran and Thunderbirds leader Arturo Corrales (Durán 2018). Members of the Thunderbirds would gravitate towards the Azetcas in the future.

As El Paso law enforcement cracked down on its street gangs, these young men increasingly populated the cells of the Texas prison system where an entirely different dynamic would unfold.

CHAPTER 2

Coffield

The Coffield Unit of the Texas Department of Criminal Justice lies some five miles outside Tennessee Colony, Texas, about a two-hour drive southeast of Dallas. Coffield, like just about every other prison in the United States, has a legacy of gangs existing behind the concrete walls and razor wire. Opened in 1965, the sprawling 20,528 square foot facility is designed to house 3,818 inmates in the facility with another 321 in the trustee camp. By the time the inmates from El Paso arrived, seeds of discord were well established, and true to their street culture, the El Paso groups unified rapidly.

Coffield served as a petri dish spawning two international gangs that would have a profound impact on crime, not only in the United States but in Mexico. Much attention has been paid, and rightfully so, to MS-13, which extended its violent reach into Central America after members completed US prison sentences and were deported back to politically unstable countries. This dynamic was replicated with the Barrio Azteca and Mexicles, all around the same time period in the late 1980s.

What is it about the prison dynamic that fosters the growth and sophistication of these otherwise unsophisticated street gang members? Much of it has to do with environment, opportunity, need for protection, racial/ethnic alliance, and the need for structure in a socially unstable environment.

PRISON GANG DYNAMIC

Prisoners join or form prison gangs for protection within the high-stakes world of elite predators who have honed their trade to exploit the lucrative prison black market for drugs, alcohol, tobacco, extortion, and sex. Controlling even a corner of that market in a prison could establish the credibility of a group and protect its members from other gangs. There is always a high price to pay.

As a veteran corrections officer, for quite some time I have been engaged on a daily basis in the unique world of prison gangs. This enigmatic subculture has a definite impact on the dynamic of prisoner-to-prisoner relations as well as prisoner-to-staff relations and ostensibly on overall facility security. "Codes" are established to maintain intra-group controls among the participants in order to keep their enterprises flourishing. These establish initiation and behavioral expectations of gang members, who typically undergo a much more diligent screening process than a street gang would implement.

The prison gang seeks loyalty and productivity. There is no ambiguity among members, who typically submit to a more militaristic hierarchical structure than a street gang, so their behavior is typically much more disciplined than that of street gang members. They may even adhere to stricter rules of hygiene, exercise, and cell maintenance. The benefits of this control to the prison facility is, on the surface, actually a mitigation in violence, since overt acts of violence draw attention to the gang and its nefarious activities. That's not to say that violence is averted, because it isn't.

Prisoner assaults occur for a range of infractions that can include cheating or stealing from a gang, whether you are a member or not. Encroaching on another gang's black market operations is another typical lightning rod. Not paying a debt is anathema. Sex offenders and child molesters are quickly "rolled out" or expelled from a unit, prior to an actual assault for failure to comply.

Protection and opportunity are the fundamental reasons many inmates align with a prison gang. Most facing lengthy prison sentences know that in the world of predator versus prey, survival often depends on alignment. Many times joining is voluntary—new inmates will seek out a particular prison gang because of an established alignment with their street gang—almost like a minor league baseball team feeding a major league team. Surprisingly, it is not uncommon for individuals to have membership in a prison gang their life's goal. It is seen as a badge of honor or validation within their barrio to be aligned with a prison gang.

Garrett Roth and David Skarbek (2014) refer to the prison gang dynamic as the *Community Responsibility System*, whereby the binds established within the organization facilitate the black market enterprises the gang is involved with—drugs, alcohol, tobacco, prostitution, etc. They cite other benefits of this system, such as tighter control over members, the ability to more easily mete out retribution to policy violators in a confined setting, and the ability to operate "in the absence of an effective legal system" (Roth and Skarbek 2014).

The relationship between the street and prison gang is apparent. Jennifer Ortiz (2018) points out the limited studies comparing these two groups and their shared dynamics. In fact, there is a linear relationship that moves in both directions, from street gang to prison gang and vice versa. For instance, an El Paso gang member may have an established reputation with his street gang. This reputation may attract the attention of a prison gang, such as the Azteca, who may decide to recruit the individual. Members are also recruited through recommendations and sponsorship of other members.

Once the commitment is made and the street gang member joins the prison gang, his membership in the street gang immediately ends. He may retain an association for the advancement of the prison gang, but he will no longer "rep" the street gang.

Where the inmate is incarcerated can also impact this dynamic. For instance, an individual from El Paso who is incarcerated in another part of the state or even out of state (if sentenced to the US Bureau of Prisons), would need to decide whom they would align with, if anyone. This can be a complex decision based on provincial differences.

Such a situation ultimately led to the creation of the BA, who refused to fall in line with the Texas Syndicate. Depending on the size of the organization, the inmate will decide who to align with if he is transferred to another state. For instance, in New Mexico we may have a street gang called the Westsiders. On the county jail level the inmate will likely stay with his gang. But when transferred to the state penitentiary, he may align with either the Burquenos or Syndicato de Nuevo Mexico. In the Federal Bureau of Prisons Syndicato de Nuevo Mexico, gang members, for instance, have been granted autonomy by the much vaunted Mexican Mafia but could still represent Nuevo Mexico, which members from less influential gangs would fall under.

An interesting dynamic emerged with the BA who were deported back to Mexico. While still considered Barrio Azetca, the *Los Aztecas*, as they are referred to in Mexico, needed to take on a different persona due to the combative atmosphere that was created during the drug war with the Sinaloa drug trafficking organization. There were cross-border allegations that the group in El Paso wasn't as tough as their southern counterparts because they weren't as deeply involved in the conflict. Membership in Mexico was predicated on committing a homicide, which was not always the case among the US-based members.

MS-13 is a prime example of extreme control over members and potential members. Primarily a street gang, MS-13 ruthlessly controls members who violate rules and teens who fail to submit to recruitment pressure. In March 2019, sixteen-year-old Jacson Chicas was stabbed more than one hundred times, then incinerated by members of his own MS-13 clique. It is with internal conflict management that Ortiz (2018) finds greater control among the prison gang members, as opposed to a "chaotic-uncontrolled" method on the streets.

The relationships Ortiz (2018) found between prison, street gangs, and law enforcement were also intriguing. It was found that street gangs have a more antagonistic relationship with law enforcement, whereas in the prison environment the relationship is more "complicated." Corrections officials acknowledge the presence of gangs and the actual value they have in mitigating violent incidents if closely monitored. It's not that any illegal activity is permitted, but the gang code is understood and can be exploited to maintain inmate control. By no means do corrections officials relinquish control of the facility to gangs. This is not always the case with facilities in Mexico.

The closed prison environment makes control over gang members particularly important. In order for a gang's enterprise to flourish it needs to be out of view of prison officials. Unruly behavior and unsanctioned violence are staunchly controlled in order to evade the attention of officials. Surprisingly, then, this control contributes to less violence in the prison setting since multiple groups will be actively involved in some kind of underground criminal activity, the type of activity usually based on racial, ethnic, or geographic place of origin.

I regularly see this self-policing by gang members in my facility, for intelligence or suspicious behavior lead to the inevitable *shakedown*, where officials diligently search through inmate's cells and belongings. This is the last thing they want.

Roth and Skarbek's Community Responsibility System describes the dynamic whereby conflicts, especially internal ones, erode the gang's influence, and community responsibility is adhered to so stringently that a gang may even serve up one of their own to a rival gang in order to maintain the status quo. It's an odd dynamic, given that loyalty is tantamount, but so are the enterprises of the gang—for these define its very existence.

When a gang member no longer *reps* a street gang, he's now all about the prison gang. The prison gang will define the inmate's life from the time he arrives at the facility until he returns to the street, which could encompass decades. On the street the member may be considered a leader or ambassador for more recruits, unifying street gangs as the Mexican Mafia has effectively done for more than fifty years, and maintaining and expanding market opportunities.

One of the reasons prison gangs are so powerful and have extensive reaches into the street gang culture is the fact that eventually a street gang member will probably go to prison. Gang members have long memories and a network of communication from the prison to the street. Street gang members realize it may be a matter of time before they go to prison, where they will be answerable for any disrespect they may have previously exhibited.

BARRIO AZTECA EMERGE

In 1988, around the time the Barrio Azteca was formed, there were 39,664 inmates in the Texas prison system, with the Texas Syndicate essentially in control of the system. Texas Mexican Mafia-Mexikanemi, Aryan Brotherhood, and much later, the Tango Blast would eventually emerge as powerful adversaries.

The dynamic for the proliferation of prison gangs doesn't emerge from internal environmental factors alone. There are institutional policies that can also contribute to the inadvertent creation of gangs, creating a perfect storm of circumstances. In 1972 a federal lawsuit was filed by an inmate against the Texas Department of Criminal Justice. Cheatham Unit inmate David Ruiz filed a federal lawsuit complaining of myriad issues, one of which included the controversial yet effective Building Tender program, where inmates who were deemed somewhat trustworthy and were not reluctant in maintaining order among their fellow inmates were given positions of authority. These positions typically would be abused at the expense of other inmates.

Prior to *Ruiz v. Estelle*, the existence and influence of gangs behind Texas prison walls were negligible. Gangs did exist, but they were controlled within the system. It would be *Ruiz v. Estelle* (William J. Estelle was the director for the Texas Department of Criminal Justice at the time) that would resolve issues surrounding mistreatment by building tenders, also referred to as "turnkeys," as well as overcrowding, inadequate prison healthcare services, unsafe working conditions, and security and safety. The Tender program ostensibly kept the expense of paying correctional officers low.

It would take eight years for the case to meander at a glacial pace through the courts and a three-month trial, which inevitably forced the Texas Department of Criminal Justice to make sweeping reforms. Among these was a dramatic expansion of facilities. Through the 1970s Texas operated just eighteen prison facilities for approximately 25,000 inmates. By the late 1980s and early 1990s, an additional eighty-nine units had been constructed around the state to accommodate more than 140,000 prisoners. This increase in prospective recruits was a windfall for the Texas Syndicate, which saw its numbers dramatically multiply, empowering it to aggressively recruit more members and resulting in its overwhelming control of prison dynamics.

One pertinent element of the *Ruiz* settlement was abolishing the Building Tender program. No longer would inmates be granted the authority to mete out discipline to other inmates. While this resulted in a controversial and deplorable abuse of inmates, it did help suppress rampant gang activity, as the tenders were neither weak in spirit or body. Once the program was eliminated, a power vacuum formed in the prisons, with the Texas Syndicate waiting impatiently in the wings.

Created in 1978 by El Paso Thunderbird (T)-Bird gang member Juan "Pájaro" Solis-Vela and Francisco "Panchito" Gonzales from the Rio Grande Valley, the Texas Syndicate arose not in Texas but at Folsom Prison in California. The two gang members mobilized Texas inmates incarcerated in the California corrections system for protection and unity against the increasingly stronger Mexican Mafia, Nuestra Familia, and Aryan Brotherhood.

Recruiting was effective among the Texas inmates in the California Department of Corrections (CDC), and they quickly earned a reputation for ruthlessness. Solis-Vela's T-Birds were from the very area of south El Paso that would spawn the Azteca. The Thunderbirds, or "T-Birds," date back to 1965 and from the mid-1970s well into the 1980s were El Paso's largest gang (Tapia 2019). The T-Birds operated under the guise of a sports club designed to keep barrio youth away from the very activities the gang was involved in. The El Paso Police Department had a different perception of what the teens were doing. In addition, there may have been barrio-related animosity between Pájaro and the mostly X14 gang members from the same El Segundo Barrio.

Eventually inmates were released from the CDC, but many found their way into the Texas prison system, where their reputation preceded them. At the time, the prison gang structure in Texas was not very sophisticated. The Texas Syndicate quickly exploited this opportunity as well as the power void that was created after *Ruiz v. Estelle*. With virtually no competition for control over the yard, the Texas Syndicate rapidly and ruthlessly swooped in, and TS would commit no less than four homicides in the first three years after the *Ruiz v. Estelle* trial.

As their power grew so did the body count, as challenges for control of the prisons emerged from such rival groups as Mexikanemi (Texas Mexican Mafia). Between 1984 and 1985 there were fifty-two gang-related homicides in the system, with most attributed to the Texas Syndicate.

Texas Syndicate was now based out of Houston and the Texas Mexican Mafia-Mexikanemi out of San Antonio. These gangs had proliferated throughout the Texas Department of Corrections. The growing number of El Paso gang members, mostly from El Segundo Barrio, had choices to make and fast: join one of the Mexican-based gangs, face retribution, or gamble on establishing their own organization, knowing full well that the cornerstone would have to be set in the blood of one of these other gangs. This was another example of the differentiation between race, ethnicity, and provincial loyalties. Despite the fact they were Mexican and Mexican American, the emerging factors in the prison system still meant that many prospective gang members found that their comfort levels required staying with their respective barrios.

In 1985, in the maximum security Coffield Unit of the Texas Department of Criminal Justice prison, the Azteca, led by José "Raulio" Rivera Fierro, began organizing Mexicans and Mexican Americans among El Paso-based inmates to oppose the Texas Mexican Mafia and Texas Syndicate. They recruited from former X14 gang members from El Paso's Segundo Barrio, who included Benito "Benny" Acosta, Alberto "Indio" Estrada, Benjamin "T-Top" Oliverez, Manuel "Tolon" Cardoza, Manuel "El Grande" Fernandez, and José "Gitano" Ledesma. Throughout 1986 Rivera and company formulated a structure and a "sacred" set of rules that would be adhered to by all members, with grave consequences for violators. January 1987 is actually considered the time of their official establishment based on completion of their rules. Their reputation as a violent prison gang in Texas and federal penitentiaries quickly spread to the streets of El Segundo Barrio and Mexico, where their numbers multiplied.

Ultimately, once their sentences were served, Mexican national members were deported back to Mexico, where they planted the seeds for the BA franchise in Ciudad Juárez.

The hierarchical structure model developed by Rivera served the burgeoning organization well in this period when groups jockeyed for positions of influence. The BA needed a structured operational model to mitigate group identity and mission ambiguities as well as to keep the typically undisciplined street-gang feeder groups in line.

In less than a year the gang had grown to about thirty-five members. That was no small task, given the tight reins the leaders maintained on membership recruitment and the overt threat from more established gangs. Strict admission rules, based on a sponsorship model, were initiated, attracting some of El Paso's most loyal sons who took a sense of pride in joining an organization that exemplified strength, unity, and culture of their barrio.

Seven years after their establishment, the BA were finally recognized by the Texas Department of Criminal Justice as a security threat group. In a correctional facility, this designation validates the impact an organization would have on facility security, whether from attacks or intimidation or introduction of contraband into the facility. To members of these gangs this designation is seen not so much as an obstacle in the cat-and-mouse world of corrections but as an accomplishment worthy of respect and attention. With this designation comes greater scrutiny by correctional officers and security threat investigators, requiring the gang to be more closely managed. With the background checks and the establishment of "Sacred Rules," the BA leadership believed it was on solid footing to launch a criminal enterprise behind bars.

These rules, or the gang's constitution, are closely guarded and venerated. The rules say that once you're a Barrio Azteca member, you'll always be a Barrio Azteca member; you will never talk to the man, "man" being law enforcement; you will do as ordered by the gang; you will attend meetings; you will not take another member's girlfriend or wife; and if you don't follow the rules, there will be consequences—assaults, death—from other members.

Jesús Ernesto "Camello" (a name given to him in his teen years) Chávez Castillo, who plays a key role in gang activities later discussed in greater detail, was exposed to the gang while serving time in Oakdale, Louisiana. Correctional departments attempt to dilute the presence of significant gangs by shipping validated members off to other facilities in the system.

His memories are most vivid of how the gang communicated behind bars.

"They send letters—they call them kites—to a bridge. Like it's a person on the streets. And from there, they send them to the other prison."

This is not a strategy unique to the BA. Inmates, even non-gang members, will communicate in this way on a regular basis. Gangs, because of their criminal enterprises behind bars, will use codes to deceive officials. In Chávez's case, it was imperative he learn those codes quickly and effectively.

Chávez recalls the Sacred Rules as the unequivocal foundation of the gang.

"One is—I don't remember all of them. But I remember one. They say that it is always going to be us first, and then family."

The other lesson he learned was that the only way out of the gang was in a coffin. Blood in, blood out, as it is referred to in gang parlance. This is not unique to the BA; most large gangs have a similar ethos encompassing a sense of uncompromised loyalty. There are exceptions: some may be eligible to walk away from the gang on their feet if they become immersed in religion or because they need to support their families, but all exceptions require stringent vetting and validation.

During the 2014 trial of Arturo Gallegos Castrellón, a high-ranking leader of the gang who was extradited back to the US to face trial, veteran El Paso Detective Andres Sanchez testified about the inner working of the gang. He said just gaining the interest of leaders would require rigorous preliminary vetting of the potential recruit.

"They're going to pretty much receive members that have done work or come from prior street gangs in El Paso, and it would be very difficult for a police officer or an agent to play that role."

In gang parlance, the reference to *work* refers to a criminal activity, typically a violent act that could be validated by a referring gang member who would ultimately be responsible for validating the recruit's credibility. On the Ciudad Juárez side, this work typically requires a homicide.

"They are going to require members that are not afraid to get in trouble. They're not afraid to get arrested, they have a criminal record, that aren't afraid to use violence when needed. They are going to be good followers, in that when they are told to do something, they are going to follow through with what they're being told."

Passing this stage will designate the recruit as a *prospectos*, prospect. It is during this phase that the recruit will be under closer scrutiny for their ability, cunning, and most importantly, loyalty.

The sponsor of the recruit is referred to as a *padrino*. This individual will already hold an esteemed rank in the organization and will vouch for the recruit as to how his membership will benefit the gang. Similar to an executive recruiting process in the legitimate business world, the BA require the *padrino* to essentially send recommendations, either written or verbally, through the chain of command up to the capo level. There must also be background checks by other criminals to validate the recruit's criminal pedigree. In the event that captains are not available or there is some communication breakdown, the gang can use a lieutenant and three sergeants to bring in people and make decisions.

A key question is whether there are any known or suspected incidents where the recruit cooperated with law enforcement—an automatic disqualifier. When it appears this process has run its course, the capo will determine if the recruit is worthy of receiving his *huaraches* (traditional Mexican sandals—a figurative reference) and being "blessed in." Once the vetting process is complete a *whila*, or secret prison letter, will be sent to the *padrino* acknowledging the recruit's acceptance into the gang.

Whilas or *kites* are tiny letters written on anything from a small piece of paper to a gum wrapper that also may be coded. These are passed around prisons as well as circulated in the outside world. This is typically accomplished through outgoing inmate mail using a *bridge*, or a person on the outside such as a spouse, girlfriend, or even parent, who will pass the *whila* to the intended gang member. Internal prison *kites/whilas* are passed through spaces in doors or by inmates who work as porters and may have more latitude of movement.

As big a commitment as joining a gang is, the actual initiation is quite informal for the BA. After being blessed in by his *padrino* before a witness or two (the availability of witnesses can be compromised by prison regulations), the new member will either hear or read the Sacred Rules from his *padrino*. The BA do not typically subscribe to the mandatory *jump in* that other gangs such as MS-13 subscribe to, where a recruit is viciously beaten for thirteen seconds by a group of other members to prove his toughness and dedication.

The Sacred Rules are closely guarded by the hierarchy in an attempt to keep them out of the hands of law enforcement. Sanchez has seen the rules and can attest to the serious nature of their effect on the organization.

"It's sacred. Only those that are in charge of a particular institution or an area will have a copy of this," testified Sanchez in the Gallegos trial.

"They definitely don't want this falling into the hands of law enforcement."

One of the rules is "Read the rules to our future brothers; every native must be aware of goings-on to prevent us from getting caught off guard for any object or reason whatsoever."

Sanchez says this is important in that the BA need to know what's going on within their own organization as well as in their rivals'. If they are at war with a particular gang, everybody needs to know this in case they get incarcerated. They also need to know who is doing what gang business in designated areas of El Paso and Ciudad Juárez, and who is in charge of collecting monies, because revenues have to be turned over to the leaders. They must know who has been arrested and who has not, and importantly who could possibly be cooperating with law enforcement.

"In other words, if a Barrio Azteca cooperates with law enforcement, gives a statement, cooperates in any way, this is a major violation of the Sacred Rules and this entails capital punishment, death."

Gaulberto Marquez has seen and vowed dedication to the Sacred Rules, which are available in both English and Spanish. He says while the foundation is solid, there are times where the rules are modified.

"Just one part that I remember, they read—they made it different so it could strengthen how people are picked up into the organization. For example, it used to be like once, two sergeants can recommend for—like, for example, me to be picked up to become a member, but they said that would no longer apply. Now it would be two sergeants and one lieutenant to be able to recruit or at least to recommend for that person to be picked up."

A typical draft of the rules is some five pages long, containing twenty-nine regulations all members must live by. On the last page is an ominous notation of the members who have been X'd or marked for expulsion in the form of murder. These names are closely guarded and historically maintained by leadership at the Coffield Unit to ensure operational security, and if they are leaked there are consequences to the violator.

Through their organizational model leaders maintain careful documentation through the use of ledgers that would include members that have fallen out of favor with the gang or have violated a regulation. This *muletl*, or "X list," will identify members that are no longer any good to the organization or have renounced the organization and have been *green lit* for death.

Ledgers will also contain *quota* money, or taxes, collected on the street from drug sales or extortion, as well as who received the payments.

Eventually this winds up in the hands of the imprisoned leadership. In order to get the money into the prisons, outside participants will convert the proceeds to money orders and send to the appropriate inmate. Many correctional facilities limit how much an inmate can receive from the outside to suppress such schemes.

"If the information gets to somebody that's an ex, it can bring consequences and damage or stop whatever—whatever active members are going to do," according to Marquez from trial testimony.

During the prospect stage, a potential recruit would become abundantly aware of the military structure of the gang and its strict adherence to the Sacred Rules.

Barrio Azteca power structure:

- Capo Mayor—Top boss
- Capos—Captains
- Tenilones—Lieutenants
- Sargenes—Sergeants
- Carnales—Soldiers
- Prospectos—Prospects
- Esquinas—Gang supporters that could include girlfriends, friends, and the street gangs that feed into Azteca.

As with any enterprise, communication is key to success. Sacred Rule 21 stresses communication within the BA. Without communication, the gang cannot exist. This communication does not solely occur within the confines of a prison, although the majority of operations are planned from correctional facilities on both sides of the border. Communication with street operatives is constant, to ensure proper management of business and tactical matters. Even with cross-border colleagues, communication between Ciudad Juárez and El Paso was virtually constant until internecine conflicts disrupted the relationship. Meetings took place via cellphone, by the handheld radios which became ubiquitous among the Ciudad Juárez operatives, or by crossing the border to meet operatives face-to-face.

By the early to mid-1990s, most of the thirty-five original gang members had returned to the streets of El Paso, where they found a fertile pool of prospective members and new business opportunities as the Colombian Cartels increasingly relied on their Mexican counterparts to transport cocaine into the US. The Colombians realized that once the United States government began choking off the Caribbean narco-smuggling routes, they would have to rely more and more on Mexican organizations who had been practicing cross-border smuggling since the alcohol Prohibition Era.

The drug explosion of the 1960s and 1970s increased the strength of these organizations and spawned super traffickers such as Guadalajara magnate Miguel Ángel Félix Gallardo, "El Padrino," who would ultimately restructure the drug trafficking cartel into the sub-organizations we recognize today. These were based in Tijuana, Sinaloa, Ciudad Juárez, and the eastern Gulf Coast. In the early years there was relative calm and territorial delineation of *plazas*, or smuggling routes, into the United States. But as the trade became more lucrative, relationships became strained and ultimately turned violent. Organizations bolstered their support staff on a military scale. Street gangs were quickly impressed into service as expendable foot soldiers, whose loss to the organizations was considered an acceptable cost of business.

These factors of expanding and autonomous control of the cross-border drug trade by Mexican organizations, plus an explosion in the US appetite for cocaine, heroin, marijuana, and methamphetamines, created a perfect incubator for the growth of gangs such as the BA, who had direct ties to Mexico, an advantage that even the Texas Syndicate couldn't exploit as effectively. This only added to the existing animosity between gangs as opportunities were gained and lost in a brief period of time.

The Texas Syndicate would remain powerful north of the border, but saw with great frustration and animus the value the BA would quickly earn in an upcoming war on the streets of Ciudad Juárez. There the Azteca would serve as the proverbial tip of the spear for the Vicente Carrillo Fuentes Drug Trafficking Organization (Juárez Cartel) in a war against the Sinaloa drug trafficking organization (DTO), who attempted to seize one of the most lucrative *plazas* in the country.

Detective Sanchez of the El Paso Police Department submitted his observations of these events. "We started seeing them pick up and get larger. As they got larger, we started seeing members parole from the Department of Corrections into the streets of El Paso. They started organizing in the streets as such as they did in the prison system. We started seeing them take charge of different areas of El Paso. And they started following our police districts, as far as how they handled their areas of responsibility, as well."

Sanchez went on to describe how the prison dynamic would continue into the county jail level.

Sanchez used the El Paso County Jail Annex as an example. There will be a gang member who is charge of the entire facility. The facility is then broken down into "Reservations," or specific housing units, each commanded by another member.

Sanchez gave the example of the 800 pod, where officials segregate validated or high-threat BA from the general population. Then there will be a leader of gang members still in the general population, known as popcorn, because they have yet to be confirmed or validated by jail staff. This member will report to the main leader about what's going on within the general population. The person in charge of each reservation will pretty much report what's going on there up the chain.

Sanchez testified that this hierarchy is broken down to the microlevel, ensuring all corners of the jail are monitored.

"The 800 pod is broken down into the different units. Each unit is broken down into twelve cells, six on top, six on the bottom, and they're segregated from each other."

So from the smallest breakdown of a correctional facility, the BA maintain control and a strict hierarchy in their correctional settings.

When a leader is about to be transferred out of a particular facility and needs to be replaced, he will recommend who he wants to leave in charge. Other gang members in the facility will send out letters and *whilas* and use jail phones to make sure this information gets to the capos in the Coffield unit, to obtain their blessings on the recommendation.

Durán (2018) discusses the relatively low amount of gang violence in El Paso as a paradox, contrasting the perceptions with the realities of gangs. One possible explanation for the relatively low amount of gang crime in El Paso, despite the presence of more than four hundred gangs there, is the possible control the BA have over street gang activity. Sanchez says that over the years many of the gangs fought with deadly consequences, but as the BA began to gel and its members were released into the streets, the prison gang began to take precedence over the street gang.

"[The gangs have] been rivals where they've pretty much committed homicides in the early and late 1990s, early 2000s. And once they became Barrio Azteca, they had to leave that street war behind because they were all now Barrio Azteca. With time, a lot of these issues between these street gangs subsided, and they started using a lot of these street gang members as their—as their *esquinas*, as their helpers, to complete their missions."

The mission is control of the regional drug trade and the establishment of *tiendas*—stores, or what they call 7-Elevens, which are houses or individuals selling drugs on the streets. Each one of these operations is required to pay a tax or *quota*. To ensure the proper amount the gang closely monitors these operations through *esquinas*. The *esquinas* can be passive, where they simply monitor the foot traffic, or more active, where they will set up buys, just like undercover narcotics officers might do, to see what drug and how much it is being sold for. In this way they can get a good estimate of how much to tax the store based on sales.

The collected money will be funneled to a member, perhaps in El Paso, called *El Banco*, or the Bank. He serves as the treasurer for the gang. As in everything the BA do, they attempt strict adherence to organization and policy. *El Banco* knows that a certain amount of the money, either on a weekly or biweekly basis, needs to be sent to support chosen incarcerated members. In order to do this, *El Banco* will convert the cash into money orders and send them to selected inmates for deposit in their jail/prison accounts for the purchase of commissary items or contraband. Since this is money laundering, the sender will use a pseudonym or put the money into other inmates' accounts. He may also attempt to throw off corrections officials by using a female sender or a family member.

The BA distinguish themselves by proudly conjuring images of pre-Columbian Aztec culture. Some knowledgeable BA used the Nahuatl language to conceal communications. There are rough similarities between the ancient Aztecs and contemporary BA. In their lore, Aztecs saw themselves as the most feared warriors. A typical Aztec became a warrior at about seventeen years old, about the same age many prospective BA advanced in street gangs prior to prison. Neither the BA nor the ancient Aztec could look forward to a long life because of their violent lifestyles.

TATTOOS

A ubiquitous designation of prison life, tattoos are intended to demonstrate a sense of permanent loyalty to the gang. They are used both in recruitment and to intimidate rivals. Tattooing is prohibited in prison facilities, but the ability of inmates to turn approved items into contraband is uncanny. Prison tattoo guns can be made with the components of a ballpoint pen,

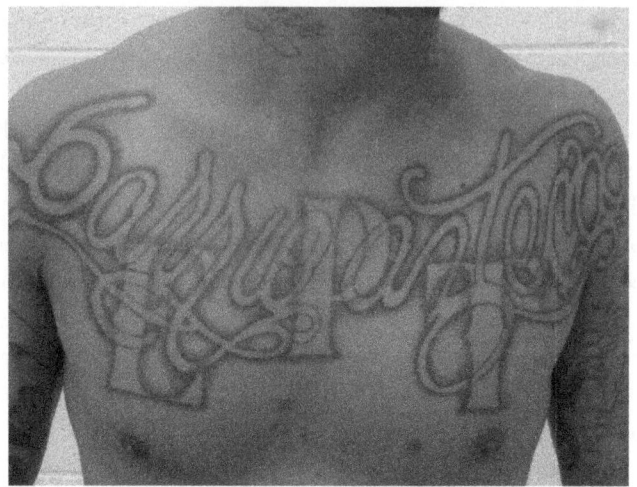

Another reference to the El Paso roots.
Courtesy of the El Paso Sheriff's Office Security Threat Group Intelligence Unit.

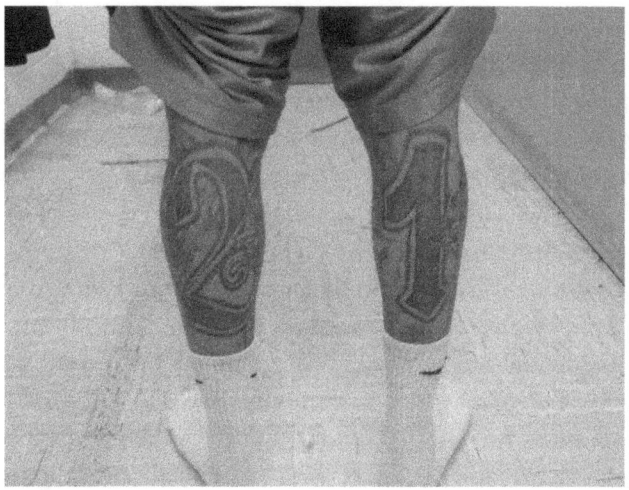

The reference to 21 correlates to the position of B and A in the alphabet.
Courtesy of the El Paso Sheriff's Office Security Threat Group Intelligence Unit.

facility-approved radio, and electric shaver. Great care is taken in making and concealing these devices. As a corrections officer, I am constantly finding the dismantled components of these tools, which are readily put back together and validated as illegal devices.

Fresh tattoos, which inmates attempt to conceal until they are healed, are obvious indicators that the gang is employing such devices inside the

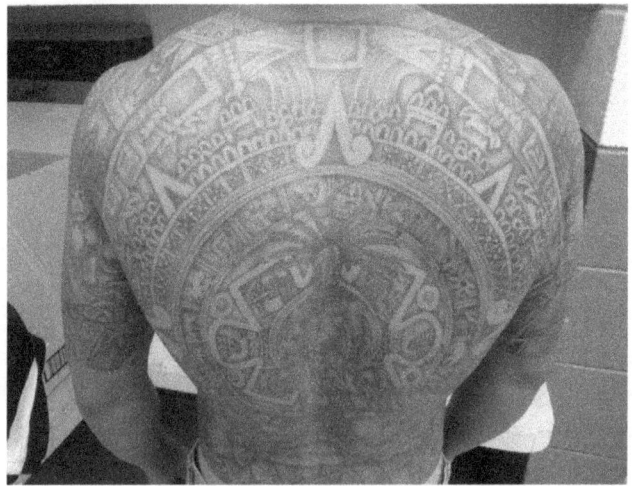

Reference to the strength of Aztec culture.
Courtesy of the El Paso Sheriff's Office Security Threat Group Intelligence Unit.

Combination of Aztec reference and "21" using Roman numerals.
Courtesy of the El Paso Sheriff's Office Security Threat Group Intelligence Unit.

prison walls. But while the gang strives to have this recognition, there are those who may attempt to downplay their allegiance.

"The ones that are being deported to Mexico and they know about it, they more than likely will not get visible tattoos," says a former member.

Among the myriad tattoos the BA are known for, most will have some reference to Aztec culture, El Paso, and 21 as follows.

- BA—Barrio Azteca
- 21, Dos Uno, or XXI—These represent the chronological order of BA in the alphabet.
- 915—This represents El Paso's area code.
- EPT—short for El Paso, Texas
- Azteca
- Aztec eagle warrior—typically adorned with a feathered plume, with or without the eagle beak
- Aztec princess
- Aztec calendar
- Indian
- Ome Ce—Nahuatl for 2-1
- The number of feathers on a warrior tattoo could indicate 2-1 (two feathers close together and one apart). The number of feathers can also represent rank. Two feathers represents a lieutenant, and a full headdress on the warrior could represent a capo.

These tattoos can be subtly located on the neck or other body part or defiantly covering the entire chest, back, or arms.

HAND SIGNS

Hand signs would typically indicate a "2-1" configuration by raising the index, middle, and pinky finger with the thumb holding down the ring finger. Most gangs have an intricate system of hand signs they communicate with on the street and in correctional facilities. Known as stacking among many gang members, the style follows some of the basic principles of American sign language and is modified based on codes and group interpretations.

To watch a full conversation using the hand signs is an intriguing spectacle. I have observed inmates converse for extended periods of time without saying a word. The conversations can be benign in nature or take on more sinister contexts involving acts of violence or other criminal activity in the facility.

CODE

Gangs survive and thrive when the outside world cannot interpret their intentions. Just like in a military operation, codes are used to confuse the opponent. Codes are used by gang members both in their kites and in external communications to thwart law enforcement. Codes are changed from time to time, but in one communication brought to light in the Gallegos trial, the prosecution presented some of the codes used by gang members to communicate drug transaction.

- *El Borla*—refers to El Paso, borderland
- Carnal—brother, and its abbreviation, CL
- *Chiva*—heroin
- *Celia Cruz*—She was a famous dark-skinned Latin singer. This reference is to the ubiquitous black tar heroin commonly distributed from Mexico.
- *Ocho*—an eight ball of cocaine
- *Soda*—cocaine
- *Sopas*—grams
- *Apartment*—quarter ounce of heroin
- *Townhouse*—half ounce of heroin
- *House*—full ounce of heroin
- *Maquila*—A house or building where the gang processed cocaine and cooked crack, primarily for La Línea.
- Code dialogue:
"The soups are already at fifty cents" means "The grams (of heroin) are already at $50." "The apartment is going for 250." Means "A quarter ounce of heroin is $250."

A RIVAL IS BORN

At around the same time the Azteca emerged at the Coffield Unit an equally sinister group was also forming. The Partido Revolucionario Mexicano, or Mexicles as they would also call themselves because of their Mexican roots, was formed in 1987 by José "El Maestro" Marquez as a means to oppose the orchestrations of the Texas Syndicate, as the Azteca did (Pacilla 2012). Like the BA, many Mexicles were in the United States illegally, and after serving their prison sentences, they would be deported back to Mexico, mostly to Ciudad Juárez, where they continued their activities. The Mexicles had strict entry guidelines. The only way to receive the coveted tattoo(s) of affiliation, one of which is the Hecho en Mexico and eagle, was through attacking a rival.

In 1991, four years after launching the gang, Marquez was ousted as leader due to his opposition to extortion. He was succeeded by Abelardo

Torres Larios. Then in 2006 David Galvez Gutierrez took the reins (Pacilla 2012).

As tensions rose in the impending battle to wrest control of the Juárez plaza from VCF, the Sinaloa DTO would enlist the services of the Gente Nueva. Similar to the way the BA aligned with La Línea, the street arm of the the VCF, the Mexicles would align with Gente Nueva and wreck a parallel swath of carnage throughout Ciudad Juárez.

CHAPTER 3

Staking Their Claim

𝔄 prison gang's reputation is based on control through violence. While a gang would prefer to stay off the radar of prison officials to ply their contraband trade, it is inevitable that members will become known by officials. This is usually in the wake of a violent incident.

The Barrio Azteca reputation for violence began shortly after their creation as they attempted to establish their power in the Texas prison system. Frequent skirmishes with opposing prison gangs such as Texas Syndicate, Mexikanemi, Tango Blast, Partido Revolucionario Mexicano, and Border Brothers established their ruthlessness and ability to establish their power base not only in the Texas prison system but in federal penitentiaries in Colorado and Louisiana. In Mexico they would be housed in the notorious CERESO Prison in Ciudad Juárez. But just as the BA meted out much violence, they also sustained many attacks, so they needed to increase recruitment both inside the prisons and on the streets of El Paso.

Following a series of skirmishes, the Mexikanemi declared war on the BA in Coffield in 1988 (Gang Intelligence 101). Five years later, the Texas Syndicate allied themselves with the Mexikanemi after the BA murdered one of Texas Syndicate's members in the El Paso County Jail. By now the BA had expanded their membership and strength in other Texas prison units, a fact underscored by the 1994 murder of a Texas Syndicate member at the Wallace unit in Colorado City, Texas.

Barrio Azteca membership rose as rapidly as its reputation, but published reports are contradictory. Data verifying the gang's actual membership is difficult to validate because of their code of silence and because of the hundreds killed in inter- and intra-gang conflicts. The following is a summary of published membership data:

2009: Source: FBI. Six hundred members (FBI 2009). However, the *Borderland Beat* reported a membership of 2,000 (*Borderland Beat* 2009).
2010: The El Paso Intelligence Center (Public Intelligence 2010) reported 3,500 inside and outside of the prison system.
2011: *Police* Magazine reported more than 2,000 members (Valdemar 2011). InSight Crime (2018) reported 3,500 active members. Texas Department of Public Safety reported 3,000 in their annual Gang Threat Assessment (Texas Department of Public Safety 2011).
2013: InSight Crime (Dudley 2013) would claim a membership of 3,000 members in the United States and 5,000 in Ciudad Juarez.
2018: The *Houston Chronicle* (Gill 2018) reported 2,500. Following the arrest of a suspect in New Mexico, the *Alamogordo Daily News* reported 3,000 members.

These numbers are purely educated guesses. This was an era when the gang experienced significant casualties on the streets of Ciudad Juárez in their battle against the Sinaloa DTO, and there were dozens of arrests on both sides of the border. What is clear is how the gang would eventually transcend the El Paso-Ciudad Juárez corridor. As prison and street crime opportunities arose, membership spread to west Texas towns such as Midland and Odessa; Las Cruces, New Mexico (*Borderland Beat* 2009c); and even Pennsylvania and Massachusetts (InSight Crime 2017a). However, the majority of their activity is centered around southwest Texas and the Chihuahua and Michoacan states in Mexico.

Animosity emerged in 2001 between the BA and the Tango Blast at Torres state prison in Hondo, Texas, and despite an apparent truce, two years later a Tango Blast member was stabbed to death at Robertson state prison, Abilene, Texas, igniting a statewide prison war and a vicious rivalry that continues as of this writing.

"After a lot of bloodshed, the families—the main capos of the families—decided to put an end to it, and they made a manifest, a pact with other—with the other organizations to stop the violence between us and focus on other things," says a former member.

In a formally ratified manifest, all of the gang's members had to sign the document verifying they knew there was a truce and not to take unilateral aggressive actions. To ensure there was no misunderstanding of the importance of the treaty, it was written in both Spanish and English.

The preamble read, "An immediate end to all forms of hostilities, aggression, disrespect, and acts of war intentionally directed towards the opposite side. This includes all forms of infiltration tactics or means utilized to obtain internal business functions information from the opposite side."

This document presents a level of sophistication not expected from a group generally perceived as uneducated. In the absence of any advanced or professional education among its leaders, the document reveals cogent pragmatism in the face of extreme violence that was not only adhered to behind prison walls but on the streets of Texas.

Efforts were taken to address any questions by incorporating a contact protocol. Inmates were instructed to contact the representative of the La Mesa Mayor (the BA leadership) in the Coffield Unit headquarters.

Over the ensuing years the Texas Department of Public Safety would release its annual Gang Threat Assessment. The gang would rise and fall between a Tier 1 and Tier 2 threat in the annual Texas DPS Gang Threat Assessment, a determination based on a variety of factors that included relationships with cartels, transnational criminal activity, level of criminal activity, level of violence, prevalence throughout Texas, relationship with other gangs, and total strength (Texas Department of Public Safety 2011). Through 2010-2011 the BA remained a Tier 1 gang behind the Mexicanemi, Tango Blast, and Texas Syndicate. Around the time of the Gallegos trial in 2014, the gang was still listed as a Tier 1 gang behind the Tango Blast, Texas Syndicate, and Mexicanemi.

AVOIDING TRANSNATIONAL CRIMINAL ORGANIZATION DESIGNATION

Recognizing the role of transnational criminal organizations in proliferating narcotics trafficking the United States government turned to recently passed legislation. The Foreign Narcotics Kingpin Designation Act (Kingpin Act) was passed in 1999 and the Transnational Criminal Organizations Sanctions Program went into effect in 2011 through the Office of Foreign Assets Control in the US Department of Treasury.

In the case of the Transnational Criminal Organizations Program, President Barack Obama issued Executive Order 13581 (E.O. 13581), "declaring a national emergency to deal with the unusual and extraordinary threat to the national security, foreign policy, and economy of the

United States constituted by the growing threat of significant transnational criminal organizations" (U.S. Department of the Treasury 2015).

According to the executive order, property and assets were to be blocked for any individual who:

- Is a foreign person that constitutes a significant transnational criminal organization;
- Has materially assisted, sponsored, or provided financial, material, or technological support for, or goods or services to or in support of, any person whose property and interests in property are blocked pursuant to E.O. 1358; or
- Is owned or controlled by, has acted or purported to act for or on behalf of, directly or indirectly, any person whose property and interests in property are blocked pursuant to E.O. 13581.

The BA would prove themselves to be prolific binational killers, and effective narco traffickers, extortionists, and money launderers, but would conspicuously avoid being officially designated a transnational criminal organization. Mara Salvatrucha 13 (MS-13), however, would obtain this designation from the US Treasury Department in 2012, around the time the BA were at their peak.

"MS-13 is an extremely violent and dangerous gang responsible for a multitude of crimes that directly threaten the welfare and security of US citizens, as well as countries throughout Central America," said Treasury Under Secretary for Terrorism and Financial Intelligence David S. Cohen under President Barack Obama. "This action positions us to target the associates and financial networks supporting MS-13, and gives law enforcement an additional tool in its efforts to disrupt MS-13's activities" (U.S. Department of the Treasury 2012).

The paradox with MS-13 is compelling. While MS-13 has proven themselves to be extremely violent, the level at which they suppressed their adversaries is only comparable to what the BA have done behind bars and on the streets of Ciudad Juárez. The defining difference between the two gangs is that MS-13 lacks the massive nexus the BA had with the drug trafficking organizations from the Sinaloa Federation to VCF, and they have not approached the BA's volume of trade.

It is interesting that the US Treasury Department has designated MS-13 but not the BA as a Transnational Criminal Organization. I suspect one reason MS-13 was designated had to do with publicity. MS-13 hit the suburban communities of Washington, DC, especially hard, so they posed a credible threat to the placid environs of Virginia and Maryland in clear view of policy makers. Multiple horrific murders in Harris County, Texas, and on Long Island merely sealed the designation. The BA, on the other hand, are more or less out of sight, out of mind. The streets of El Segundo Barrio and Ciudad Juárez are a comfortable distance away from most politicians, who have likely never heard of the Barrio Azteca.

MS-13 was designated a transnational criminal organization under President Obama's 2011 National Strategy to Combat Transnational Organized Crime, which saw MS-13's threat to include the crimes of drug trafficking, kidnapping, human smuggling, sex trafficking, murder, assassinations, racketeering, blackmail, extortion, and immigration offenses (U.S. Department of the Treasury 2012), all of which are proficiently conducted by the BA, and likely on a grander scale, especially during that time.

"This designation allows us to strike at the financial heart of MS-13 and is a powerful weapon in our fight to dismantle one of the most violent transnational criminal organizations operating today," said then ICE Director John Morton. "History has proven that we can successfully take down organized crime groups when we combine sophisticated investigative techniques with tough street level enforcement, cutting off cash flows, contraband, and collaborators to ensure they no longer find safe haven in our communities" (U.S. Department of the Treasury 2012).

I do not argue that MS-13 is not vicious and, since it is present in more than forty states, is more prolific in the US. I have seen the result of their depravity on Long Island and even in El Salvador. The amount of revenue the BA controls, however, and the instability they create along the US-Mexico border should bring them under much closer scrutiny by the US Department of Treasury.

Even the more applicable Department of Treasury Foreign Narcotics Kingpin Designation Act (Kingpin Act) of 1999 ignores the BA and La Línea but did list Vicente Carrillo Fuentes in 2000 and the Carrillo Fuentes Organization in 2004 (U.S. Department of Treasury 2020). The act, however, stipulates that operatives could also be culpable. In this case members may be implicated but not specifically because of membership in the BA.

CHAPTER 4
CERESO Prison

The contrast between correctional institutions in the US and those in Mexico is stark in terms of facilities, management, staff training, and level of corruption. Recent history is replete with multiple incidents of corruption resulting in prison violence and national embarrassment for Mexico.

The saga of Joaquín "El Chapo" Guzmán is the most notable. He not only escaped once but twice from the country's highest security prisons. A disputed account states that the first time, in January 2001, he escaped from Puente Grande prison by being pushed out of the facility in a laundry basket with the help of heavily bribed prison officials (Saviano 2015). Anabel Hernandez (2013) found El Chapo was actually led out of the prison by officials wearing police officers' uniforms. Arguably the most dramatic incident occurred in July 2015, when he disappeared into a hole dug in his prison cell shower at the Altiplano federal maximum security prison, then fled the facility on a motorcycle that ran on a rail through a sophisticated mile-long tunnel (Shoichet, Payne, and Melvin 2015).

In Ciudad Juárez the primary correctional facility is CERESO 3, located in the far southern desert reaches of the city. CERESO is the Mexican abbreviation for Centro Readaptacion Social. There are 284 state-run facilities and twenty-one federal facilities called Federal Centres for Social Reinsertion (CEFERESOS) in Mexico (Prison Insider 2017). Rising three stories, the white edifice of the Juárez CERESO, surrounded by barbed wire and with an imposing guard tower, was designed to hold 2,300 inmates.

The National Human Rights Commission (CNDH) conducted a study, "National Diagnosis of Prison Supervision 2014," and found that most facilities—seventy-one prisons—followed a model of inmate self-government (Prison Insider 2017).

"This implies that inmates who imposed themselves by the use of violence take control of common spaces, possess the keys to the cells, and compel other inmates to pay in order to access certain rights (space to sleep, calls, receive visits, entrance to the toilet, among others). In certain prisons, these inmates own weapons and sell drugs. The main causes of this phenomenon are overcrowding, lack of staff and low staff salaries" (Prison Insider 2017).

This dynamic was abundantly clear to Melissa del Bosque, a reporter for the *Texas Observer*, who penned an article in 2011 titled "In Juárez the Prison Inmates Run the Asylum."

In her piece del Bosque pointed to the absence of institutional control, whereby prostitutes, including underage girls, were permitted into the prison for the pleasure of the inmates, particularly the gang members who essentially controlled the facility (del Bosque 2011).

"Criminals run the Juárez jail and money can get you anything you want. The nicest part of the prison is run by the Sinaloa Cartel. Inside the white stucco fortress are two restaurants, a hair salon, a store, carpentry workshops, and even a cockfighting ring. The Sinaloa wing of the prison is overseen by a man the prisoners refer to as 'The Assassin,' alleged to have killed at least 200 people," reported del Bosque (2011).

Inside this cauldron would be some of the most violent men in the Western Hemisphere. Separate wings for the Artistas Asesinos (Doble A), Mexicles, and Barrio Azteca would do little to mitigate acts of violence between them to control the guards and prison. Flashpoints had occurred essentially since gang members had been deported and incarcerated in CERESO 3. Not only were these confrontations inter-gang but intra, as well.

The BA had no reservations about viciously killing their own as well as their rivals, especially in the confines of the prison. In 2006, gang member Alejandro "El Veneno" Ferrer Perez was killed by his own gang for allegedly cooperating with law enforcement. Ten other inmates would be killed in the melee. His wife, Magda Núñez, suspected it was corrupt guards who planted the seeds among the inmates that ignited the assault (Eaton 2006).

Months prior to the attack, after taking over as the director, Juan Fernández Ordóñez knew and saw firsthand the dire condition of the facility. By his own admission the prison was the "biggest shooting gallery" of narcotics in the city (Eaton 2006). So he launched a massive attempt, albeit futile, to rehabilitate the prison. In the course of this effort more than five hundred weapons and twenty cell phones were seized and thirty guards were dismissed (Eaton 2006). One of his strategies was to break up the influence of the BA in the facility.

Just weeks after the Ferrer murder, the public saw that Fernandez was serious. He had 1,090 officers converge on the prison and remove four hundred BA inmates, who would be transferred to other facilities (Eaton 2006b).

Separating gang members intra- and extra-facility is a common practice in the United States (Trulson, Marquart, and Kawucha 2008). The theory being that the more diluted the gang is in a facility, the weaker it will become. The author has observed the advantages and disadvantages of this policy. While separating prisoners does alleviate the potential for gang dominance in a given facility, moving the inmates into other facilities gives gangs the opportunity to lay recruiting seeds in their new prisons, thus allowing the gang to proliferate on a grander state or national level.

In the case of the BA, something had to be done, but few lessons were learned. One practice that is implemented in El Salvador is creating entirely separate prisons for rival MS-13 and 18th Street gang members. Quezaltepeque and Ciudad Barrios prisons were designated for MS-13 prisoners, while Chalatenango and Cojutepeque were designated as Barrio 18 prisoners (Dudley and D'Aubuisson 2017). This strategy does little to mitigate intra-gang violence, however, which occurs regularly with those who violate gang rules or who attempt a violent leadership change.

For Ciudad Juárez, a city that was literally hemorrhaging from gang and DTO violence, the move of those four hundred inmates from the prison did nothing to stanch the violence behind the pale concrete walls of the facility.

The next major flashpoint occurred almost exactly three years later, at 7:00 a.m. on March 4, 2009, when fourteen BA, who were being escorted back to their cells following their conjugal visits, overtook the guard escorting them. Brandishing knives and other weapons, they jumped the guard and stole his keys, then opened cells freeing one hundred seventy of their fellow gang members who began a two-hour rampage against Mexicles and Doble As who were in a visiting area, many enjoying conjugal visits. The BA then beat their rivals with clubs, rifles they had somehow obtained, and other objects. Some victims were even thrown from the roof (Tuckman 2009).

"The external conflict is being transferred to inside the prisons," Enrique Torres, spokesman of the federal government's security operation in Ciudad Juárez told the Guardian newspaper. "Organized crime looks for any space it can fill" (Tuckman 2009).

As fires started by the BA burned throughout the facility, more than two hundred federal police and fifty soldiers with air support arrived at the prison. The violence was quelled within two hours.

A violent attempt by the BA to take control of the prison was repeated two years later, in July 2011. In this incident, prison officials were more complicit in the uprising.

Inexplicably, the BA were permitted to hold a large party that included teenage girls, one of whom spent the night in the jail with an inmate (Corcoran 2011). Officials were unsure as to the cause of the violence, but following the party, two armed members of the BA wearing white hooded sweatshirts were caught on surveillance cameras talking with three guards, who then left. The inmates then grabbed keys and opened a door (Ibarra 2011). Once the door was open, two men wearing masks armed with automatic weapons entered the frame of the video. They walked into the doorway and opened fire on the occupants, reloaded, and entered the room. When the smoke cleared, seventeen lay dead and twenty wounded, with 729 shell casings littering the floor. Among the dead would be Nicolás "El Nico" Frías Salas, the leader of the Doble A (Corchado and Kohcerga 2011).

The deplorable state of corrections in Mexico, where inmates were able to come and go as they pleased depending on what criminal organization they belonged to, came under scrutiny.

"Obviously, in the case of Ciudad Juárez, there are things that have to be cleared up. Fundamentally, as we have said, security at the state and local jails all across the country has to be reviewed and strengthened, and everything has to be done to avoid tragic events like the one we had there (in Ciudad Juárez)," said Federal Security Spokesman Alejandro Poire after the shooting (Ibarra 2011).

A week after the shooting Lucio Cuevas Sanchez, the prison director, was arrested on suspicion of illegal public service and of a crime committed within a prison. Also taken into custody were four guards who were charged with an array of offenses that included the corruption of minors, illegal public service, and alleged favoritism (*Albuquerque Journal* 2011b).

The general management of the facility has also come into question. The absence of either policy or adherence to a policy would prove deadly in August 2018, when BA and Doble As clashed in the hallway outside the medical department. Reportedly, one group was leaving while the other was entering, which should have immediately sent up a red flag. The clash left one dead and four wounded (Borunda 2018c). The murdered inmate was Azteca Daniel "El Pelon" Queen Calderón, who was implicated in another party massacre earlier in the month when eleven Doble As and Mexicles were killed in a dispute over crystal meth sales.

THE MICRO CERESO PRISON EXPERIENCE

When Jesús Ernesto Chávez Castillo was taken into custody by the military, he was taken to CERESO 3 prison in Ciudad Juárez. This location has a long history as a flashpoint for the city's gangs. Although the gangs occupy separate wings so that authorities can try to stem their violent clashes, the effort is futile. Fortunately or not, the military took Chávez-Castillo to their camp outside the prison, where he stayed for about two weeks. There he alleges he was tortured with beatings and electrical shocks.

Officials were hoping to get information on who was leading the BA and where the leader was located. He was surprised that they asked a separate line of questions regarding *Camello,* not realizing he was the same person. Following his stay at the camp, Chávez was transferred to the PGR—federal prosecutor's office—where he was charged for having fourteen kilos of cocaine in his truck and for an attempted escape—of course denying all of these accusations. While his case was pending, Chávez was sent to Unit 6 at the CERESO prison.

When he was placed in the unit, a gang member called high-ranking member Rafa Díaz on the outside to validate Chávez's membership in the BA.

"Rafa Díaz tell him that—that I was working with—with the BA outside."

His accusations of torture are supported by the fact that when he initially arrived in the BA unit, he was not required to do any "work" because he was so battered.

After a two-week recuperation Chávez began putting in his work, but because of the call from Rafa, he was treated with a higher level of respect.

"I don't have to work like everybody else. I receive, we can say, a check per week, because of Rafa tell them to do that," Chávez said. "He (Rafa) tell them because I was working hard outside, they give me a break, and so—and tell *Roñas* to give me a paycheck per week."

After about four months in the prison, when his predecessor and some other members were transferred out by the warden, Rafa Díaz would put Chávez in the vaunted leadership role of the prison. His primary duty was ensuring the flow of drugs continued into the prison. At the time this was around four ounces of heroin, five or six ounces of cocaine, and about a pound to a pound and a half of marijuana per week, making the gang forty-five to sixty-five thousand pesos every week. The system was simple, especially when officials' eyes were looking the other way because of bribes and threats. The members who snuck the drugs in also snuck the proceeds out.

There was retaliation planned against the warden because he was responsible for the transfer of the members out of CERESO. Chávez received information on the type of car the warden drove and passed it on to Rafa on the outside.

"I tell him at what time he get out. And then twenty-five minutes later, he called me again, and he tell me, 'Hide your radio, hide everything, the warden is done.'" The next time Chávez heard anything about the warden, his murder was being described on the news. Even inside the prison, inmates had access to cell phones and radios to communicate with the outside.

In a surprising display of entrepreneurship, Chávez also started a concrete-block business in the prison to generate seemingly legitimate revenue. This was extremely lucrative, given the expansive use of blocks in Ciudad Juárez for buildings and walls around virtually every property in the city. But there was more to the arrangement. Evidently he worked with the new warden by paying her 15,000 pesos a week. This allowed him unfettered visitors and sand for the brick business. There was also an ulterior motive for having sand delivered. Mixed in with the sand was beer and liquor, not only for personal use but for resale among inmates.

Through the new arrangement with the warden Chávez's visitors were no longer searched. That allowed them not only to sneak in drugs but also weapons. These were typically unassembled rifles that would be reassembled when needed. Chávez admitted deliveries also included bulletproof vests, 5.7 millimeters, M-1s, AR-15s, AKs, and grenades.

Chávez's lawyer, whose fees were covered by the gang, would prove the "cocaine" was actually marijuana when he inquired about the purity of the so-called evidence, which voided the initial cocaine charge. Mysteriously, after Chávez spent eight months in prison, all of his charges were dropped.

His story is just one of hundreds of tales of how broadly corruption spread throughout the Mexican prison system and how the gang used their positions to further the profit potential of the organization. Membership also grew as more gang members were deported from the US, many of whom would land in CERESO at some point in the future.

CHAPTER 5

Crossing the Line

I refer to the *line* as the literal border between the US and Mexico, as defined primarily by the Rio Grande River. The border line has historical relevance for local residents and law enforcement, who have seen generations of businesses sprouting in response to human and economic migration patterns, some lasting longer than others. There is also the figurative line separating criminal from non-criminal behavior and how the border has been exploited by criminal organizations smuggling contraband and humans into the US, and money, weapons, and even criminal suspects hoping to evade American law enforcement by heading south. It is a unique dynamic that has transcended generations.

The El Paso-Ciudad Juárez corridor has been one of the most contentious sectors for decades, attracting opium smugglers, outlaws, sex traffickers, bootleggers during Prohibition, then human smuggling and narcotics trafficking. It would not be unreasonable to assume that generations of family members utilized many of the same smuggling routes but for different commodities.

In 1993 US Border Patrol El Paso Sector Chief (later US Representative) Silvestre Reyes implemented an aggressive strategy that would thwart waves of illegal crossings into downtown El Paso. Operation Blockade, which eventually gave way to the softer Operation Hold the Line, resulted in stepped-up placement of agents, stadium-type lighting, and barriers in the immediate vicinity of downtown El Paso. This strategy put an agent every one hundred yards, resulting in a 72 percent drop in apprehensions. The strategy choked off the massive stream of individuals who stormed the border in the hope that sheer numbers would increase the chance that some would evade Border Patrol (Dowd 2013). This had little impact on the Barrio Azteca, however.

Between returning to the streets of El Paso or deportations back to Ciudad Juárez, the BA fell under what Felson (2006) describes as the influence of specific and tangible events, their specific sequences, and their specific settings. The tangible events coinicided with the growth of the Mexican DTOs; the settings were the mutual cross-border relationships members had through family and friends. The sequence of events can be described as the informal associations from previous criminal activities that led to more sophisticated networking with burgeoning DTOs amid escalating tensions over control of the lucrative El Paso-Ciudad Juárez plaza.

As the BA were establishing their rule over the drug trade on the El Paso side, their strategy of exploiting binational relations and circumstances likely required some strategic alterations on the part of the Vicente Carrillo Fuentes DTO (Juárez Cartel). With the criminal knowledge of border vulnerabilities on both sides, operatives were able to exploit and establish new trafficking routes, or *plazas*.

Immigration law would serve as the catalyst for these opportunities to gel. Immigration law has come under extreme scrutiny in recent years for its haphazard enforcement, and a lack of operational understanding even by lawmakers.

The US history of immigration laws dates back to the country's founding with the Naturalization Act of 1790. It is not just a contemporary issue: there have been catalytic waves of racism, xenophobia, and paranoia that have sparked laws. The first aggressive immigration law passed by Congress targeted the Chinese in 1882 with the signing of the Chinese Exclusion Act. "The Yellow Peril" was touted in the media and among politicians as the cause célèbre for limiting Chinese immigration. There was concern over the numbers entering the US to work on the railroad, their emerging cottage industries, and the introduction of opium into American communities. The Immigration and Naturalization Act of 1952 and its amended version in 1965 sought to incorporate equity into what country's citizens would be admitted into the US, and how many.

The Refugee Act of 1980 put an annual cap of fifty thousand on the growing number of refugees from around the world that were increasing due to regional conflicts that made life untenable.

The Immigration Control and Reform Act of 1986 was an attempt by the government to ensure the elimination of illegal immigrants in the workplace. This targeted employers, who had to ensure their workers were in the country legally and could prove it with valid documentation. This act has been dismally enforced over the years, especially in hospitality, farming, ranching, and other low-wage jobs that are not necessarily attractive to American citizens.

The flow of Mexicans across the border continued. The Bracero Program went into effect in 1942 through executive order by President Franklin D. Roosevelt as a means to meet labor demands during World War II. The Mexican Farm Labor Agreement would extend into 1964, well past the 1945 surrenders of Japan and Germany. The program would ultimately invite some five million workers from Mexico into the United States for low-wage jobs. This opened a floodgate of illegal immigration, prompting the US to launch a sweep of over one million illegal immigrants in Operation Wetback in 1953-1954.

The Immigration and Nationality Act 8 U.S. Code 1227 forms the basis for the removal of criminal aliens and has been in place for more than a century. This is the statute most frequently used in removal of gang members. Sections (A) and (B) of Criminal Offenses names such deportable offenses as aggravated felonies, narcotic convictions, drug use/abuse conviction, and firearms-related offenses.

These offenses are all potentially deportable acts. In most cases, the suspect will serve out his or her sentence in the United States and be handed over to Immigration and Customs Enforcement (ICE) Enforcement and Removal Operations for deportation from the US. Despite what is portrayed in the media, this is not an easy nor automatic process. It is now becoming even more complicated, given the existence of sanctuary cities, where municipalities will not place an ICE hold on inmates who have entered the US illegally without a judicial warrant.

A major infusion of deported gang members began around 1996, when the US aggressively pushed to deport criminal aliens who had completed their sentences (Dudley 2013).

El Salvador and Mexico were among the prime recipients of deported criminal aliens.

In 2010, Ciudad Juárez Mayor José Reyes Ferriz drew a stark corollary between US immigration policy and crime in his city. He estimated that 100,000 illegal immigrants from Mexico had been deported into Ciudad Juárez, with the expectation that they would filter back to their home regions. This wasn't always the case. The war between the DTOs was in full swing, and the potential to make more money with a criminal organization in Ciudad Juárez than with a legitimate job was attractive, especially to teens (Valencia 2010c).

"We did a study of the killings during an isolated period recently, and cross-referenced to the date we have of deportation," said Reyes. "We found that 10 percent of those killed in previous months from the time we made this study actually had been deported within the last two years from the US to Juarez" (Valencia 2010c).

It was US policy to deport thousands of gang members back to Mexico, where they could proliferate gangs such as the BA and Mexicles, or to Central America, where MS-13 and 18th Street gangs would prosper and essentially control their respective countries from the shadows.

Once imprisoned BA had served their sentences in the US, they were deported back to Mexico, usually to Ciudad Juárez, where they had established family and gang networks. The Ciudad Juárez faction of the gang would come to be known as Los Aztecas. Tapia (2019) contends that the early concentration of these members was situated in and around the Ciudad Juárez gang hotbed in Bello Vista Colonia, around 1990.

A tight operational communication network was established for gang members who were deported.

"One of the things is, when somebody get out from prison and they are going to be deported, they have to let—in that time, they have to let *Chino* Valles know that he was heading that way," said Jesús Ernesto Chávez Castillo in testimony at the Gallegos trial.

Two members who testified at the 2014 trial of Arturo Gallegos Castrellón in El Paso, Texas, were Gualberto Marquez and Chávez, both of whom painted one of the most vivid pictures of the membership dynamics of the BA, thus violating one of, if not the most vaunted rule: cooperating with law enforcement.

Marquez, who went by the nickname *Bird*, had a string of arrests beginning around 1992 that included charges of aggravated assault, falsifying his identity to police, and drug charges. He first joined the BA while in the Coffield Unit in 1996 under the auspices of his *padrino*, Manuel "El Grande" Fernandez. Upon his release from Coffield the following year, he was to report to *Tolon* Martinez, a capo, on Idalia Street in El Paso.

Once he hit the streets of El Paso Marquez immediately started selling drugs, primarily marijuana and cocaine. Unlike a typical street dealer, Marquez was more of a distributor, selling as much as one hundred pounds of marijuana and 350 to 500 kilograms of cocaine a month, brought into El Paso from Ciudad Juárez.

"In 2004, we received $11.8 million, and we were expecting some more, but it never showed up," Marquez says. "The operation extended all the way up to Chicago."

It was back to jail in 2004, when he was sentenced to the Smith Unit of the Texas Department of Criminal Justice. While far from the streets of El Paso, Marquez felt right at home with the eighty or so BA members incarcerated there.

Chávez, also referred to as *Camello Joroado,* is just one example of hundreds of BA members who have exploited the cross-border relationship. Chávez joined the organization in 2006. He first arrived in the United States from neighboring Ciudad Juárez when he was seventeen years old on a border crossing visa which he overstayed by some fifteen years. During that time he married an El Paso woman, thereby establishing residency but not citizenship.

His first arrest dealt with the sale and distribution of fifty pounds of marijuana. Although he briefly spent time in the El Paso County Jail, he ultimately received probation. Despite the quantity of drugs he had, Chávez was able to avoid deportation. It wouldn't be until a subsequent drunk driving conviction—on four counts of intoxicated assault with a deadly weapon (a car)—that he would be deported, but once again avoid prison time.

Like thousands of other deported criminals, Chávez turned right around and entered the United States illegally the same day he was deported. It wouldn't take long for him to be found by law enforcement, who charged him with illegal reentry into the United States. Ironically, it wasn't the possession of drugs or the drunken driving incident with injuries that put Chávez in prison; it was the federal immigration charge. He would spend three years at the minimum security federal penitentiary in the tiny town of Oakdale, Louisiana, with a population of less than ten thousand people, an area a little over five square miles, and a world away from the border.

This experience would mark a significant turning point in his life. He eventually gravitated toward the other El Paso inmates, who happened to be BA allegedly led by "Sleepy" Ramirez.

"I started associated with them, exercise with them. I live with some of these guys," he says. This opportunity was bred not only out of a local/

ethnic association but also the protection it afforded from other non-El Paso inmates. He would say there were many gangs in the penitentiary, and failure to associate would have consequences. "It is more easy to be a target. The other gangs—every single gang, they bully you and target you."

This draw to the BA served him well. He began "helping" them in their prison activities and was actually referred to as a gang helper, which is essentially the more formal designation of a *prospect-esquina*. As part of his initial duties Chávez would exploit the prison job he had working in the paint shop, where his activities transcended painting in the facility.

"When I take the (paint)cart, where I handle all the paint—we made shanks (jail-made knives made both with metal and with strong plastics as seen typically in meal trays), weapons, and we deliver it to the units where the BAs are."

His duties would also include smuggling contraband such as cigarettes, radios, and stamps, which could be sold at inflated prices to other inmates.

"I sell it and help the BA members with the [postage] stamps that I collect from the selling. Every week, we're supposed to give certain amount of stamps. As the prospects and the BA members, they have to give some stamps also."

Another popular unit for contraband was the Special Housing Unit. Correctional facilities around the United States are getting away from designating units as segregation units, opting for the softer and more compassionate Special Housing designation. These are used for disciplinary cases as well as high-profile cases or for inmates who need protection because of their charges. Informants are also typically housed in these units.

"Like sometimes I take that to the special housing unit or the gang unit where you do your program, supposedly, to get out from the gangs."

Chávez said he was able to smuggle shanks into both units on his paint car.

"I put it on the cart when I take my paint. So they register me, but they just look over the cart. Sometimes I hide those things inside the paint or under the cart."

Inmates in most correctional facilities around the country attempt to make homemade alcohol or *hooch* by fermenting fruit or potatoes. Chávez quickly became adept at creating this commodity as well.

The issue of drug sales behind prison walls is a bane for any facility and ultimately becomes a sophisticated game of cat and mouse between inmates and security officers. The BA were adept at exploiting this opportunity both for financial gain and for personal use, not only in Oakdale but virtually all facilities they were incarcerated in.

"They use certain type of drugs. Not all of them, but most of them do." Chávez said this is violation of a fundamental rule of not using drugs in prison. "Because when the people are on drugs, they don't know exactly what they're doing. They can be an easy target from another gangs."

During this period Chávez learned the major tenets of the gang, of which family is highly valued, in which a mutual protection circle of trusted associates is developed, even among those meting out violence.

In April 2005, with his release from prison and deportation to Matamoras imminent, Chávez said Sleepy Ramirez told him to go immediately to Ciudad Juárez as soon as he could. Rather than check in with the local BA, Chávez opted to find employment to get settled. He found a job with the prominent beer company Carta Blanca de Juárez, where he worked as a forklift operator. This was legitimate work, but Chávez was drawn to more lucrative criminal opportunities as well. He began stealing cars with friends, averaging anywhere from four to six vehicles a week. This went on for about a year until he was arrested and sentenced to the notorious CERESO prison, the site of numerous violent outbreaks between the BA and their rivals, the Artistas Asesinos. Because of this long and bloody history, BA were housed separately, where they enjoyed control of their part of the facility.

Chávez went straight to Unit Number Six, *El Templo*, the BA wing of the prison, where he quickly hooked up with a fellow gang member nicknamed "Cantinflas." The name is based on the famous Mexican comedian Mario Fortino Alfonso Moreno Reyes, who did skits as a drunkard.

In CERESO Cantinflas was selling three to four ounces of heroin a week, smuggled in from the outside by the man in charge of the wing. Chávez helped Cantinflas count the money, and eventually began selling heroin himself to a multitude of his own gang members as well as the general prison population. "All the inmates in there," he says when asked who his customers were.

Selling to fellow gang members who knew this was a direct violation of the rules put Chávez in a tenuous position. Gang members on the Mexican side were forbidden to use heroin. If caught, they would be given the opportunity at rehabilitation, but subsequent violations would prove fatal, for a cloudy mind had a negative impact on business and organizational security.

"Because I was a prospect. So they approach me to buy from me, and they tell me to shut up, don't say nothing."

This combination of productivity and discretion propelled Chávez's standing, with the endorsement of Cantinflas in the gang eventually earning his *huarachas*.

"Cantinflas talked to the guys that were in charge, and they talked to somebody outside, and put his word that I was going to be a BA member."

Chávez underwent the required background check both inside and outside the CERESO prison.

"Because when you became a member, they have to do a background check on your name to see if you're clean. 'Clean' means that you're not a sex offender or things like that. It come back okay."

With that, he was validated by a lieutenant named Tyson (likely a reference to boxer Mike Tyson) who was also housed at the time at CERESO. Entry for Chávez into the BA was somewhat anticlimactic, void of any formal or secret ceremony. It's a simple gathering with the newly initiated, the *padrino*, a leader, likely a lieutenant or capo, and witnesses. In his case there was Cantinflas and another member nicknamed *Mexico*.

As part of his initiation Chávez was asked a series of simple questions that carried a significant lifelong obligation. They asked why he wanted to join the gang, and was he sure. His answers were based on his desire for financial and physical security.

"Because I was already working a lot with them, so I was—I was thinking that I was going to make money like that too."

With his membership ensured, Chávez continued selling drugs throughout CERESO, with one caveat: now that he was officially in the gang, he abided by the rule of not selling drugs to members of the gang. Not only would he be held accountable for it, but the purchaser would be as well.

"Because I was a BA member now. So if I sell drugs to another BA, they're going to punish me, too, not only the one who buy the drugs."

Even behind prison walls, the drug trade was flourishing. Chávez employed lessons learned from Cantinflas. He would obtain large quantities of drugs, divide them into sellable doses, and sell within his growing network. Since these were drugs owned by the gang, Chávez obtained a percentage of sales averaging around six hundred to seven hundred pesos per week, which he would send to his wife on the outside.

Upon his release, it was expected that he would continue with his criminal enterprise. Tyson, his padrino, didn't make it to the outside. During one of many riots Tyson was fatally shot. As an homage, Chávez got a tattoo with Tyson's name.

Immediately after his release from CERESO, Chávez was instructed by Luis Rosales to report to "Margarito." Back out on the streets of Ciudad Juárez, Chávez got a known supporter of the gang to help locate Margarito.

"I met Manny Lam. He was a guy who brings the drugs inside the CERESO, and he was from the area where I grew up in Juárez. So I contacted him because he works for the BAs."

When he did hook up with Margarito, Chávez told him he was just released from CERESO and was looking for work. Doing his due diligence, Margarito checked with the incarcerated leadership, who confirmed Chávez's story. Chávez promptly started selling crack and powder cocaine in the La Chavena section of Ciudad Juárez, and fellow gang member Borrego found him a place to live.

Averaging the same six hundred to seven hundred pesos a week he was making in CERESO, Chávez accepted his role as a recently admitted soldier. Chávez's life and standing in the gang would soon take a turn when he committed the first murder he could recall committing for Margarito.

"I was cleaning the territory for Margarito. Like, he wants to expand his sales. And we got—we get into it with these guys, and we kill—we hit them with the baseball bats and knives. We kill them like that." These duties quickly increased in number. "Sometimes it was only two persons. And I remember one time, it was up to six, seven persons."

This cold-blooded behavior was explained in vivid detail, and such incidents happen with greater regularity in Ciudad Juárez than the general public on either side of the border realizes. Chávez said his weapon of choice was a baseball bat that he used to beat his victims to death. His accompanying gang members might have guns and knives.

Margarito would send them to an alleged competing drug house. "So we got into the house, and whoever was in there, we kill them."

The victim's alleged indiscretion was selling drugs in Margarito's territory.

"He wants to have control of his territory, full control." Chávez elaborated as to what "cleaning the area" meant. "Make sure that nobody else is selling drugs, just Margarito or the people that Margarito put to sell the drugs."

In addition to these duties, Chávez was also used to conduct surveillance in the area surrounding the gang's *tiendas*—"drug stores"—essentially neighborhood houses they sold drugs out of. In a city with numerous potential competitors it was important to observe suspected rivals planning on raiding the store or chicanery among the gang members running the store.

"I was in one corner watching if the police or somebody else, you know, that look suspicious come into the store or whatever that sells the drugs."

It's not known whether he received permission or was doing it surreptitiously, but Chávez was also selling drugs for Borrego at the same time he worked for Margarito.

"In the morning, I sell for Margarito. In the night, I sell for Borrego."

Eventually Chávez would have an opportunity to meet the gang's leadership at a "church" meeting at a ranch on the outskirts of the city. This was a big moment in the burgeoning gang member's career but could be nerve-wracking, to say the least.

"Church" is the gang's code for meetings which could be large or small but in either case were mandatory. This particular meeting, which Margarito told Chávez he needed to attend, was for the leadership to meet the newest ten members, Chávez included. As Chávez rode in a twenty-vehicle caravan with four or five people in each vehicle, the importance of the meeting was clear.

Once at the location, Chávez observed a gray Jeep Liberty with tinted windows pull up. Cantinflas, recently released from CERESO himself, turned to him and said it was *Tablas* and the other leaders. *Tablas* was Eduardo Ravelo, who would be on the FBI's Ten Most Wanted list until his arrest in Mexico in 2018. Ravelo was the alleged leader of the gang's Ciudad Juárez faction.

The other lieutenants who emerged from the vehicle that day were Luis Mendez; Arturo Gallegos Castrellón, who would go by aliases such as Tury, Farmero, Benny, Guero, Manon, and 51; and Boots. With their arrival, the meeting came to order as the aroma of carne asada being cooked by a team of veteran gang members wafted in the air.

The new members lined up and began introducing themselves to the four leaders. That's when Chávez's excitement likely turned to abject panic, which he struggled to outwardly repress.

"I gave them my name, my nickname, and who my padrino (Tyson) was," Chávez says.

The response Tablas had was incredulous.

"Tablas say that Tyson, he cannot give me my—I cannot be an associate—a member because Tyson didn't have the power to do it at that time."

Tablas promptly pulled Chávez aside and had two gang members guard him. Chávez knew how serious the situation had become, with no apparent validation of his membership or reason to be at this vaunted meeting. Was he an infiltrator from an opposing gang? Or worse, law enforcement? He had no idea what was running through Tablas's mind.

"I thought that they were going to kill me. They were carrying guns, and I know what leaders—I hear already by that time what the leaders do to people like that, who try to fake that they're members."

As dangerous as it was, Chávez knew that people stupidly faked membership, perhaps for a brief moment of street credibility, intimidation, or profit. The end result was always the same: death. But despite the administrative snafu, Chávez knew he was legitimate because of all of the work he already put in for the gang. This did little to assuage his tension. Tablas was brandishing an AK-47, and the other leaders were carrying handguns in their pant waists.

Chávez's issue would wait for what seemed like an eternity, until the relatively short line of new members made their introductions. It was then that he received something of a reprieve. His former leader at CERESO, Luis Rosales, was there and vouched for him.

"He talked to Tablas, and he told him—he explained why Tyson was my padrino, because at that time there was no lieutenant in the CERESO."

Tablas was satisfied with the explanation given to him by Rosales.

"I feel better. I feel that it was not going to be my last day. I went with the rest. They were drinking beer. I drink a beer."

The leaders then called the meeting to order and stood in the middle as the others gathered around. Tablas said there were going to be quick response teams formed to pick people up. At first Chávez didn't know what this meant.

"I knew that it was—like it was a quick response, just in case they need something, like go and kill somebody or helping in something, deposit money, whatever they need."

Tury and Alberto Núñez Payan, whose aliases included Fresa, Fresca, and 97, began picking team members. Tury selected the newly reprieved and formally accepted Chávez.

"I feel all right. I thought that it was going to be a good thing."

Despite the close call, Tury handpicked Chávez.

"When he picked me up, he—he just—he look at me and he told me, 'I want this *vaquerito* with me.'" That means "this cowboy with me."

Chávez had actually known Fresa from his childhood, both attending the junior high school *Secundaria Catedral de Juarez*.

The leadership stayed at the meeting about another thirty to forty minutes, then left the teams to do their bidding. Before officially hitting the streets, the newer team members were required to undergo a training period of about two to three weeks. A key component was their response time when Fresa called, since hits may not always be intricately organized. Sometimes they arise when an issue needs to be dealt with immediately. The expected response time to Fresa's "office" was less than five minutes.

"So whenever they need us, we can go and—that was the purpose of the first response teams, to go and kill people."

The primary targets were members of the Mexicles and Doble A— Artistas Asesinos (Artist Assassins), both of which supplied street soldiers for the Sinaloa Cartel. Even at CERESO, where there have been multiple homicides and uprisings, these groups are separated from the BA.

Upon completion of the training the new recruits were given a vehicle and a weapon. Rafa Díaz, one of the lieutenants who was essentially the leader at the time, gave Chávez a chrome 9 mm Beretta with an ivory grip.

Chávez would go on to continue his murder spree at the behest of the gang. There were no boundaries to his or their depravity. He admitted to having killed two men in front of their wives, who cried and screamed from the house as Chávez hit them in the head with a baseball bat some fifteen times, a number he couldn't recall, while another member repeatedly stabbed their prey.

When it was all over the bodies were left battered and mutilated, the victims' wives cowering in the house, fearful of coming out.

Ernesto Padilla had also been picked to be on the team with Chávez. Despite being committed to their duties, the team essentially fizzled out due to lack of work.

"We don't need a team like that to go and persecute gang members."

Chávez was reassigned to the downtown area to work under *Cosas*, where the pay was better than what he had been earning under Margarito and Borrego. Now he only had to work during the days, earning around a thousand pesos a week ensuring that drug and prostitution enterprises were running smoothly and that there were no competitive incursions.

"I make sure that the prostitutes don't steal from the customers or they don't have to call the police and bring the heat to the area. The deal is, they (prostitutes) can work in the area. Nobody bother them. Nobody bother the prostitutes, but they have to buy the drugs and alcohol from the BA members."

He was unequivocal in stating that anyone caught selling drugs that were not authorized by the crew would be killed. Period. This contributed to an unparalleled homicide rate at the time, as the Sinaloa DTO led by Joaquín "El Chapo (Shorty)" Guzmán Loera brazenly attempted to wrest the plaza away from the Vicente Carrillo Fuentes DTO. Violators of lesser infractions would receive a baseball bat-wielded "beat-down."

The downtown Ciudad Juárez drug market of marijuana, crack cocaine, cocaine, and heroin was flourishing, and it was up to the *Cosas* crew to ensure that gang members were not harassed by police and were resupplied to meet sales demands.

Opportunities arose faster than he could have realized, and when Chávez saw that the new job, while paying better than what he had earned before, still was not where he wanted to be. He jumped at the opportunity to be the right-hand man of Jesús Alfredo Martinez Mendoza, whose aliases were *El Ferro* and *El Freddy*, the *jefe de grupos*. Freddy was in charge of all the groups in the gang. Members were grouped according to where the Azteca members lived, so each group was from a particular area. Chávez estimated there were between twelve and thirteen teams. The leader of each reported to Freddy. This was a significant jump in Chávez's career.

"He just picked me up because I was—I was ready all the time. I believe that's why."

The job expectations were more demanding than he had ever had in the gang. He was not only ensuring street security but the behavior of his fellow gang members—an area that had to be strictly enforced because of the unwanted attention irrational behavior could draw to the gang.

"If you let them do drugs, they're just going to be lost. They're not going to be there whenever they need it, or they're going to start doing crazy things, like stealing. And it's—it's—part part of the—of the rules." One thing that had to be quelled was any drug use within the ranks. It happened regularly but was not condoned.

Being in a high position of responsibility, Chávez saw firsthand the income potential he had before him but had yet to reap because of his standing. Now, he felt, was the right time to ask permission for his own drug "store," where he would have much more autonomy. He approached Rafa Díaz and asked if there were any available areas in Ciudad Juárez to open his own store.

Ironically, the way the gang divided its stores was based on designated police districts such as Aldama, Babicoa, Benito Juarez, Chihuahua, Cuahtemoc, and Delicias. After speaking to Tablero, the leadership determined that Chávez could have the area around Rancho Anapra. This is an extremely poor and violent area directly across the border from Sunland Park, New Mexico.

"So they tell me that if I cleaned Rancho Anapra and put order over there, I can take over."

And take over he did. "The first thing, I got my gun. I got my baseball bat. And I went and I start getting all the people—or knowing where the people that they were selling drugs over there in Rancho Anapra and to see for who they work."

For some two months Chávez did his due diligence on the area. The current store was run by a man nicknamed "El Alacran," whom Chávez met in CERESO.

"So I went with him, and he's the one who helped me. Then we went to the addicts, the drug addicts, and we start asking who is the one who sell."

Within about two weeks the store was established and earning money. He asked Freddy for his own team, and Freddy confirmed with Rafa. Chávez's team of seven would go into Anapra to tax every one of the six or seven stores in the town.

"Everybody was armed. So we went to the places where they are selling drugs. And we get into the places, got the drugs, the money, and tell the people that if they want to sell drugs, that they are supposed to buy it from me and don't work for nobody else."

Acquisition of the Rancho Anapra store was relatively quick but required Chávez and his newly established team to demonstrate their seriousness in taking over the small area, which included about seven stores. A concerted strategy of hitting all of the stores simultaneously was planned to prevent any warnings going out.

With guns and baseball bats at the ready, Chávez and his team hit the local operators swiftly and violently. This strategy proved successful, with the majority of stores relinquishing control to Chávez, except for one man who was the supplier for more than half the stores.

"I get into a little fight with him—not fight, but—we got into a shootouts," Chávez said. These shootouts were repeated three more times over the course of a month.

The conclusion of the business dispute set a brutal tone for any further competition.

"I kill part of his family. I kill his brother in one of the shootouts. And one time, I went to the house that he is supposed to live, and a person was there. And it end up that it was his uncle." Chávez and his partners put about fifteen bullets into the man.

With his store established and drugs fronted him by gang leaders, Chávez went on to flood Rancho Anapra with cocaine, marijuana, and crack cocaine. Rafa kicked in a pound of marijuana and Tury gave him two ounces of cocaine to launch the enterprise. It wasn't a donation. Payment was fully expected upon sale of the product.

This new position of responsibility provided Chávez with greater insight into the gang's narcotics trafficking from Mexico into the United States.

"Freddy told me that whatever drugs come to the United States, it was from the leaders. About that time, I knew that Rafa Díaz was the one that was handling the heroin, and Tury and Mendez, they were in charge of marijuana and coke."

Eventually Chávez was asked to participate in trafficking drugs over the border.

"Mendez asked me to help another person nicknamed Zorro to help him smuggle—he was going to tell me how and from where to smuggle the drugs to the United States."

Vaguely familiar with Zorro from a few meetings, Chávez did know he spent a lot of time in El Paso.

"I believe—well, this is what I hear, that he was sending back—he was taking back money, and he would make sure that everything—all the drugs got distributed here in El Paso."

One reality of the border is that not only do the narcos control the drugs crossing north but also do the majority of human smuggling and trafficking. Both are lucrative collateral revenue streams for the organizations. Chávez would come to learn that Zorro was also involved in smuggling aliens across the border, and he made an alliance with him. As a cover, Zorro had a busing business in Ciudad Juarez called *bruteras*.

The drug smuggling operation is one played out virtually the same way thousands of times across the border.

"He was crossing the Rio Grande. He sent people with backpacks to the Rio Grande, and then get into the canal on the Anapra side."

The people, mostly men, with the backpacks were not full-fledged gang members. They were the most expendable prospects or people who wanted to make a few hundred dollars, usually local teenagers. Occasionally Zorro would take the illegal aliens on the journey into Sunland Park, New Mexico, and surrounding remote areas. There was a strategic element to this concept.

"A couple of times that he send the illegals for one side, so they can—the Border Patrol go to one side and [this opens] the other one, so they can cross the drugs."

The relationship with Zorro was short-lived. Chávez would only participate in five operations with him because of expanding responsibilities within the gang.

"I was—I have a lot with Freddy as a jefe de grupos, and I was busy with the response teams and in Anapra."

In 2007 these responsibilities would greatly expand with the incursion of the Sinaloa DTO into Ciudad Juárez and a declaration of war against all cartels by the newly elected president, Felipe Calderón.

On December 11, 2006, the newly elected president from the Partido Accion Nacional announced his administration would take the drug trafficking organizations head-on with a full-scale military operation that would result in the deployment of forty-five thousand troops and five thousand federal police to eighteen states (Jimenez 2010), including Chihuahua and most specially Ciudad Juárez, where armed vehicles with heavy machine guns patrolled the streets and sandbagged or dirt-filled tire checkpoints were established around the city. One of these was near the entrance to Rancho Anapra.

Five years later and tens of thousands of dead in his country, Calderón would admit he was somewhat naïve in his strategy. He admitted he had little comprehension of the breadth and grasp the drug trafficking organizations had on his country.

"The cancer was there, and as we confront it, we see the dimension it has," he would admit (*The Cartel War* 2011). Then as he saw the carnage unfolding in a city such as Ciudad Juárez, which would eventually be designated the "Murder Capital of the World," Calderón, who still had two years left in his administration, said, "To me, this will be a very long and bloody war. It will implicate lots of time, money and unfortunately, human lives" (*The Cartel War* 2011).

Contributing to this carnage were the eight hundred murders Chávez admitted he was responsible for between January and August 2009 alone. Comparing the 2009 Ciudad Juárez homicide rate of 2,754, Chávez's nine-month total of eight hundred represents close to a third of all these murders. Since he stopped counting, that number was likely higher.

ALL IN THE FAMILY

Fernando Carrillo, a nephew in the hierarchy of the Vicente Carrillo Fuentes Organization, would join the BA while incarcerated in the US.

"Two of my uncles are relatives to the main guy, Vicente Carrillo Fuentes," he would explain to authorities.

After he was released from prison in the US, he too was deported back to Ciudad Juárez, where his first obligation was not his family but to report to gang leadership there. The first person he would report to was *Fresa*, whom he met in prison and who was also deported. His early impression of the gang was unimpressive.

"It was like a prison gang, not a big deal. It wasn't organized like the way it is right now."

As a result, he gravitated more toward work with La Línea, because it was better organized than what he observed among the BA. He felt, perhaps because of what he was exposed to growing up, that the BA were not truly organized crime. At the time La Línea, which had a closer relationship to his uncle's operations, was required to have a tighter management system.

It didn't take long for Carrillo to start moving drugs for La Línea. He started trafficking cocaine and took in around five thousand dollars a week. It is unclear whether La Línea authorized it or not, but Carrillo started smuggling large quantities of marijuana on the side. This was short-lived. After ten months, in 2006, Carrillo arrogantly went deeper into the US, finally getting arrested in Oklahoma en route to Memphis, Tennessee, with two hundred pounds of marijuana. This venture was not for the cartel but his personal gain.

Carrillo pleaded guilty and was sentenced to thirty-seven months in prison, which took him on a whirlwind journey of transfers through the Texas correctional facilities in Fort Worth, then Bastrop, then back to his old stomping ground in Pecos. All of these moves required him to check in with the reigning BA members, who checked his background both internally and externally, despite Carrillo's pedigree. This process is required of all members when re-entering the system.

"Well, if you got a rank over there, he can check all your background with your name. And if we don't have a rank over there, we've got to send your name out to a rank and he can check you out."

After being cleared through his association with his padrino Tolon, Carrillo went right to work for the gang. He readily admitted to inmate assaults on behalf of the gang, violence being the means to prison dominance.

After serving out his sentence, Carrillo was deported again back to Mexico, where he was surprised at the changes that Ciudad Juárez had undergone during his absence. The war between the VCF and Sinaloa organizations was raging, and there was an escalated alliance between the BA and La Línea. The prison leadership was well aware of the escalating violence on the streets of Ciudad Juárez and attempted to brief the soon-to-be-released members with what to expect when they returned to Mexico.

"Well, we got to know about everything. Actually, before I got out, they let us know what was going on everywhere. They gave us a phone number or some people who we need to get in touch with them."

With a sense of déjà vu, Carrillo reported to Fresa, and the leadership on the streets once again had to validate his credibility as a member. It was up to Chino Valles to conduct Carrillo's background check. Essentially a telephone interview, with probing and nerve-wracking questions, was conducted.

"Where I was coming from, how much time I did, if I was clean. There was—they were going to check my background. And if I came out dirty, I'm going to be up to some kind of disciplinary action."

Once his background check came back clear and no disciplinary action was to be taken, Fresa briefed Carrillo on the status of the situation in Ciudad Juárez. It was 2006; President Felipe Calderón had declared his war on the drug trafficking organizations, and El Chapo Guzmán's organization had endeavored a violent takeover of the Juárez Plaza into the US.

"We are at war right now. We're helping out the Juárez Drug Cartel. We got to watch out for enemies and government looking for us. People who has tattoos got to be covered up," Fresa told Carrillo. The purpose of covering the much-vaunted tattoos was to better conceal themselves from both law enforcement and their rivals to avoid becoming unneccesary walking targets. It was made clear to Carrillo that they were "just doing the dirty work for La Línea."

The purpose of the war in the corridor was clear. "It was a major port of traffic to smuggle drugs into the United States," says Carrillo.

An important figure in the Juárez organization was Jota Ele, who was the cartel manager of Ciudad Juárez. Carrillo knew Jota Ele because he hung out at a Ciudad Juárez bar his cousin owned. One day Jota Ele had nonchalantly asked about Carrillo, who was in prison at the time. When he returned to Ciudad Juárez after his deportation, Carrillo met up with the inquiring leader.

The meeting occurred at a ranch on the outskirts of the city. Jota Ele was there along with members of his crew and some Azteca members such as Camello, a hit-squad leader; Rafa Norte, a lieutenant; and Tablas, whom he knew as a capo. Carrillo was surprised that Jota Ele didn't realize he was a member of the BA and tried to introduce him to people he already knew. This was embarrassing to his host but also perplexing. Once this faux pas passed, the participants sat down to business, but strangely, Jota Ele asked Carrillo to go to another room while the members talked.

"Well, Jota Ele told Tablas—like, he don't want him to put me on the hit squads and get more heat than the one I have already, because I just barely got out from prison. They don't want me to be in some kind of danger. He just spoke to them."

Tablas was incredulous at this instruction but acquiesced.

"I spoke to Tablas like three days later," says Carrillo. "He asked me first how did I know about Jota Ele."

Carrillo told Tablas that he used to work with him in the past. He went on to say that Jota Ele wanted to take over. Tablas attempted to manipulate the conversation because Carrillo was close to Jota Ele, and perhaps he would help him "take him (Jota Ele) out of the game."

"No, I don't want to be in that position. I told him, if he's not real connected on the top—the top boss in the Juárez Drug Cartel, they are going to send some people to kill him up," replied Carrillo.

When he returned to Ciudad Juárez, Carrillo was acquainted with prevailing hierarchy. He knew Tablas was a capo. Chino was a sergeant. And then there was "Farmero," one of many aliases used by Arturo Gallegos Castrellón. It was well known that Farmero was a lieutenant in charge of the gang's main squads in Ciudad Juárez.

He described how the main source of communication, almost for rapid response, was handheld radios, a standard piece of equipment for nearly all leaders and most soldiers. They would dial in a frequency and would use codes rather than their real names. This was designed to shroud the gang's primary mission, which was to kill opponents of the gang and the Vicente

Carrillo Fuentes Organization. Carrillo did admit that other activities included extortion, money laundering, and collecting and enforcing the *cuota*.

It wasn't long after that Carrillo returned illegally to El Paso where his wife, a US citizen, was living. Upon his arrival back in El Paso, Carrillo promptly reported to "Flaco," a leader of a crew in El Paso's Lower Valley. While in El Paso Carrillo kept in touch by radio with Fresa, who was still across the border. In one conversation the two expressed concern over Gallegos, whom Carrillo had never actually met but had seen. It wouldn't be until Gallegos's trial that the two would come face to face with Gallegos and point him out from the witness stand.

"This guy is getting crazy. He's been killing a lot of people, and it's heating up," Fresa told Carrillo.

Heating up was an understatement for what was brewing in Ciudad Juárez.

CHAPTER 6

Deadly Marriage

The use of street, prison, even outlaw motorcycle gangs as proxies by sophisticated criminal organizations such as Mexico's drug trafficking organizations is not unusual. Proxies can be used to insulate the main organization from criminal culpability while still reaping the financial rewards of the enterprise. They can also serve effectively as cannon fodder in fights for territory or to exert retribution when the occasions arise to protect core leadership from law enforcement and adversaries. These "soldiers" are seen as valuable in accomplishing the mission of the organization but are nonetheless expendable, since typically there are many willing to take their places in the hopes of moving up the lucrative criminal ladder.

For the Vicente "El Viceroy" Carrillo Fuentes DTO, their front-line surrogate would be La Línea, whereas Gente Nueva, with the Sinaloa DTO, was their rival. Through the machinations of Ángel Félix Gallardo and the shutdown of Columbian cocaine routes in the Carribean by the US Coast Guard and US Customs Service, predecessor to US Customs and Border Protection, Mexican narcotics trafficking blossomed, setting up the perfect situation for the Barrio Azteca to gain a foothold in this lucrative enterprise.

Amado Carrillo Fuentes obtained the Juárez Plaza by killing Rafael Aguilar. Carrillo had proven his worth largely for his dedication to Miguel Ángel Félix Gallardo and his ability to move massive loads of drugs into the US with his mini air force, garnering him the sobriquet *El Senor de los Cielos*—Lord of the Skies (InSight Crime 2017b).

In 1997 Carrillo, facing mounting pressure from both US and Mexican law enforcement, underwent unsuccessful plastic surgery that left him dead on the table. The organization was then taken over by Amado's brother, Vicente, giving the drug trafficking organization its more contemporary name: Vicente Carrillo Fuentes (VCF) Organization (InSight Crime 2017b).

The ever-expanding operation required a close and trusted association with a more grassroots level organization. This is when the VCF turned to La Línea.

La Línea, led by Juan "JL" Pablo Ledezma, had an ignominious beginning in former officers from the Juárez Municipal Police Department who saw a much more lucrative source of income in the local drug trade. It would not be long before a formal alliance as street enforcers was established (*Reuters* 2010).

While deported BA flooded the streets of Ciudad Juárez, leadership of La Línea siezed an opportunity that would further benefit them in the eyes of VCF. In 2000 the two organizations united to further insulate VCF and bolster the plaza for trafficking cocaine and heroin (*Milenio* 2019).

At a time when the Mexican cartels were superior to the Colombian cartels, who were successfully suppressed but not completely eradicated with that country's increased utilization of American resources, the BA expansion into the cartel strata was fortuitous and timely. With the death of Pablo Escobar on December 2, 1993, the Mexican cartels quickly saw their fortunes change for the better. In order to enhance their markets they needed distribution networks and security staff. Being from the El Paso-Ciudad Juárez corridor was a natural opportunity for the BA, whose strong familial and criminal ties on both sides of the border had them crossing the border on a regular basis.

The initial organizational framework in Juárez was surprisingly ambiguous for the BA. The Guadalajara Cartel was rebranded as the Sinaloa Federation, and up until 2004 El Chapo and VCF operated under its umbrella. That is until the two had a violent falling out causing support groups like the BA to choose sides. By 2008, the gang switched allegiances exclusively to VCF (Burton and West 2008). Open source literature is scant when it comes to information on the era when the BA worked with the Sinaloa Federation. It is not unreasonable to contend that during this era the BA actually contributed to El Chapo establishing a foothold in Ciudad Juárez, only to fight against them come late 2008.

During the months of the Calderón initiative, the bodies began piling up on the streets of Ciudad Juárez, and the military was impotent in stanching the flow of blood. The Sinaloa DTO and its soldiers in the Gente Nueva mounted an aggressive offensive throughout the city and the smaller villages in the Valley of Juárez. La Línea was in dire need of tactical support. Growing up, living in, and even being incarcerated in Ciudad Juárez, the BA and everybody else in the city's underworld knew that La Línea's violence would be led by José Antonio Acosta Hernández, who also went by the nickname "El Diego."

For the street soldiers of the BA, the announcement of the alignment with La Línea in 2008 was logical.

"I hear Tury on the radio one time, saying that everybody now is going to be—is going to consider as La Línea. All the BAs that they were working—they were able to go and kill people and help La Línea to the war to the Sinaloa Cartel," Chávez said during the Gallegos trial.

The announcement validated the gang's alignment with the Vicente Carrillo Fuentes Organization. It was expected this would be mutually beneficial. There were already close ties being established because this was the organization the gang essentially purchased bulk orders of narcotics from. But clear sales delineations were established.

"We were supposed to give up all the sales of crack cocaine and powder cocaine to people of La Línea. And the BAs, it will be able to sell only heroin and marijuana and pills. They give us certain time to get rid of whatever we have, a week, ten days. And after that, only La Línea was going to sell crack cocaine and cocaine powder," Chávez recounted.

There was one major drawback to this arrangement: La Línea had very little experience in processing and moving cocaine. The BA would cook the crack cocaine and make the doses of the powder cocaine for La Línea, but would not be involved in the sales.

With this changed affiliation, the BA were set loose on the streets of Ciudad Juárez. Murders came fast and furious. As previously noted, Chávez estimated that by 2009 he was responsible for more than eight hundred murders, and eventually he stopped counting. He was told by leadership that they required him to kill eight people per day to send a stronger message to their rivals.

"I tell them that it was too many. And Rafa told me that if I put each group to kill one, it was going to be more than eight. I received a call from Farmero and then Rafa, telling me that I was supposed to follow those orders, that they were Tablero's orders."

This activity has escaped any real scrutiny in the American press. There is a legacy of Americans ignoring compelling crises such as this in Mexico or linking it to issues directly affecting American public health and safety.

These murders, often just across the border bridges, drew little attention. The El Paso and Ciudad Juárez media are the only ones who extensively report and analyze these issues. Farther north, people argue that this kind of violence does not affect them. In reality it does.

In a budding alliance between the fledgling Zeta DTO and the more established VCF, the BA were receiving professional, efficient, and deadly training from the Zetas at a camp in Torreon, Coahuila, Mexico.

In 2009 Chávez was ordered by Farmero to increase the efficiency of the killing by sending fifteen of his soldiers to train with Los Zetas in Torreon, Coahuila. Los Zetas was composed of defectors from the Mexican Special Forces known as Grupos Aeromóviles de Fuerzas Especiales (GAFE). This unit was trained at the School of the Americas by American Special Forces at Fort Benning, Georgia (El Parece 2020), for the specific purpose of thwarting the cartels under President Ernesto Zedillo as well as the insurgents in the Zapatista uprising in the mid-1990s.

The training the BA would receive included how to use AK-47s, how to throw hand grenades, and how to kill somebody in a moving vehicle (*El Diario* 2014). This training would have dire consequences in the very near future. After Los Zetas successfully trained the one group, Chávez sent a second, but ended it there.

"The Zetas want to keep all the members over there, and that's what the second group told me when they come back, that they don't want to let those BA members go, that they want to stay over there with the Zetas and fight with the Zetas."

The evolution of these special forces soldiers to cartel security and then to a free-standing cartel occurred in a relatively short time for the Zetas. In 1997 the Gulf Cartel led by Osiel Cárdenas Guillén required increased security forces as it expanded its control of the narcotics trade in eastern Mexico. Rather than follow the model of most other DTOs, which recruited poorly trained and undisciplined street gangs, he went for the cream of the crop and approached members of GAFE through his personal bodyguard Arturo Guzmán Decena (Logan 2012). Initially, thirty chose the DTO over government service and created Los Zetas (Zeta simply referring to the letter Z in Mexican military radio code). Guzmán would assume leadership of what would be the first actual specialized military group working with a DTO.

Tamaulipas state would be the main area of operation for the Zetas, but their sphere of influence would steadily increase. Their sophistication in weaponry, intelligence, counterintelligence, and communications was unparralled. So was their efficiency in killing.

By 2010 their relationship had all but ended with the Gulf DTO, and the Zetas would establish their own DTO, challenging their former bosses for control of the region.

Heriberto "The Executioner" "Z3" Lazcano, a former GAFE commander, was debonair but ruthless, resembling a character from a *telenovela*. He would now assume control of the organization. To further bolster his security forces he recruited members of the notorious Guatemalan special forces—Kaibiles, all of whom were also trained by US Special Forces. Lazcano would be killed in a firefight with government forces in October 2012 (InSight Crime 2016).

The BA and La Línea became very adept at torture and dismemberment, with the intention of leaving messages for their rivals and even law enforcement, who were not immune to the same consequences. A typical example of eliciting information and disposing of the source in the most macabre fashion occurred one day when Chávez received a call from Farmero to meet him at the El Toro Quintaco restaurant next to the Parque Central. When Chávez arrived, he parked his burgundy-colored four-door Ford F150 behind Farmero's truck, which was the same model save for its pearl-white color. One desirable material item among cartel-related criminals is a high-end, well-accessorized pickup. These two vehicles likely stood out amidst the beat-up vehicles that were usually found on downtown streets.

The target was abducted and left in the hands of Chávez, who was told by Farmero to take the victim somewhere and interrogate him. Chávez took the restrained man to one of the gang's downtown Ciudad Juárez houses, about a ten-minute drive away from the restaurant. As soon as Chávez arrived he took the man from the bed of the pickup and brought him into the house. There Chávez and another gang member, Caudillo, immediately started beating him, first with hands and feet. Chávez asked for a baseball bat, his weapon of choice in these circumstances, and was given one by an *esquina* standing watch outside the house.

The victim endured this punishment for about an hour until the desired information was elicited and passed on to Farmero, who was not satisfied with the fulsomeness of the victim's answers.

"Every time that I call him and tell him what information that I have, he tell me to ask him for more. He was on the phone with me, and he's telling me, 'Ask him about this, ask him about this other person, about a dude named Wallace.'" This exchange was repeated two or three times.

When Chávez heard from Farmero that he was finally satisfied with the man's answers, he ordered Chávez to kill him.

"He told me to kill him, to decapitate him and put a message. And he told me—I asked him where does he want the body. He told me, 'Surprise me.'" Chávez and his crew decapitated the man and amputated his hands.

These homicides are typically designed to send a message to Farmero's rivals. Chávez put the body in the back of a Transito (Traffic) Police station in downtown Ciudad Juárez.

"I put him in a position like he was sitting up with—with the message on the floor, the head on top of the message, and his right hand on top of his [decapitated] head."

The macabre scene was punctuated by the blood-soaked message. "It say that that's what's going to happen to all the people who help the rival cartel and *Chapo*." The letter was not signed by the BA but La Línea, acknowledging their place in the expanding narco war.

To maintain stringent lines of communication, the gang established a sophisticated communications network using cell phones and handheld radios with multiple frequencies. Chávez said he eventually would have a Kenwood radio, a Nextel radio, and as many as three phones.

"I have like the Nextel, I have it for the jefe de grupos and direct with Farmero. Or the radio that we have with attack teams and they are with the leaders and La Línea. We just change the frequency button to the next frequency, and it was a frequency for La Línea."

The relationship with La Línea would have its challenges. Facing mounting market pressures to distribute cocaine, the BA were pressed immediately into service in a sophisticated network of cocaine processing sites throughout Ciudad Juárez.

MAQUILADORAS

Maquiladoras formed the foundation of Ciudad Juárez growth in the early 1990s. With the passage of the North American Free Trade Agreement (NAFTA), factories began popping up all over the city as international corporations sought cheap Mexican labor. Low pay and long hours, usually involving female laborers, also coincided with the savage murder of hundreds of women that brought unwelcome attention to the city as it attempted to attract businesses as well as workers from the southern part of the country. There are more than three hundred maquilas in the city, employing some quarter million workers, mostly women.

In interviews I had with the previous Ciudad Juárez Mayor Héctor Murguía, the city was ill-prepared to absorb and service this population explosion. He argued there was little infrastructure and few social and educational services available to the new residents. This contributed to many young people turning to drug trafficking organizations.

La Línea and the BA exploited this perfect storm by establishing maquilas of their own that produced more nefarious products.

Much to his dissatisfaction, Chávez was ordered by Ernesto Padilla, also a member of the quick response teams, to work with La Línea on crack production. This involved the establishment of houses, which they called maquilas, where the powdered cocaine was cooked into crack. These large houses in upscale neighborhoods of Ciudad Juárez became efficient labs. Cocaine was delivered by Padilla, quickly processed, then put on the streets for sale. An average of ten BA members would work three-day shifts in the maquilas. Very few people in these upscale neighborhoods had tattoos or looked like gangsters, so the "employees" were stuck in the houses for their entire shifts to avoid creating suspicion among the neighbors. This was an insult, since the BA were essentially relegated to cooking crack for La Línea without reaping the large profits of street sales.

"One time Padilla called me because his truck transmission burned. And I went where he told me, and he was picking it up, a lot of coke, like 80 kilos, and he took my truck to put them inside the maquilas," Chávez says.

Chávez also suspected the arrangement was influenced by Gallegos's relationships with La Línea. Gallegos kept tabs on the maquilas regularly. Before arriving at a maquila, he would call ahead so that the garage door could be opened as he arrived in his bulletproof truck. Brandishing an AK-47, Gallegos would make the rounds of the house, checking on progress.

When it was time for the crack to hit the streets, the process was just as meticulous as the production process. It was expected that the BA would produce some eighty thousand "doses" each week. Gallegos would call Padilla, for instance, inquiring about the available quantity. The "doses" of crack would be packed into black trash bags and placed in a truck for delivery. Chávez came to learn that the large quantities of crack being produced were not just for Ciudad Juárez, but for the entire Chihuahua state.

Eventually La Línea member *Chepe* took over the maquilas, and Chávez and Padilla were directed to run security. As the violence in Ciudad Juárez escalated, so too did the number of military deployed to the troubled city. As part of President Felipe Calderón's war against the cartels, Operation Chihuahua was launched (Borderland Beat 2010e). In 2008 Ciudad Juárez was dubbed the "City of the Future," but that sobriquet soon changed to the "Murder Capital of the World." It was with the realization that the city was under siege, with the rampant corruption and attacks on the Juárez Municipal Police, that the Mexican military and federal police were deployed to the city.

The roving patrols of ominously armed military vehicles and the less-than-tolerant military put the criminal organizations on heightened alert, but at the same time the local citizens began accusing the military of crimes and human rights violations.

Chávez and Padilla had maintained their vigilant patrols for about four months when Padilla was arrested by the military, elevating Chávez to supervising the surveillance groups. This de facto promotion didn't last long. Attrition, whether through violence or arrest, is always a management challenge for criminal organizations in maintaining structural continuity.

"One of the days that I was off, I was resting in my house, and I receive a call from Margarito. And they tell me that a lot—a big caravan of militaries in white trucks were headed my way. When—I was laid down in my bed. When I get up and looking through the window, the whole street was full of militaries already."

Chávez immediately realized how he had been identified. He drove his brand new 2008 Dodge Durango home. In this particular middle-class neighborhood, nobody had new SUVs, and this stood out like a beacon in a Ciudad Juárez dust storm. After an eight-month stint at the CERESO prison, he was released.

Upon his release he was picked up by a fellow gang member who drove Chávez to his house to pick up his wife and kids. They would stay at a hotel by the old US Embassy where it was "calm" because of the presence of visitors and pedestrians. Upon arriving Chávez called Freddy for instructions, which included renting or buying another house close to where he used to live. Once that was accomplished, he could get back to work as the jefe de grupos and would still be answerable to Freddy.

Chávez's new house would only be two minutes from the gang's leadership houses, which proved advantageous. He contacted Fresa, who was in charge of security for that part of the city, and was told they would also be responsible for keeping the neighborhood secure for the leaders, which was a bonus for Chávez since he lived there. This security wasn't just against rivals.

"People—males that they were selling door to door things, let's say, chocolates or *mazapanes* from a rehab or—they don't want nobody knocking on the doors. So whenever that happens, they call me—Fresa call me to help them and we go and beat these guys up so they can get out from that area and tell them to don't come back," he says. "Because they don't want—the—the leaders, they don't want nobody in their area looking around in their houses."

Chávez would also now find himself put in charge of gang prospects by Freddy and Rafa.

"I would make sure that whatever—whenever they needed or I send them to do something, that they have a lot aggressivity, that they were savages to do the things, because sooner or later, they're going to become BA members."

These lowly but enthusiastic hopefuls, many in their teens and early twenties, would be called upon to bolster Chávez's leader-community patrol and test their mettle in "cleaning stores" or the elimination of an unauthorized drug operation. Some of these youngsters would be paid as little as fifty to one hundred dollars to kill someone.

When Freddy was killed Rafa put Chávez in charge of that unit.

"It didn't affect me bad. It was just more responsibility."

Chávez would split his duties in Rancho Anapra across from Sunland Park, NM, to work closer with Rafa in downtown Ciudad Juárez, where Chávez would sell the marijuana and Rafa the pills and heroin.

A daunting task he would have to assume, especially given the constant temptation, was to ensure that members weren't abusing drugs. If they were, he was to see that they were put into rehabilitation. One rehabilitation facility, ironically, was owned by Rafa Díaz. If the addicted member wouldn't rehabilitate he had one last chance to come clean. Failure to do so would be fatal.

Proving his worth, Chávez would be put in charge of a hit team by Arturo Gallegos Castrellón, a distinguished position in the gang.

"A hit team is a group of BAs that we have in a house. They have weapons and a car. And whenever we need them or somebody else need them, they come out especially to kill."

The hit team only existed to commit murders. The primary target of the BA at this time was the Artistas Asesinos, a gang that was working for the Sinaloa organization.

"They have a plant A and plant B, that they were houses—stash houses, and they have weapons in there too."

The hit team model expanded across the city, expediting the carnage while saving resources.

"Whenever we need somebody—it depend on what area. Instead of the old plants, A and B, that they were in downtown area and travel all the way to the other side of Juárez to go and kill somebody, now we have hit teams everywhere in Juárez."

Each of these new and more efficient district operations would have its own leader. The gang's districts coincided with police districts, and were much more efficiently run because neighborhood squads had a more intimate knowledge of the streets and landmarks and could better approach targeted victims, then quickly escape law enforcement. An added benefit was that most local residents knew who these men were and were less likely to cooperate with police trying to investigate their homicides.

There was also a relationship with police in this model.

"We can ask the police—the police will give information. Now they know the area—if a killing happens, then we know to who they are going to call."

The district leaders were as follows:

- Aldama District: Chabez and Farmero
- Babicora: Quintan
- Benito Juarez: Maguro and Pac
- Chihuahua: Zorro
- Cuauhtemoc: Tury, Chávez, and part Zorro because it was between Chihuahua and Delicias
- Delicias: Zorro—José Díaz Díaz

This strategy was established by Gallegos to ensure operations stayed covert, especially after an incident that occurred downtown with Chávez.

"I have a problem when I was working in downtown. One of the prostitutes was giving information to police—to police officers that don't work with us. So I report her to Freddy and Rafa, and they tell me to kick her out of the area of downtown. So I did that," he says. "I tell her that she cannot work there no more. I grab her clothes from the hotel that she's staying in and threw them out to the street and tell her to don't come back."

The woman made the grave mistake of challenging Chávez and was murdered the next day. This was not well received by Gallegos because of the unwanted attention it drew from police. While Chávez asserted his innocence and believed the killer was actually Gallegos, Chávez was still interrogated by Gallegos, beaten, and nearly killed.

"I explained what happened. And Tury, the defendant, he's one of the ones who believe in me, and he tell Tablero they were going to investigate. So that's why I don't end up dead at that time."

Rather than lose his life, as a compromise Chávez was required to surrender to police but was afforded a lawyer provided by the gang. He appeared before the special prosecutor for crimes against women, a post that was established because of the city's notorious reputation for the murder of women—*feminicides*. He would learn that the woman was raped and a nipple bitten off. He was required to provide DNA and a bite sample to prove his innocence. The tests came back in Chávez's favor.

Even though he was exonerated in this case, Chávez admitted to contributing to the city's history of feminicide that would claim hundreds of victims.

"One was a bartender that she turn—she turn in one of the BA members that was real close to Rafa Díaz. So the BA member end up dead. So Rafa Díaz give me the order to go and pick up the bartender and kill her," he says. "I send a group to pick her up—pick her up. And they drive her to one of the streets of Juárez. They put her on her knees and shot her in the back of the head."

Chávez said he was not the trigger man but did take responsibility within the gang.

This incident underscored the gang's other source of revenue—prostitution. The core of the operation was run out of the Hotel Verde on Calle Samiengo, just a six-block walk from the Santa Fe Bridge. The run-down beige three-story building had wraparound patios on the two upper floors and Club Verde painted on the street level walls.

The BA were directly involved in the deplorable plight of the city's females. Between 2008 and 2011 the gang would randomly kidnap attractive young girls, then turn them into sex slaves with the complicity of the federal police and army, who were known to have sex with underage girls (Winter 2020). Some of the kidnapped women would also be brought to

Club Verde was a focal point of Barrio Azteca prostitution and human trafficking activities. Courtesy of the *El Diario de Juarez*.

the United States. After being shuttled to stash houses, the girls, some as young as fifteen, were put to work in the hotel and around the city. The gang was so brazen they advertised in the daily tabloid *PM* (McGahan 2017), which graphicaly chronicled the city's homicides amid provocative photos of nude women.

A turned gang member who was a key witness for the prosecution implicated Jesús Damian Perez, aka "El Patachu," and Pedro Payan Gloria, aka "El Pifas," as the leaders of the prostitution operation. He said that many of the girls would be lured into stores in the Reform Market with the promise of nonexistent jobs or kidnapped right off the street as they changed buses. Businesses were also complicit in the scheme. The extortion ring the Azteca ran was profitable, but they gave businesses the opportunity to have their quota waived if they helped recruit girls (Borunda 2017).

A witness testified to Payan's intimate relationship with the military and their complicity in the sex operation. "Because it was another point where women were kidnapped from, sometimes they asked to keep them a day or two for pleasure, if you will, or to hold the girls, it was also a point where the women were held en route to being transported to the United States or wherever it was they were being taken to," testified the gang member (McGahan 2017).

As disposable as the trash that litters Ciudad Juárez, girls who violated or refused any orders were summarily killed, but likely not until they had been brutally raped and tortured.

"Once the women were no longer 'useful' in their illicit activities, they decided to take their lives and abandoned their bodies in the vicinity of the Navajo Arroyo in the Valley of Juárez," the Chihuahua state prosecutor's office said in a statement in 2013. Payan would ultimately be convicted and sentenced to 430 years in prison for the murder of eleven girls whose remains were dumped in a dry stream bed—Navajo Arroya, some eighty miles outside the city in the Valley of Juárez. That January 2012 discovery actually yielded twenty-one sets of remains, but only the eleven were confirmed through DNA.

In another incident a woman made the egregious mistake of turning in Rafa Díaz to kidnappers. The woman was the daughter of a heroin dealer who worked with the BA.

"After torturing her. It was a few BA members, including myself in that house. And Zorro is the one who put the tape around her head to suffocate her."

According to Chávez, teams would scour the city looking for rivals either to kill or interrogate—the latter a euphemism since those interrogated ultimately died. Chávez emphasized that each district leader was responsible for interrogations, which not only kept the process compartmentalized but also sent a message to other rivals in the district.

"I show up at whatever house that they have him and start asking the guy about what his—with who he works, how they work. And most of the time, when they picked up somebody, it's because they knew already that they are working with a rival cartel," Chávez recounted.

The rival would be questioned. There was no doubt among the captured what their fate would be. It was a matter of how long and painful the process would be. Chávez admitted to torturing his victims, usually by relentlessly battering them with his baseball bat. Being fulsomely truthful was fruitless.

"Most of the time—99 percent of the time, they are going to die."

The murder usually ended with decapitation, and the head and body were dumped in places that would leave an unmistakable message to the Sinaloan faction. Chávez admitted to ordering at least eight beheadings, three of which he did with his own hands.

One such victim was a man named Gilberto Ontiveros-Lucero, known as *Greñas,* a renowned drug dealer in the eighties in Mexico who had become affiliated with the Sinaloans while serving a prison sentence in Mexico City. It would come to Chávez's attention from fellow gang member Casitas that he knew where Greñas's adult son Gilberto lived. Casitas, who lived in Guadalupe, El Barrio de Juárez, was believed to be a reputable source because he was the brother of "Popeye," whose real name was Martin Perez Marrufo, and the brother-in-law of Lentes.

At the time it was more convenient for the gang to pick up Gilberto as a way to send an unequivocal message to his father. Chávez ordered Casitas to pick Gilberto up (kidnap him). Gilberto was an overweight man in his late thirties. When he was brought to an abandoned house in Ciudad Juárez, the torture started immediately.

When Chávez arrived at the house his cohorts had already tied Gilberto's hands and legs. The helpless victim had already been beaten and was lying on the floor when Chávez entered. He left Lentes and Popeye outside to act as lookouts. Already inside the house was Shorty Palacios and Casitas.

Chávez immediately launched into a brutal forty-minute baseball bat attack on Gilberto, eventually getting the young man, who was completely covered in bruises and suffering extensive internal injuries, to give up information which was passed up to Arturo Gallegos Castrellón. Gallegos then ordered Chávez to get rid of Gilberto. The message was clear, but the method was left up to Chávez.

"I cut him in pieces," he coldly admits. As if completely dismembering Gilberto wasn't gruesome enough, the men desecrated the body. When the head was removed, Shorty Palacios talked to it as if holding a conversation.

When this macabre ritual ended, they had to dispose of the body. They decided to put it in a sewer near the intersection of Zempoala and Panama Streets. Message sent and received. Gilberto was not the first and would not be the last dismembered body to be found in the city.

CHAPTER 7

War Footing

Between Calderón's declaration of war and El Chapo's gamble of expanding into and consuming the Juárez Plaza, a perfect storm was created in which the Barrio Azteca could expand their reputation and sphere of influence. As with any military conflict, this required a steady flow of weapons, soldiers, and money, as well as efficient logistics.

A violent tit-for-tat would evaporate any relationship Sinaloa had with VCF. In 2004, El Chapo allegedly had VCF's brother assassinated; VCF in turn had El Chapo's brother killed while he was serving a prison term. El Chapo's bloody declaration of war and incursion into the Juárez Plaza unofficially occurred on January 5, 2008, when gunmen targeted rival gang members in Ciudad Juárez. Murders mounted in the ensuing months, culminating in one of the first of multiple bilateral massacres.

At 7:15 p.m. on September 2, 2009, four hooded members of Gente Nueva, the street soldiers of Sinaloa DTO, stormed through the front door of the El Aliviane rehabilitation center and killed seventeen recovering drug and alcohol addicts, most of whom were associated with the BA (Lacey 2009b). The victims were lined up against the wall of an internal courtyard and systematically gunned down in a fusillade of AK-47 fire. More than one hundred rounds were reported to have been fired in ten minutes (Schapiro 2009). One additional victim would die the next day in the hospital. Investigators were unable to avoid the thick coat of blood that covered most of the facility's tile floors as they made their way toward the bodies. Just the previous month the city had experienced a record-breaking 326 homicides (Schapiro 2009).

Sprinkled around the city were drug rehabilitation centers where gang members were "encouraged" by their leadership to escape the clutches of the very drugs they were trafficking in Mexico and the United States. A standing rule among the BA was that their members should avoid those drugs, since drug use would compromise discipline and mission effectiveness. The massacres continued, largely unmitigated by the police, since many were complicit in some capacity.

Nonetheless arrests were now up 300 percent, and the criminal organizations were not having it. On May 26, 2011, forty-one-year-old Captain José Manuel Rivas López was riddled with bullets in his own home on the 1103 block of Joaquín Soto Mendoza and Teniente Daniel García Streets, in the Oasis Revolución neighborhood. Investigators found sixty-four shell casings at the scene (Borderland Beat 2011b).

Julián Leyzaola took the reins as chief of the municipal police in Ciudad Juárez in March of 2011 and quickly garnered the ire of the DTOs there for his aggressive policing style and reallocation of officers to enhance police response times. The no-nonsense chief also fired four hundred officers suspected of being corrupted by the local criminal organizations (*Albuquerque Journal* 2011a).

The attacks against police intensified, even against the new chief himself. In June 2011 his vehicle was fired upon in the La Chaveña neighborhood by a twenty-four-year-old suspect, Roberto López Valles. Six more attempts would be made on his life. The next year was no better for police as the VCF DTO amped up its campaign to control the city. Banners, otherwise referred to as Narco Mantas, appeared all over Ciudad Juárez calling for the resignation of the chief. Julián Leyzaola stubbornly refused.

One banner read: *"This is for Leyzaola. If you continue supporting the imitators and only arrest our people we will kill one officer daily so that the citizens will know how corrupt you are. Leyzaola = a criminal with a badge. Sincerely, Nuevo Cartel de Juarez"* (Gibson 2012). Between October 2010 and January 2012, sixty-four Juárez police officers were murdered (Gibson 2012).

The wave of violence forced police to abandon their homes and live in secure hotels.

"We are more like soldiers living in barracks than police officers," one female officer said. "I don't want my family to become collateral damage if I become a target" (Fox News 2012a).

Ciudad Juárez Mayor Héctor "Teto" Murguía joined Leyzaola in the chief's defiance of the crime wave against police.

"We pay no attention to the banners. If we did, we wouldn't even get out of bed," Murguía said (Fox News 2012a).

With his contract set to expire in October 2013, Leyzaola told reporters in December 2012 that the best efforts of law enforcement and the military were steadily improving public safety for his country's citizens, but his own prospects were bleak.

"There is no safe place in Mexico for me," Leyzaola told the *El Paso Times*. "Mexico is prohibited for me" (Cárdenas 2012).

These words would prove to be prophetic. On May 8, 2015, after leaving the department two years before, Leyzaola dropped his wife and son off around noon at money exchange business in Ciudad Juárez near the Zaragoza Bridge. While he waited in the front passenger seat of his Jeep Commander, a man exited an SUV and shot the ex-chief three times at close range, leaving him paralyzed. The shooter, Jesús Antonio Castañeda Alvarez, alias "El Güero," and the driver, Hugo Alonso Serenil Luna, alias "El Cabezón," were caught a few blocks away by a roving police patrol (*Mexico Daily News* 2015).

"When I turned to the side, he ran to the front of my window on the left, I saw that he was aiming at me already and he pulled the trigger," Leyzaola told Mexican media. "Fortunately, it did not work the first time because if it did, I would have been shot in the head. He pulled back and then pulled, I heard him tell me, he said to me very clearly: 'message from director Reyes,' he told me" (Borunda 2015).

While recuperating, Leyzaola said he vividly remembered the words of the would-be assassin as he repeatedly shot at him—the shooting was a "message from director Reyes." Jesús Antonio Reyes was the incumbent chief of the Juárez Municipal Police Department who, as expected, would deny any complicity (Borunda 2015).

Further fueling suspicions that Reyes was complicit was the fact that Leyzaola had fired Reyes, squashing his prospects of being hired by the state police, because Reyes was a "malandrinazo," a bad guy (Borunda 2015).

It was evident that the battle lines were being clearly defined. Although DTO and their minions continued to face off against each other, they were effectively unified against law enforcement. In order for the various sides to launch effective campaigns in this arena, recruits and weapons were going to be needed on an enormous scale.

But it wouldn't be the rival gangs or even the police that the DTOs and their surrogates would have to face on battlefield Ciudad Juárez, it would be a more imposing opponent. Pursuant to his declaration of war against the drug trafficking organizations in December 2006, President Felipe Calderón felt the most effective way to fight this war was with the Mexican military.

Joint Operation Chihuahua was the first bold step in the administration's strategy to eradicate the drug trafficking organizations and address the country's mounting death toll, especially in Ciudad Juárez. Between 2008 and 2010 more than seven thousand soldiers would be deployed to the besieged city (Borderland Beat 2010e). The results were controversial. Not all his strategies would contribute to the positive outcome Calderón had anticipated.

The military armada arrived both by land and by air, in a movement reminiscent of a Baghdad-like occupation. The first deployment occurred on March 29, 2008, with three C-130 transports and one 727 landing with 392 troops at the city's Abraham Gonzalez International Airport, while another eight hundred five troops entered in 116 vehicles.

This was an imposing spectacle. Olive drab trucks with soldiers in the back, mostly carrying semi-automatic weapons, poured into the streets. Interestingly, the uniform of choice was the standard forest camouflage, out of place in the arid urban setting of Ciudad Juárez. Later units would adopt the desert tan uniform. Some of the units deployed in the operation included the Twentieth Motorized Cavalry Regiment, Third Independent Infantry Brigade, Seventy-Sixth Infantry Battalion, and the Parachute Rifle Special Forces Brigade (Borderland Beat 2010e).

These units maintained sandbagged and dirt-filled tire bunkers, checkpoints around the city, and regular patrols of heavily armed vehicles. In a suprising and controversial early strategy, the military disarmed sixteen hundred members of the Municipal Police Department, which only heightened local cynicism about where the department's loyalties rested. The military units were also augmented by more than a thousand federal police, who arrived in their blue and white Ford pickups with officers standing in truck beds surrounded by roll cages. The officers wore balaclavas to cover their faces as did some, but not all, of the military.

When Arturo Gallegos Castrellón was interviewed by the FBI after his arrest in Mexico, he laid out for the agents the scenario by which his gang was called to active duty at the behest of the Vicente Carrillo Fuentes Drug Trafficking Organization. In the early days of the conflict, he was informed that El Chapo Guzmán's Sinaloa DTO was launching a violent takeover of the lucrative VCF drug plaza into the US. A trigger occurred when Sinaloan soldiers murdered members of Jota Ele's crew. In response Jota Ele began providing the Azteca weapons to retaliate against their enemies.

The need for weapons was tantamount, and gang members obliged, turning their steady incoming trickle of military-grade weapons into a flood. One member had a drug connection in Midland, Texas, who had a connection with a licensed gun dealer to buy weapons from Texas gun shows in bulk. Just from this connection the gang obtained fifteen thousand rounds of much-needed ammunition. Weapons and ammunition began traveling from Midland to El Paso in an F-250 pickup truck, which made the return trip loaded with drugs. No cash was exchanged in the transaction. The wares were purchased with about twenty pounds of marijuana.

The weapons and ammunition were stored in the garage of a gang member's eastside El Paso house until they could be transported into Mexico.

"The [Carrillo-Fuentes] cartel decided to give their 'work' to the Aztecas, which was mostly killing," said Fernando Carrillo, an Azteca member and nephew of the cartel boss in trial testimony. "Alberto '*Fresa*' Núñez Payan said 'we are at war right now, we are helping the Juárez drug cartel.'"

Arturo Gallegos Castrellón would also provide the FBI with a succinct account of the historical alliance between the BA and La Línea as well as a history of their alliance against the Sinaloa DTO and their proxies, which included the Artistas Asesinos (Doble A).

The Artistas Asesinos would become comparable in their depravity to the BA. They also had a prison-based genesis, but in this case on the Mexican side. Around 2002 Jorge "El Dream" Ernesto Sáenz, who hailed from the Morelos II barrio, was incarcerated for killing a police officer while Éder Ángel "*El Saik*" Martínez, from Villas de Salvarcar, shot up a vehicle with three occupants (Santiago 2019).

El Saik was as talented in art as he was in killing. While imprisoned he won a national prisoner art contest—an accomplishment that would ultimately spawn the name of the gang (Salazar 2016). (I have personally been awed by the quality of art I have seen imates create from such rudimentary materials as the insides of potato chip bags, soap, strings and the like.)

The whole gang had a propensity for jail art and graffiti (Borunda 2018d). Before long officials would observe their art around Ciudad Juárez in the form of graffiti, or tagging, as it is also called. Even their tattoos were less ominous looking than those of their rivals. The Doble A would come to be identified by such banalities as stars and music notes.

Early on, the Doble As were generally perceived as "tagging crews," and little attention was paid to their exploits. Gradually they escalated their level of street drug sales and accompanying violence. Their activity caught the eye of Sinaloa operatives, who knew they were going to need additional street soldiers to support the Gente Nueva in their war against the VCF DTO. The Doble A would emerge as one of the prime criminal antagonists in Ciudad Juárez. The Mexicles would ultimately align themselves with the Doble A, bolstering the street soldier ranks for the Sinaloa DTO, a relationship that would eventually erode.

Barrio Azteca leadership talked about the possible need for rocket-propelled and hand grenades as well as for armored vehicles. Gallegos said there were inquiries but ultimately no need to purchase these items, since his rivals were not driving armored vehicles, and the weapons his organization had cached were more than sufficient. Military-grade weapons are illegal in Mexico, so much of their arsenal was obtained in the United States and transported illegally across the border.

In one case, the former mayor, police chief, and trustee of the tiny border village of Columbus, New Mexico, were among fourteen charged in a not-so-sophisticated smuggling ring that sent more than two hundred weapons and other tactical gear across the border to La Línea. Angelo Vega, the disgraced lawman, said he was paid "well over" $10,000 to perform a variety of activities such as surveillance for the smugglers entering nearby Palomas, Mexico, and even stopping federal agents to ask what they were doing in the dusty, barren border village (Romo 2011).

It would be revealed that the conspirators used a police pickup to drive the spoils directly into Mexico (Romo 2011). These included body armor, AK-47 pistols, and 9 mm handguns. Among cartel operatives the AK-47 is euphemistically referred to as the *cuerno de chivo*, goat's horns, because of the bent magazines of these rugged weapons.

The operation was conducted between January 2010 and March 2010 through gun shops in the towns of Chaparral and Deming, New Mexico (Haussaman 2011). The scandal would ultimately force the Columbus Police Department to be dissolved by July 2011, with law enforcement duties being assumed by the Luna County Sheriff's Office (EIDEARD 2011).

Seven years later, two other men in Columbus began not only running weapons into Palomas but smuggling human contraband north. The duo, twenty-four-year-old Josias Garcia and twenty-year-old Eduardo Chávez, who lived on the Mexican side but was an American citizen, purchased a cache of weapons in El Paso, Texas, and Las Cruces, New Mexico, that included forty-seven high-capacity rifle magazines, four thousand rounds of ammunition, an AK-47 assault rifle, and two AK-47 magazines, all earmarked for Mexico (Gallagher 2018).

While weapons poured into Mexico from organized and makeshift crews looking to capitalize on the warring cartels, the US government ostensibly contributed to the carnage in a failed effort to better track and interdict the smuggling networks.

Operation Fast and Furious would become a debacle for the Bureau of Alcohol, Tobacco, Firearms, and Explosives. The brainchild of the ATF Phoenix office, the operation was launched October 31, 2009, when agents received a tip of possible straw purchases from a gun shop owner. More than two thousand weapons were purchased under the tacit approval of the ATF, who thought that by monitoring the puchasers they would be able to track them to larger operations in Mexico (CNN 2019). This failed dismally when agents tasked with monitoring the weapons lost track of them as they crossed the border. The blunder probably wouldn't have seen the full light of day had it not been for John Dodson, an agency whistleblower who penned his experience at the ATF's Phoenix field office in *The Unarmed Truth; My Fight to Blow the Whistle and Expose Fast and Furious* (Dodson 2013). Dodson recounts his frustration with the policy and the attempted coverup that would ultimately hold US Attorney General Eric Holder in contempt of Congress for his refusal to release information on the operation.

One major consequence of this blunder contributed to the murder of US Border Patrol BORTAC team member Brian Terry on a remote Arizona mountainside December 14, 2010, as his team was attempting to apprehend a notorious Mexican "rip crew" that opened fire on the team, killing the forty-year-old agent (U.S. Customs and Border Protection 2019a). On February 15, 2011, Immigration and Customs Enforcement agents Jaime Zapata and Victor Avilla were attacked in a diplomatic SUV by members of the Zetas organization. Avilla survived his wounds; Zapata did not (Attkisson 2013). Both were assigned to the US Embassy in Mexico and were driving through San Luis Potosi state when gunmen pulled them over, believing they were members of a rival criminal organization. US law enforcement working in Mexico are not permitted to carry weapons, giving the pair of federal agents no chance to defend themselves. A Fast and Furious weapon was implicated in this attack.

It would also be uncovered that a weapon used in the massacre of sixteen young people at a party in Ciudad Juárez was also linked to Fast and Furious (Robillard 2012). This massacre is discussed in more detail later in the book.

Most of the targets of this weaponry were members of the two gangs supporting the Sinaloa faction—Artistas Asesinos and the Mexicles. This murderous duo became formidable foes of the La Línea/BA alliance.

Another group that emerged in alliance for the VCF organization was a trained hit team that lurked in the shadows even darker than those veiling the BA and La Línea. Los Linces (The Lynx) were hired hit men (*sicarios*) contracted by La Línea. Their unique talents, unlike those of the street thugs that roamed the city, were honed professionally, through special forces military trainers.

"[*Los Linces'*] sole function is to execute people they have been ordered to kill. They move around in different types of vehicles and are always driven by someone else. We always met them in homes inside gated communities and saw them with a vast number of equipment such as ballistic vests, helmets, long rifles, assault weapons and even grenades," said Martin Hugo Valenzuela Rivera, who was arrested on December 26, 2008, by the army in Chihuahua (Borderland Beat 2009a).

These cartel special operations units average less than one hundred members and typically operate in cells of five—similar to most special operation units. They are very well insulated and only take orders from the upper VCF hierarchy. Even La Línea and the BA have virtually no interaction with these men (Borderland Beat 2009a).

CHAPTER 8
Death of a City

For decades, it was a rite of passage for young people from the southwestern United States to party in downtown Ciudad Juárez. It was also a destination for tourists looking for good deals on Mexican knickknacks, an exotic lunch or dinner, and for elderly people on fixed incomes looking for low-cost prescription drugs and dental work. There was regular bus service from El Paso to Ciudad Juárez to make the trip faster and more convenient, without the worry of obtaining Mexican car insurance, finding parking, or running the risk of being pulled over by an unscrupulous Mexican police officer looking for a bribe.

Even before the DTOs and street gangs essentially took over Ciudad Juárez, the border city became internationally infamous with an inexplicable rise in female homicides. Journalists and advocates descended on the city, which was experiencing a boom in its new role as a manufacturing center under the North American Free Trade Agreement. With the rise in job openings came a flood of female applicants from all over the country, mostly from repressed southern agricultural regions, to work in the maquiladoras. By the mid-1990s the mutilated bodies of dead women began appearing, and the number of the "disappeared" rose.

I observed the instability of the social order firsthand while on assignment for FoxNews.com in 2012. Chamizal Park is an expanse of grass and trees just across the border. On one particular day while I was in the city, the body of Perla Cristal Garcia Ponte, a seventeen-year-old runaway, was found in the park. She had been strangled. Just another female found dead on the streets of Ciudad Juárez.

Garcia's death underscored the ongoing, albeit quiet, crisis of females being found dead and discarded throughout the city. Her case was somewhat different in that her body was not mutilated and was found in a well-traveled area.

As part of the assignment, I interviewed frustrated officials who had seen little change in the plight of the females in the city, which had been struggling with this scourge for more than twenty years.

Irma Casas, director of Casa Amiga Esther Chávez Cano, a woman's rights advocacy and counseling center, expressed her frustration in how these cases were managed by the police. There was always an ambivalence toward feminicide investigations, especially as the death toll mounted during the drug war.

The following is an excerpt of an article ("Violence Against Women Worse Than Ever in Juárez, Experts Say") I wrote for Fox News.com in 2012 (Kolb 2012):

> Perla Cristal Garcia Ponte, 16, was released to her mother after being arrested the day before for public intoxication. Shortly after being returned to her family at 3:30 p.m., June 17, the teen ran away.
>
> The next morning, her body was found in Chamizal Park, a well-traveled oasis in this city of brown and gray shades. Officials said she was strangled to death and found beneath a sign that said access to the area was for municipal use only.
>
> The case of Garcia Ponte highlights a problem in Mexico that has been quietly pushed out of the public eye thanks in large part to the country's ongoing drug war—that women are being murdered in the city at an alarmingly high rate.
>
> "Murders are rarely investigated and only one percent are even decided upon," said Irma Casas, director, Casa Amiga Esther Chávez Cano, a woman's rights advocacy and counseling center. And the situation seems to be getting worse, Casas said.
>
> Ciudad Juárez received worldwide attention in the early 1990s not only for an inordinate number of women missing, but the sadistic manner in which they were murdered.
>
> And while the headlines have disappeared, the problem has not.
>
> Cecilia Espinosa of Red Mesa de Mujeres said officials have used the war on drugs to deflect attention from a problem that has actually worsened after the insertion of the military and federal police into Ciudad Juárez.
>
> Human rights organizations have been tracking the murder and disappearance of women in Juárez for nearly twenty years, and the

numbers are staggering, despite officials boasting the lowest murder rate in three years.

According to statistics provided by Casa Amiga, between 1993 and 2007—before Mexican President Felipe Calderón escalated the war against the cartels in Ciudad Juárez—there was a total of three hundred eighty five women reported murdered. From 2008 through 2011, there were 789 women officially reported murdered, a more than 100 percent increase, despite a saturation of military and federal police in the city.

Not included in this data set are the hundreds of disappeared. Flyers about missing women dot the city. Much of the effort to find them has been in the hands of family members, many of whom scour known body dumping sites hoping to find a shred of clothing or a piece of a bone that could lead to their loved one.

To meet this crisis, Chihuahua state launched a program exclusively to address crimes against women. The Chihuahua State Prosecutor for Attention to Women Victims of Crime by Reason of Gender has shined a light on the crisis and has yielded modest results. They speculate that the higher number of deaths and reports of missing women are not because more women are being kidnapped or killed, but because more people are reporting it.

"I'm sad and hurt as a woman," said Silvia Najera. "But fortunately, there is an increase of women who are complaining and denouncing to the authorities all the abuses such as rape, abuse, and murder. From the past ten years to the last three, you can see an increase of complaints not because more women are being abused, but because more women are making complaints to the proper authorities."

Najera said there has been an exhaustive effort to raise awareness of the crisis women face in Ciudad Juárez and that their rights are protected. But critics say the increase in violence against women is because of a long-running culture of corruption and impunity toward the law in Ciudad Juárez.

There's no doubt that the majority of these women are the victims of domestic violence and sexually driven kidnappings and exploitation, but there have also been a growing number killed because of their involvement in the drug trade. The majority of women are operating on the street level, making them more prone to violence; however, there are some who accede to the upper echelons of drug trafficking organizations.

The Council on Hemispheric Affairs drew a direct correlation to feminicides and women involved in the drug trade (2011). This is generationally evident when looking at the legacies of such female narcos as La Nacha and others. There is also an erosion of the macho mentality that asserts that women can't function in the drug trade's trademark violence. This has been proven false on multiple occasions. Because of the same ingrained macho mentality, however, women are seen as more expendable when their usefulness to the DTO has expired.

The overall death toll in Ciudad Juárez, mostly perpetrated by the plaza-grabbing gangs, increased exponentially with Calderón's declaration of war and Guzmán's attempted hostile takeover. In 2007, the first year of Calderón's initiative, there were 310 homicides recorded. As the military's efforts gained traction and the battling criminal organizations escalated their efforts, the murder rate jumped to 1,587 in 2008; 2,643 in 2009; and 3,111 in 2010. As we will see, these numbers, while appalling, slowly decreased in the years subsequent to the removal of the army and with more coordinated law enforcement efforts from local, state, and federal agencies, at the core of which was the controversial Chief of Police Julián Leyzaola. There is also argument that there was a lull in violence because the Sinaloa faction had achieved victory.

In a staggering admission after his 2010 trial, Arturo Gallegos Castrellón admitted to Mexican officials that he was responsible for 80 percent of the recent murders in Ciudad Juárez (Malkin 2010).

The city was in a tailspin.

Commercial extortion exploded as the ever-larger, more organized gangs looked for enhanced revenue to buffer their coffers and help support their war. This came at great cost to the Ciudad Juárez economy even as it bolstered the economy of El Paso. Between 2009 and 2011, three hundred bars and four thousand restaurants shuttered their doors in Ciudad Juárez due to the violence that evaporated most foot traffic around the city, especially at night, but also because extortion from the criminal organizations flourishing at this time had become unsupportable (Borderland Beat 2011a).

By 2008, extortion of legitimate businesses large and small—including sidewalk food stands, junkyards, corner stores, the tortilla factory, and funeral homes—was rampant. Local businesses were low-hanging fruit for the criminal element in the city. Illegal businesses such as bordellos or hotels known for prostitution were also targeted. The *cuota* was imposed on businesses to ensure "protection," which ultimately became a double-edged sword. Failure to pay the required amount for protection resulted in property damage, physical injury, or death from the "protectors."

The more prosperous businesses were shuttered and reopened in the safer confines of El Paso, which experienced an economic upturn in the midst of the national recession even as businesses closed their doors in Ciudad Juárez, which lost $140 million in investments and a third of the work force. Residents who lost their jobs as a result of the economic collapse were vulnerable to criminal recruitment just to survive (Corchado 2016).

Losing faith in their leadership and fearing for their safety, residents fled the city. Mayor José Reyes Ferriz would admit that more than twenty thousand homes were abandoned as residents fled to safety. It was estimated that one hundred thousand people fled the city, with a third of them relocating in El Paso.

According to the El Paso Hispanic Chamber of Commerce, this resulted in the opening of four hundred new businesses in the city, many of them once well-established clubs and restaurants in Ciudad Juárez (Grissom 2010).

The truest indication a city is collapsing is when its chief of police resigns and the mayor moves his residence not only out of the city he runs, but out of the very country. The situation had become so dire in his city that after receiving death threats, Mayor José Reyes Ferriz moved across the river to El Paso. First to go, on February 20, 2009, would be Municipal Police Chief Robert Orduna, who faced relentless threats. More than one hundred of his officers had been murdered the previous year, and just prior to Orduna's resignation, so had his chief of operations, Sacramento Pérez Serrano. Orduna was credited with firing some eight hundred corrupt officers from a force of sixteen hundred (Estrada, Ware, and Rodriguez 2009).

"The police chief has resigned, saying he did not want to be responsible for any more police dying," Mayor Reyes said in an interview. "We have not blinked," he said. "We will continue to fight organized crime . . . he has done a good job, but we will find someone else" (Estrada, Ware, and Rodriguez 2009).

Reyes had welcomed five thousand troops to the city hoping it would quell the violence. That did little to mitigate the attack on a Reyes motorcade in the city that resulted in the death of one of his bodyguards and the wounding of two others (Lacey 2009a).

The forty-six-year-old Reyes had a legacy to uphold, however. His father, José Reyes Estrada, had also been mayor (in Mexico the title is municipal president) from 1980 until 1983. Nonetheless, by the end of the month, Reyes had seen the writing on the wall. He moved his family across the border into El Paso after repeated threats on narco mantas, most likely written by the VCF, who would have been using the BA as their soldiers.

He was met with jeers and a lot of finger pointing for abandoning the city he was elected to protect. Reyes made the announcement at a public meeting at his city hall in Ciudad Juárez, and it was not taken lightly by the embattled residents.

"It's absurd for the mayor of the most violent city in the world to live on the other side when we live daily as hostages to criminals who extort from us and murder with impunity," said a protester (Garcia 2009).

The pall over Ciudad Juárez was evident. Residents observed self-imposed curfews. They deserted the streets, restaurants, and parks for fear of being caught in crossfire. And the ever-reliable tourism industry evaporated.

Part of Reyes's decision to abandon residence in his own city was likely his lack of confidence in his own police department. In a cable from the US Consulate released by WikiLeaks, Reyes would say to consulate officials that 100 percent of his officers were corrupt in one form or another (Ramsey 2011). The strategy of infusing the military into a law enforcement role was not without its controversies, either, for there was also concern over the military's loyalties.

Although he kept one foot on each side of the border, Reyes attempted to appear proactive. In September 2009 he announced the appointment of 1,150 new municipal police officers who were reportedly better vetted and trained than their predecessors. They would augment the already growing presence of the military and federal police. Reyes would attribute a "turning point" in the city's violence to this increase in manpower, maintaining that more positive momentum was imminent.

However, a cross-border political scientist told CNN he was much more cynical about the city's prospects, as gunshots could be heard from the campus of the University of Texas at El Paso, which faced Ciudad Juárez (Castillo 2009). "I think that the mayor is more optimistic than most people in the city and most analysts," said Tony Payan, PhD (Castillo 2009).

"We received information that the Juárez mayor lives in El Paso, and that possibly [the gangs] were going to come to El Paso to get him," said Detective Carlos Carrillo of the El Paso Police Department, who expressed concern there might be cross-border violence as the antagonists pursued their prey. "He has not asked us for our help, but it's our duty to protect any resident of our city who may be under threat" (Valdez 2009).

By the end of the year Reyes had moved yet farther away, from Ciudad Juárez to Las Cruces, New Mexico, about fifty miles from downtown El Paso.

Police interventions in Ciudad Juárez remained less than aggressive, a situation exploited fully by the Barrio Azteca and other criminal organizations in the city. They knew full well the control they held over police, and so did the public. And yet Reyes remained adamant. In 2010 he said, "It's irresponsible to suggest the cartels have control of this city. Their actions indicate signs of desperation. It shows their backs are against the wall" (Valencia 2010e).

Reyes and Calderón had to contend with a desperate public's perception of public safety. Not only were the street gangs and DTOs running the city at this point, the residents knew there were fault lines in the structure of law enforcement. Massive firings followed when officers of the municipal police force failed integrity tests. Then there was dissention among the federal police when allegations of corruption in their own ranks emerged.

These officers were put under extreme pressure by the DTO's application of their Plato o Plomo philosophy. Law enforcement faced a gut-wrenching choice: either take a bribe, be murdered, or have family members murdered. While many leaders of drug trafficking organizations were current and former law enforcement officers, there are hundreds, if not thousands, who are confronted with this dilemma when they try to help quell drug violence. Americans are very cavalier in indicting all Mexican law enforcement as corrupt. I have seen firsthand the circumstances these officers face on a daily basis. Imagine facing daily threats associated with investigating crime in Mexico on a salary of six hundred dollars a month. An individual approaches you and offers one thousand dollars to look the other way. And by the way, if you don't take the bribe—Plato (silver)—the individual and his colleagues will kill you or your family—Plomo (lead). Of course this does not imply endorsement of corruption. It does shine light on the fact that officers of the law in Mexico often face dire circumstances.

In August 2008 elements of the federal police held three days of demonstration which devolved into physical confrontations between officers (Valencia 2010e). One federal officer's colleagues allegedly believed he was falsely accused of "drug crimes." The incident sparked a massive demonstration of some two hundred heavily armed officers in front of the La Playa Hotel, where many were housed. The incident sparked another investigation that resulted in the recalling to Mexico City of four commanders for misconduct (Valencia 2010e).

Following Reyes's three-year tenure Héctor "Teto" Murguía, who had served from 2004 to 2007, was elected to a second term. Murguía's stark approach was unambiguous if perhaps overly simplisitc. In a 2012 interview with the author, Murguía questioned the benefit of the Merida Initiative to his city.

Murguía said that the $1.4 billion Merida Initiative, a US aid package intended to support Mexico's war on drugs, failed to make an impact at the local level. The aid package, signed by Congress in 2008, stipulated that no money would be sent directly to Mexico; rather the aid would come in the form of training and equipment. The initiative also called for Mexico to enact judicial reform, strengthen government institutions, respect human rights, and respect the rule of law—reforms that many argue have yet to occur. Improvements have taken place at a glacial pace, if at all.

"We don't see any benefit of Merida," Murguía said from his third floor office, two blocks from the US border at El Paso, Texas, one of the safest cities in the US. "The US is the biggest consumer of drugs, and their aid package is not enough for us to do what they expect us to do—yet the American media is so critical of Juárez," said a frustrated Murguía. "These people need to be more responsible and not criticize what they don't know."

Murguía said his city needed jobs and better social services, if there was any prospect of mitigating violence. "I have sympathy for the seventeen-year-old who chooses a very bad option because they are filled with anger and hate because they have no opportunities," said Murguía.

He pointed in the direction of El Paso and said that city has less than 50 percent of his 1.8 million inhabitants but has an operating budget nearly four times his city's. At the time, Ciudad Juárez operated on an annual budget of $228 million. Its municipal police department consumed 60 percent of the budget, he said, adding that Ciudad Juárez receives only 4 percent of every taxed peso to cover costs while it needs 20 percent just to provide basic services.

"We don't have the resources to fight the delinquency here," Murguía said. "That is where we need the aid—give us jobs."

At the time, former presidential candidate and El Paso resident Beto O'Rourke agreed with Murguía about the Merida Initiative. "This $1.4 billion has been a waste of US money, because the 'war' metaphor perpetuated the mentality of resolving violence through further violence," O'Rourke said.

But the coauthor of the Merida Initiative, Congressman Silvestre Reyes (D-TX), who took to politics after a career with the US Border Patrol and helped implement Operation Blockade, stands by the initiative.

Murguía says it would be better to use an aid package like the Merida Initiative to supplement municipal law enforcement agencies and bolster social services to deter the recruiting efforts of the Sinaloa and Vicente Carrillo Fuentes DTOs. The DTOs compete for recruits among street gangs that have turned much of the city into a ghost town.

Adding to the erosion of trust in police and local government that the DTOs exploited was the exponential increase in human rights violations and other allegations against the military. The Washington Office on Latin America issued a scathing report against the Mexican military stationed in Ciudad Juárez since their deployment in 2008. Issued in October 2010, the report alleged multiple incidents of torture, forced disappearance, and sexual harassment of women (WOLA 2010).

Ciudad Juárez, Chihuahua state, and federal officials knew the DTOs had their tentacles deeply embedded in all levels of law enforcement, and they exploited every opportunity to strengthen their battle plans. If there was an incident involving police, the gang would call the respective police station to have the officers on scene back off so the gang could handle the situation. The driving forces behind the enforcement of the extortion "contracts" were Chino Valles and Farmero.

When Chávez ran the extortion operations in Ciudad Juárez, he initially had a unique approach.

"At that time, I did not ask for *cuota* to the businesses. I make a meeting with the guys that they have business, and I ask them for help so I can pay the police. And I was going to give them protection with that. So in a way, it's *cuota*, but I ask them nicely." The message was begrudgingly received, with Chávez raking in 15,000-20,000 pesos per week for the organization. Other members collected *cuotas* north of the border in El Paso and southern New Mexico. Chávez put the proceeds to effective use by paying off the police in his district.

"I give it to—when it was to pay the Federal police, I gave it to one of the La Línea workers. When it was for the municipal police, I give to Zorro. Zorro was the one in charge to give it to somebody." He made it clear that law enforcement—municipal, federal, and traffic police—received a take of the extortion proceeds.

The federal police were apparently double-dipping in 2009 by taking bribes from both the VCF DTO and Sinaloa DTO. A dangerous but lucrative proposition, it held only until 2010, when the financial agreement between the BA and federal police became strained.

A cable obtained by WikiLeaks from the US Consulate in Ciudad Juárez on March 16, 2011, painted an ominous picture of life for residents (Ramsey 2011):

> 4. (SBU) Perhaps more than a fear of being in the wrong place at the wrong time when cartel hit squads go after a target, Juárez residents are troubled by the increase in the levels of kidnapping and carjacking. Prior to mid-2008, kidnapping was rare in Ciudad Juárez. Around mid-year, reports of kidnappings of junkyard owners began to hit the news. While there was commotion in the press over this phenomenon, there was also a perception that cash-strapped, cartel-affiliated gangs were going after soft-target individuals who were operating on the fringes of legality anyway. [Note: many of the junkyards are "chop shops" for cars stolen by the gangs themselves.] Ransoms also tended to be relatively low; families could often retrieve a loved one for 30,000 dollars or less. Over the past few months, however, as the twin crimes of extortion and kidnapping became more widespread, the level of concern has increased. The kidnapping on Junary 13 of a Lear Corporation manager, as he left a Juarez maquila plant at 7:00 a.m., and the subsequent reported demand for 1.5 million dollars in ransom, appears to have taken this crime to a new level. [Note: the Lear manager was reported rescued by Mexican army troops on January 19.]
>
> 5. (U) The other crime that most concerns law-abiding Juárez residents is carjacking. Figures for nonviolent and violent [that is, carjacking] car theft over the past twelve months paint a troubling picture.

Murguía, who would serve as mayor from 2010-2013, was never ambiguous as to what he felt about the criminal element in his city. He wanted results and wanted them fast, hiring the controversial Julián Leyzaola as his new municipal chief of police.

"These delinquents are beasts and we will catch them," the Ciudad Juárez mayor said. "Chief Leyzaola said he is not resigning and we don't expect him to" (Kolb 2012a).

"Morale is higher than it has been in years because Leyzaola is a hands-on manager," said one eight-year police veteran who only wanted to be identified as Patrolman Francisco. "We are much more professional and getting results" (Kolb 2012a).

Officials believe this reborn police effort has been a source of antagonism among many of the mid- and lower-level street gangs.

CHAPTER 9

Matanza

Animosity between the Barrio Azteca and their Sinaloa counterparts, the Artistas Asesinos, had been escalating since 2008 with multiple brutal murders on the streets of Ciudad Juárez. Villas de Salvarcar is a community in the southeast section of the city. The working-class neighborhood was able to avoid much of the carnage enveloping the rest of the city. That was until late one brisk January night in 2010.

On Friday, January 30, 2010, eighteen-year-old Jesús Enríquez celebrated his birthday with some sixty people in the small, pale yellow house-turned-pseudo-community center at 1310 Villa de Portal Street. Teens and young adults from around the neighborhood, many of whom played on a local football team, joined in the party.

While the word of the party spread, an informant notified La Línea that members of the Doble A, prime targets, had converged on the party. José Antonio "El Diego" Acosta Hernández, thirty-three, second in command behind La Línea leader Juan Pablo Ledezma, dispatched a team of *sicarios* to send a pointed message that the Doble A would not be accepted on the streets of Ciudad Juárez. Many alleged gang members in one confined place was a target-rich environment. It would later emerge that three of the adult partygoers were street-level drug dealers (Borderland Beat 2010a).

Acosta had been dismissed from Chihuahua's state investigative police force and its anti-kidnapping unit in 2007, after failing a polygraph test. He wouldn't be the lone former police officer implicated in the Villas de Salvarcar massacre.

Early in the evening, between seven and eight o'clock, the hit team would meet at a restaurant to hash out and confirm the final details of the raid. It was determined that a scout vehicle would drive by the house and survey the area, then return around fifteen minutes later with the last reconassaince report prior to the assault.

Around midnight some twenty operatives silently moved six vehicles to both ends of Villa de Portal Street to block it from incoming and outgoing traffic. With the street secured and lookouts in place, the gunmen walked toward the house at a nonchalant pace and began shooting. AK-47 and AR-15 fire was sprayed around the house hitting cinder block walls, furnishings, and human occupants, who scrambled over furniture and each other to avoid the fusillade. It only lasted a few minutes. When satisfied with their attack, the assailants fled the scene.

Luz María Dávila, who lived nearby, knew her two sons, José Luis, fifteen, and Marcos, nineteen, were at the party. She had assumed it was safe for them to be at a neighboring house on the typically quiet street. When the gunfire erupted around 11:30 p.m., she knew her sons were in danger. She arrived at the house to find Marcos, a worker at a local maquiladora and a college student studying international relations, lying on the ground. Then she saw José Luis. "The bodies were scattered everywhere," she says. "I yelled to my husband, 'They're dead!'" (Beaubien 2010).

It would take ambulances two hours to gain access as families and spectators descended upon the neighborhood to assess the condition of their loved ones and futilely attempt to render first aid.

When officials arrived, they found a scene reminiscent of a horror movie. Blood-covered bodies lay next to each other. Footing was tenuous because of the blood-soaked tile floors. Blood splatter was all over the walls of the small house, and hysterical families clamored to see their children. Neighbors waded through puddles of blood attempting to sweep away the tragedy which would garner international attention for the sheer brutality of the incident.

When the final count was taken, sixteen young men ranging in age from thirteen to forty-two years old were dead. Many of the eleven teens murdered played on a local American-style football team intended to keep youth away from the violence that consumed the city.

While it would emerge some Doble A were at the party, the majority of those killed had no connection to the narco organizations. This intelligence disaster caused great consternation with the La Línea leadership, who knew there would be broad outrage and a media-fueled police investigation.

Especially incensed was El Diego, realizing the attention the massacre would draw to the organization. He held the informant personally responsible and had him summarily executed.

"They informed me there were Doblados (Artistas Asesinos) there that belonged to the Sinaloa Cartel. I sent the guys and they said they had located them. I gave the order for them to go to work. Some victims were members of rival groups. They recruit students and the very young to avoid detection on the streets. Because they were all underage, there was a lot of publicity. The truth is several of them were innocents," El Diego told investigators in a taped interview after his subsequent arrest.

When alleged conspirator Israel Arzate Meléndez, who served as a lookout as the massacre unfolded, was arrested, he told investigators his orders were clear.

"We were looking for a young guy . . . who was with the Artistas Asesinos," Arzate said. "*El Rama* [the leader of the group] told us to kill everyone, including women" (Valencia 2010a).

Acosta, who would also admit to orchestrating fifteen hundred murders in and around Ciudad Juárez, told investigators that it was not uncommon for the Doble A to attend large parties in an attempt to recruit more members.

Officials would ultimately attribute the massacre to Los Linces, the special forces-trained hit squad that worked closely with La Línea and the BA (Borunda 2016). Officials went on to say that the attack was masterminded by Adrian "El Rama" Ramirez of El Paso, José Dolores Arroyo Chavarría, and Israel Arzate "El 24" or "El Country" Meléndez, who then trickled the orders down the chain of command (Borunda 2016). There was speculation the organizers had been subordinates of Eduardo "Tablas" Ravelo Rodriguez, the BA leader in Ciudad Juárez.

The massacre drew the same level of international attention and scorn that had been garnered by the disappearance of hundreds of women from Ciudad Juárez over a twenty-year span. The city's reputation had received one more blow. Its infamy would be hard to escape, especially after the president made an erroneous assumption that would cause his administration significant embarrassment.

The initial public response made by President Felipe Calderón was that since they were targeted, the partygoers likely had some connection to the city's crime scene, a pronouncement that caused nationwide outrage. The president was compelled to quickly retract his statement. Two weeks later he arrived in Ciudad Juárez to address the families and apologize for his insensitivity. What he likely wasn't prepared for was the hornet's nest he kicked during the town hall-like meeting with residents and family members, who were fed up with the unrelenting violence in their city, where even teens trying to avoid crime were violently sucked into it.

One gathering of families in front of the house where the killings occurred displayed a banner saying "Until we find who is responsible, you Mr. President are the assassin!" (Cardona 2010).

The president's words hit Luz María Dávila like the many bullets that killed her sons. Standing in front of the dais that held a seated and humbled Calderón, who kept nodding his head in affirmation as she spoke, Davila excoriated the president in a voice cracking with emotion. "My two sons were students; one was in college and the other was in high school, they both worked to pay for school and they hadn't time to be involved in gangs. Mr. President, how do you explain and how do you justify saying that the youths that were massacred were gang members? My children and their friends were students, not gang members!

"Mr. President," she continued, "if you had lost your two sons and I lost them, I assure you that you would move land and sea to find the murderers. . . . Please do that for my children" (Borderland Beat 2010b).

Facing daunting pressure, law enforcement and the military, which had occupied the city as part of Calderón's offensive on the narco traffickers, had to move fast to secure arrests, most under typically dubious circumstances that would strain the Mexican constitution and violate human rights.

Regret came from an unlikely source. Acosta told officials after his arrest that he realized most of the victims were innocent and that he felt "bad" about what happened. This did nothing to assuage the pain the victims were feeling. They wanted arrests and accountability—often a paradox in Mexican criminal justice.

On February 3, José Dolores Arroyo Chavarría was taken into custody following a firefight with the military that claimed the life of another suspect in the massacre, *El Doce*. Arroyo would say that the military coerced his confession by torturing him.

Within a month, authorities had an array of suspects, including Aldo Favio "El 18" Hernandez Lozano. This arrest would be a mixed blessing for law enforcement. On the positive side, it was an arrest in the case. On the embarrassing side, Hernandez was a member of the Juárez Municipal Police Department from July 2000 to October 2008. CNN reported at the time that Hernandez had failed a lie detector test, which might have been an indication he was working for the DTO while in uniform. His next occupation would be that of hitman—Sicario—where he was paid $2,000 per week (Valencia 2010b). Israel "El 24" or "El Country" Arzate Melendez; Heriberto Martínez, an Azetca who was suspected of committing four of the fifteen murders; Juan Alfredo Soto Arias; and Aldo Favio "El 18" Hernández had been taken into custody while another suspect was killed by the Mexican army in a gun battle in the southern part of the city.

Aldo Favio Hernandez Lozano informed investigators that Alfredo "Arnold" Arias was the leader of Los Linces, had coordinated the attack, and had supplied the weapons. The last suspect was Luis Alberto "El Shoker," or "El Flaco," Camacho Ramos.

It wasn't long until Arzate also complained that his confession was obtained after he had been tortured by the military. He alleged the torture included electric shocks, asphyxiation, and threats that his wife would be raped and killed. A Mexican judge found his complaint to be legitimate, but it wasn't until November 2013 that the Mexican Supreme Court decided that testimony obtained under torture was a violation of the constitution and ordered him released from prison, where he had been held in isolation for nearly three years.

In July 2011, José Dolores Arroyo Chavarría, Heriberto Martínez, Juan Alfredo Soto Arias, and Aldo Favio Hernández were found guilty of the attempted homicide of eight other people. Each was sentenced to two hundred forty years in prison.

The arrest of Acosta in July 2011 in the Colinas del Sol neighborhood of Chihuahua City was a pivotal event in crime fighting on the border. After a brief shootout with military and police, Acosta was taken into custody. Not only was his arrest another important piece of the massacre puzzle, he had also ordered the murder of US DEA agents in Ciudad Juárez and Chihuahua, a threat officials took seriously but which never materialized. Interestingly, the Central Intelligence Agency had a hand in intercepting information that contributed to Acosta's arrest (Justice in Mexico 2011).

Another embarrassment that emerged from the tragedy was the hand the United States government inadvertently played in the massacre. When Acosta was arrested, he had in his possession weapons that had crossed the border as part of the ATF's botched "Fast and Furious" strategy.

Villas de Salvarcar was not Acosta's first ordered massacre, nor was it the first to use weapons from Fast and Furious. The first occurred when he ordered the killing of nineteen drug addicts El Aliviane drug rehabilitation center on the night of September 2, 2009 (Reyes and Wills 2012).

"I instructed them to go and murder some groups of opponents in two rehabilitation centers," Acosta said, presuming the occupants were from a rival gang (Reyes and Wills 2012).

Acosta may not have been aware that the ATF gave tacit approval for these weapons, which included multiple AK-47s, to cross the border, but he took full advantage of the agency's debacle.

In a little-known footnote to the massacre were reports that four survivors of the tragedy had allegedly been kidnapped by police investigators less than a week after the shooting. It was reported that late at night on the Wednesday following the shooting, agents from the Chihuahua State Police, wearing hoods and driving unmarked vehicles, barged into the still-shocked victim's homes and took them out by force.

Frantic parents ran to the police headquarters inquiring about their children, only to be told they would not learn where their children were until the morning. Around 3:30 a.m. the youngsters were released (Garcia 2010). Everyone in Ciudad Juárez knew by now that hit teams would stop at nothing to finish the job. Masked men could pose as police officers—a ruse that had been employed on previous occasions, so there was a credible threat the parents would never see their children again. Or, in a worst-case scenario, legitimate police, corrupted by the DTOs, would kill them.

Almost ten months to the day following the Villas de Salvarcar massacre, a birthday party was interrupted by gunfire and bloodshed at the hands of the La Línea/Barrio Azteca alliance. At around 11 p.m. on October 23, 2010, two minivans parked outside a house in the southeast Ciudad Juárez neighborhood of Horizontes del Sur, where a birthday party for a fifteen-year-old boy was being celebrated. Some ten gunmen wearing hoods and dark clothing, mostly teens themselves, approached the house with automatic weapons drawn. The attack was similar to the Villas de Salvarcar massacre, which was about a mile away from this scene of carnage, in that the approaching cross streets were guarded and effectively closed down by gang members. Gunmen were looking for an individual connected to the Artistas Asesinos, and nobody at the party appeared to have any knowledge of gang connections. Indiscriminate shooting started outside, continued inside the house, then spread to a neighboring house where many had fled the fusillade.

When the shooting ended eleven lay dead at the scene. Another three died at the hospital, and twenty were wounded. Seven of the mostly teen fatalities were members of a traditional Mexican dance group. Nobody was ever prosecuted for this massacre, emboldening the BA further.

In the wake of the party massacres the BA continued their reign of terror, which caused many collateral casualties not associated with the drug trade. There were two subsequent incidents in 2010 that would finally begin to unravel the organization as it was known, splitting it into two factions and causing what some felt would be an irreparable rupture in the binational structure of the BA. One eroding factor leading to these two high-profile attacks was the violation of the one of the gang's major tenets: that no gang member may cooperate with law enforcement.

Gallegos would later fill in some of the blanks associated with the Villas de Salvarcar massacre when he was interviewed by FBI agents after his arrest. Telling them he was fully aware of what had happened, in a surprise twist he claimed the massacre was actually carried out by La Línea and not the BA, which contradicted previous assumptions and media reports. He did confirm that the attack was based on the intelligence that Doble As were there.

Whether he was being truthful or merely trying to mitigate the already monumental evidence against him, it's likely that Gallegos's crews at least had their fingerprints on the tragic miscalculation that raised the national ire of an increasingly exhausted Mexico.

Even with Acosta and Gallegos serving federal prison sentences in the US, the BA continued their shooting sprees.

In August 2018, eleven people were murdered at a house party attended by both Mexicles and Doble A gang members in the Pradera de los Oasis neighborhood of Ciudad Juárez. Police officials said the raid was revenge for the Doble A green-lighting the death of an associate of the BA. The victim, Jonathan Rene Hernandez Perez, was reportedly set up to be killed by his girlfriend because he had been stealing the proceeds from narcotics sales (Borunda 2018b).

The twist came when Hernandez's father, a reputed Doble A and heroin and methamphetamine dealer, switched allegiance to the BA to obtain revenge for his son's murder. At the father's behest, the Azteca hunted down those responsible. The bodies of the alleged cheating girlfriend,

Meibi Oyuki, and Amador Estupiñan Ibarra, who was a former partner of Hernandez's father and the culprit in setting up Hernandez's death, were found tortured and dead in the trunk of a Honda Accord (Borunda 2018b).

The Villas de Salvarcar massacre was a prelude to an incident that would rock the borderland as much as the murder of DEA Agent Enrique "Kiki" Camarena did in 1985 when he was tortured and murdered by the Guadalajara Cartel.

CHAPTER 10

Americans in the Crosshairs

On Saturday, March 13, 2010, Tanisha End was assigned to the El Paso sector as an enforcement specialist for the US Border Patrol. Although End was relegated to an office, her job was no less important in monitoring suspicious border activity. Among her duties were running warrants on apprehended individuals, vehicle inquiries, and monitoring fifty cameras trained on both sides of the border. The cameras had infrared capability for night monitoring, and End and her colleagues could manipulate the cameras one hundred eighty degrees and zoom in and out. When End observed any suspicious activity such as attempts at illegal entry, fires, accidents, or people loitering by the border fence, she would radio the appropriate USBP agent to investigate. She could also observe activities in Mexico.

This was a period of high alert for officials like End along the border. The narco war was already claiming a body count in the thousands, and errant rounds would occasionally find their way into El Paso. Even though Operation Hold the Line mitigated illegal border crossings, attempts were still made. These would be facilitated by teens throwing rocks at agents as a diversion at one end the the border, while migrants and/or drug smugglers would cross farther away.

"We were on alert because we had a lot of shootings that were coming into El Paso. We had a lot of people that were fleeing Mexican authorities. Anything that happens close to any of our POEs (Ports of Entry) and close to the United States, we're told to keep a better eye on it," she said at the Gallegos trial.

Standard procedure was to notify Mexican authorities if USBP picked up anything on the Mexican side. Surprisingly, this system was usually effective.

Arturo Gallegos Castrellón orchestrated much of the chaos perpetrated by the Barrio Azteca in Ciudad Juárez. Courtesy of the *El Diario de Juarez*.

On this particular day End was working the day shift when at 3:13 p.m. she received a call from a field agent reporting smoke on the Mexico side. End swung tower-mounted cameras thirteen and fourteen in the direction of the Ciudad Juárez City Hall, just yards from the northbound entrance of the Stanton Street Bridge. Immediately scanning the area, End saw what appeared to be an motor vehicle accident.

"I'm watching to see if there's an accident. If so, if there's anyone getting out of the vehicle. If not, I can call Mexico and let them know they have an accident."

Over the course of the ensuing twenty-one minutes, End would see multiple vehicles converge around a white SUV and a red Pontiac GrandAm.

"I figured it wasn't really an accident because there was a lot of law enforcement present. We had federal, you had military, and you have local Mexican authorities on the scene."

End was surprised that despite the law enforcement and military response at the scene there were no fire or emergency medical personnel. Nothing and no one was moving.

For most of the gang's existence, the Barrio Azteca enjoyed relative public anonymity in the United States, perhaps even in El Paso itself, save for the RICO (Racketeering Influenced Corrupt Organizations) indictments.

The gang's exploits were perceived as an isolated gang matter. A cartel matter. Or even a Mexican matter. That all changed, albeit briefly, in March 2010.

Organizations, whether licit or illicit, can make poor corporate decisions that can render them vulnerable to competitive and legal consequences. In March 2010, the BA made a pivotal error in judgement, likely based, as with the party massacres, on poor intelligence. Not since the torture and murder of DEA agent Enrique "Kiki" Camarena, during an undercover operation in Guadalajara in 1985, had the full weight of American law enforcement fallen on individuals across the border as it did when the BA attacked US consulate workers and their families on March 13, 2010.

Even in the wake of the Villas de Salvarcar massacre, which only yielded five suspects out of a supposed twenty, the BA had continued to enjoy relative freedom from large-scale prosecution from Mexican law enforcement, who were able to apprehend only the inexperienced lower level—most expendable—members of the gang. In the infamous consulate attack, BA were once again pulling the triggers. While the actual reason for the attack is subject to speculation, what can reasonably be assumed is that it was the result of another BA intelligence blunder.

It's hard not to be paranoid in the narco world. As the competition and violence escalated during the early part of 2010, VCF capos ordered more pressure to be put on Sinaloa operatives in the city. During this period El Paso saw an influx of cheaper heroin from Sinaloa, raising questions among the VCF about how it was getting into the city. Operational intelligence gave way to supposition by VCF, and they wanted answers and accountability immediately.

TARGETS

There was speculation among BA leadership that a white SUV was conducting surveillance in the neighborhood many of them lived in, perhaps preparing an attack. Another theory held that the only way for Sinaloa to increase the shipment of cheaper heroin into El Paso was with the cooperation of consulate officials.

Gallegos called the shots, and the BA would be the willing executioners. During Gallegos's 2014 trial, Chávez, the star witness for the prosecution, said Gallegos told all BA members in Ciudad Juárez to watch for a white Honda Pilot. Conspicuously missing from the gang's intelligence information was identification of the vehicle's driver.

Around 2:30 p.m. on March 13, thirty-four-year-old Arthur Redelfs, Lesley Ann Enriquez, thirty-five, and their seven-month-old daughter left a party for another consulate employee at the lemon-yellow Barquito de Papel in an upscale Ciudad Juárez neighborhood in their white 2009 Toyota RAV4 with Texas license plates. Lesley Ann was four months pregnant with a boy.

Later that afternoon radio chatter identified two white SUVs, referred to as "white jackets," that were spotted behind a party hall near some apartments on Bustamante and Insurgentes.

Gallegos was in close radio contact with Popeye, who was the eyes in that vicinity. Two blocks away, Popeye positioned himself by the Benavides Pharmacy. In the meantime, Gallegos was on the radio with Chino, asking if the team had been deployed.

"Affirmative, affirmative, yes," came Chino's reply.

El Chino left Mexico with his family when he was six years old and moved to El Paso, where he lived for some thirty years. His criminal orientation was initially through El Paso's Las Fatherless gang. During a stint in La Tuna federal prison in nearby Anthony, Texas, he was introduced to the BA by David Almaraz. In 2007 he returned to Ciudad Juárez to work for the Azteca, where he tallied his own large and gruesome body count against the gang's main rivals (Borderland Beat 2010c).

Wanting to satisfy his boss, Popeye repeatedly radioed "*86*," which was Gallegos's other nom de guerre.

"I'm there in the area in case they wanted me to help them locate them. I'm telling him that I'm on—well, I'm saying the word *people*. *People* is in reference to *Avenida de la Raza*, that's the street, and that I'm there to locate them, and to tell the other guys who were going to arrive." The mobilization of gangsters left little doubt what the mission was: eliminate the occupants of the white SUV.

Other key players at this point in the operation included Fresa, also known as Tio. When Gallegos contacted him over the radio, he was instructed to bring "little tools," meaning weapons. Luis Mendez contacted Camello and said he would need more "32s," referring to men, in order to launch the operation.

Outside the party, where children were celebrating a birthday and parents conversed on the side, a second parent arrived in another white SUV. Miguel Ángel Nevarez radioed to his commander that he was down the block on Bustamante Street looking right at them.

"I reported that to Benny. While I was giving him this information, some people came out, a couple [the woman is referred to as a "20" in the gang radio language] with a child. And I tried to tell him what they were wearing, the people I'm looking at. And these people were trying to leave. They were about to leave in one of the SUVs that were parked there," Nevarez says. "It's not necessarily someone with money but someone who dresses like fashionable, casually, with jeans and shirts and athletic shoes and the like."

As soon as the white RAV4 SUV with *parque* (El Paso) license plates pulled away from the sidewalk, Nevarez began tailing it. It proceeded north along Bustamante, then made a right turn onto Insurgentes. When the SUV got to Plutarco Elias Calles (locally abbreviated to *Plues*) street, prey and predator turned left, now heading north. At this point Zorro joined Nevarez in the pursuit. It is not clear at what point Redelfs noticed he was being tailed, but when the vehicles arrived at Costa Rica after turning off Ribereno, the situation became clear.

"That's when the first attempt was going to be made to shoot," says Nevarez of the order radioed to him by Gallegos.

Since there were two white SUVs in play at this point, a mission clarification was made by Popeye. The reply from Gallegos was to kill all of them. At one point before the attack was launched two military vehicles pulled in front of the pursuers, temporarily delaying the attack. The gang's slang for the military was *abuelo*, grandfather. Around this time doubts began to arise among the attackers. Zorro reported to Gallegos that the vehicle he was surveilling was a Toyota and not the white Pilot they were looking for.

"Well, shoot him anyway," Gallegos coldly responded.

Nevarez says his mission was to stand watch around the white SUV while Zorro killed the occupants. Zorro formulated and radioed the getaway plan following the shooting. They were to drive to Sunland Park, New Mexico, across the border from Rancho Anapra, Zorro's stomping grounds.

As the military peeled off the route, Zorro decided he had a shot.

"Zorro is telling us to keep an eye, to keep a close eye, because he was going to try to make the hit at Costa Rica—at the light on Costa Rica. He's saying 'Costa,' which is Costa Rica Street," Nevarez said. But when they got to Costa Rica, the light changed to green, so they had to continue waiting for an opportunity. Zorro is asking us to stop next to the SUV, to box him so that the white SUV would not be able to escape."

It wouldn't be much longer before Zorro had his chance.

"We got to—to a U-turn on Ribereño—to a place where you can make a U-turn on Ribereño. And then vehicle that was in front stopped, and then a white—the white SUV. And since I wasn't able to stop next to it, I stopped behind it, and then Zorro got next to it. He got out of the vehicle and he shot."

By now there was no doubt Arthur and Lesley knew they were in trouble. The first shots were fired on Ribereño in front of the Ciudad Juárez municipal building, toward the passenger's side, at an angle. Several shots were heard. The SUV sped up, then Zorro got back into his vehicle and followed them. It didn't take long for them to catch their prey. When they reached the RAV4, Zorro leaned out of the window and started shooting. Then there was quiet, followed by Zorro's triumphant radio transmission to Gallegos, "That's it. That's it. The person tried to escape, but we got him right in front of City Hall."

In one of his last living actions, Redelfs had crashed into a vehicle stopped at the intersection. The red four-door GrandAm was idling at the red light at 3:15 p.m. when the SUV crashed into it. A sixteen-year-old in his first semester in high school emerged from the passenger side. His mother was behind the wheel, driving the boy and his sister home, proceeding east on Heroic Colegio Militar, a busy thoroughfare that runs along the border.

"[The SUV] struck us and then it struck another vehicle, and then it stopped," the teen reported.

Sensing something beyond an ordinary accident was dreadfully wrong, the teen's mother backed out of the intersection but eventually had to pull over due to the damage their vehicle had sustained. The incredulous teen exited his car and walked toward the white SUV to confront them about the accident when he was shocked to see the bullet-riddled bodies of Arthur Redelfs and Lesley Ann Enriquez in the front seat. Arthur and Lesley's daughter would be taken out of the rear child seat of the vehicle by a female police officer upon her arrival.

Speculation was rampant about the incident. The arrested suspects attempted to deflect blame for their actions, and a shroud of intrigue surrounded the crime that briefly made for scintillating reading. But there was no evidence that Redelfs or Enriquez were involved in any wrong-doing—the logical motive for such an attack. The botched operation hadn't achieved any retribution for the BA, and the long-term consequences of the attack would be unrelenting pressure by US law enforcement.

There was speculation about other possible motives for the attack. Redelfs was a ten-year veteran officer employed in the El Paso County Detention Center, a long-standing depository for arrested BA. One of the first suspects arrested in the case by Mexican authorities, forty-five-year-old Ricardo "El Chino" Valles de la Rosa, claimed that the attack was retribution for Redelfs's mistreatment of incarcerated gang member El Chano in the El Paso County Detention Center (McKinley 2010). The statement by El Chino, who sported BA tattoos on his torso with a large El Paso tattoo on the back of his neck, was met with cynicism by US officials.

"It must be remembered that he is a career criminal whose credibility may be suspect," said El Paso County Sheriff Richard Wiles in a statement upon hearing the allegation made against his murdered officer (McKinley 2010).

Redelfs's pregnant wife Lesley worked in the US Consulate in Juárez, a singularly important border facility where individuals obtained visas to enter the US. The theory that garnered little public traction was that Enriquez was the specific target because the gang had tried and failed to corrupt her in her position as an assistant in the American Citizens Services Department, where she would have dealt with transborder visas. Jesús Ernesto Chávez, who would later be arrested in connection with the attack, floated the idea that the hit was because Lesley was giving preference for visas to the BA's rivals (Lee 2010).

"An individual approached [Enriquez at least twice in consulate-related settings prior to her murder] and tried to get her to do something with a document without the proper paperwork," one law enforcement official claims. "Her murder was ordered because she refused to go along with it."

Chávez would later testify that Gallegos received intelligence that a white Honda Pilot SUV was being used by the Sinaloa group to ambush Juárez Cartel and La Línea members, so an all points bulletin went out to locate and eliminate those in this vehicle. Another reason Gallegos may have wanted this vehicle targeted was that his wife had recently been followed by such a vehicle. On March 13, 2010, the Redelfs had the misfortune of driving a white SUV in Ciudad Juárez.

Thirty-seven-year-old Jorge Alberto Salcido Ceniceros married his wife, Hilda Antillon, in 1997. She had worked at the consulate as a Foreign Service National Employee since 1996. Jorge was late for the party because he had to run errands that morning. He arrived about an hour after Hilda.

When the couple left the party Hilda followed Jorge in the family's other vehicle. Jorge left the party with his two, four, and seven-year-old children in his white 2003 Honda Pilot. They departed around the same time as the Redelfs.

Hilda would recount how she and Jorge left the party and were driving the short distance to their Ciudad Juárez home along Insurgentes. At a red light on Plutarco Calles, she pulled up to the side of her husband's vehicle, not realizing the vehicle that was creeping up behind him. When the light turned green and Jorge began driving away, the occupants in the trailing vehicle began firing at the Honda. Hilda could hear her husband's screams amid the fusillade. The attacking vehicle briefly pulled away, but made a U-turn and began shooting into the Honda again, as if they wanted to be sure they had hit their target. Hilda got out of her vehicle and implored the shooters to stop. Inexplicably, she was not harmed. The shooting ceased, and the attackers drove off (CBS News 2010a).

Hilda quickly ran to the vehicle and told her gravely wounded husband to be strong, but he did not respond.

"I saw my kids. They were crying and bleeding and screaming."

Hilda called her sister to come quickly while a woman whose house was nearby took the children in. Hilda stayed with her dead husband. Hilda would later testify that, "The kids used to go always in that car [the Honda Pilot], because he [Jorge] felt it was more safe for the kids to ride in that particular car."

The synchronized attacks, which occurred ten minutes apart and several miles from each other, indicated the type of tactical training the BA allegedly had learned from Los Zetas—how to shoot at a moving vehicle.

The incidents sparked immediate outrage and microscopic attention on the BA as well as the Mexican criminal justice system, which faced pressure from the US government.

Gallegos's 2014 trial and subsequent conviction resulted in his being sentenced to life, and testimony at the trial—largely from Chávez—opened a window into the Barrio Azteca organizational structure, tactics, and relationship to La Línea and VCF. This in turn appeared to open an irreparable rift between the BA and VCF.

Just as it did in 1985, after Enrique "Kiki" Camarena was tortured and murdered in Guadalajara, the US government aggressively launched a campaign to bring those responsible for the murders to justice, a case that would both alienate the BA from the VCF and begin to destroy the gang from the inside out, as their most cherished value of silence had been shattered.

It's unusual for the BA to demonstrate remorse following their murders, but the hit teams almost immediately felt there was something wrong about this particular mission. Nevarez said that as soon the news broke they knew it was a mistake. There was an implicit order from Tablas, the current head of the organization, not to discuss the mission over the telephone or radios. An angry Vega took a bold stance by agreeing the ambush was a mistake. It's unclear if they were angry because they realized they killed innocent people, rarely an issue in the past, or because they knew how much heat would come down on them when the victims became known.

THE INVESTIGATION

In less than two weeks Mexican officials began rounding up suspects with the full support of the US Drug Enforcement Administration and the Federal Bureau of Investigation. The initial investigation into the ambushes was handled by the *Procuraduría General de Justicia,* essentially the Chihuahua state attorney general's office, but a few weeks later, for unpublished reasons, the case was taken over by the federal attorney general's office, the PGR (Procuraduría General de la República), out of Mexico City. Down the road this would complicate matters since all suspects arrested in Ciudad Juárez would be transferred to the capital.

Among the first significant suspects to be arrested was Ricardo "El Chino" Valles de la Rosa. Two weeks after the attack the military in Ciudad Juárez took him into custody (Valencia 2010d). In July 2010, Jesús Ernesto Chávez Castillo, forty-one, was also picked up (CBS News 2010b). He would later admit at trial that after personally killing more than eight hundred people he stopped counting (*Daily Mail* 2014). Gallegos is said to have ordered the murder of Chávez's wife in retribution for his giving too much information about the gang to officials (Malkin 2010), although Chávez alleged his confession was elicited after three days of extreme torture by Mexican police.

Throughout the remainder of 2010 a steady stream of gang members was taken into custody, but it wouldn't be until late November that Gallegos, the reputed ring leader and ultimate target of the case, would be arrested in Ciudad Juárez. Prior to his extradition to the United States in June 2012 Gallegos also alleged he had been tortured by federal police while in custody in Mexico City. He alleged his testicles had been electrically shocked and that he was hung by his arms and beaten. He also claimed that his wife had been raped (McCormack 2013).

"He is in charge of the whole organization of Los Aztecas in Ciudad Juárez," said Luis Cárdenas Palomino, chief of the regional security division of the federal police at a press conference in Mexico City. "All the instructions for the murders committed in Ciudad Juárez pass through him" (McCormack 2013).

On March 11, 2011, a year after the ambushes, the US Attorney's Office unsealed a third superceding RICO indictment against thirty-five gang members, ten of whom were charged in connection with the ambushes (FBI 2011). This led to eventual extraditions and prosecution in the United States, including José Antonio "El Diego" Acosta Hernández, who was extradited in March 2012 and would plead guilty to his role in the murders. These cases were resolved in relatively short shrift.

Of the thirty-five defendants charged, twenty-four pleaded guilty, twenty-two of whom were US-based gang members. Ramon "Spooky" Renteria, a capo on the US side of the border, committed suicide while incarcerated during his trial. Luis Mendez and Eduardo Ravelo remained on the run, and the latter would join the ranks of the FBI's Ten Most Wanted until his arrest by Mexican officials in Uruapan, Michoacán, June 26, 2018.

Prior to his extradition to the US on June 29, 2012, Gallegos had a cordial interview with FBI agents in Mexico City. Although he would allege he'd been tortured over the previous few days, he made no mention of this to the FBI, who found Gallegos to be relaxed and unintimidated.

A request was made and granted for FBI Special Agent Carlos Hernandez, Supervisory Special Agent Rodolfo Ortega, and Special Agent Lorenzo Perez to interview Gallegos November 29, 2010.

Hernandez was scheduled to interview the thirty-two-year-old Gallegos on the third floor of the PGR offices in Mexico City. The FBI team went into the interview with Gallegos cold. They did not read any of the reports provided by Mexican officials, perhaps to have a clean unbiased canvas upon which to paint their own picture. At the time, the agents didn't even know whether their prime suspect had made any statements to either Mexican state or federal officials.

After the agents were settled in, at 6:38 p.m. Gallegos, in handcuffs and wearing a polo shirt and Docker pants, not the stereotypical appearance of a gang member, was escorted into the interview room by two members of the *Agencia Federal de Investigaciónes*, the federal investigative agency.

Once in the room the Mexican agents removed the handcuffs from Gallegos and left, closing the door behind them. As he settled into an office chair the agents noticed Gallegos was red around his face and had a limp. The room was a simple office with a glass wall allowing a view into the rest of the facility. The agents noticed that the ebb and flow of work continued unabated while the interview was being conducted, with few curious glances toward the glass from office personnel.

Gallegos paid close attention to the agents' questioning during the initial interview, which lasted about two hours. The agents presented Gallegos with a document explaining his rights, which he signed "firmado" where it indicated nombre (name).

"Mr. Gallegos indicated that he was familiar with the document; that he had seen that document before, because between the years 1998 and the year 2000, he had been incarcerated in the United States at the La Tuna Federal Correctional Institution in Anthony, Texas, and that he had seen that document before," testified Agent Hernandez.

Surprisingly, Gallegos said he was willing to discuss at great length his introduction into the gang. It was during his two-year sentence in the US that he became familiar with the BA through a fellow inmate—*Casitas*—finally becoming a full member in 2005. Gallegos was deported back to Ciudad Juárez, where he began working with his father selling *tortas*, meaning sandwiches. When *Casitas* was released from La Tuna in 2005, he too, was deported back to Mexico and became reacquainted with Gallegos. Once firmly entrenched in the gang Gallegos told Hernandez he would attend the "church" meetings twice a month. For about a year Gallegos had met various members, but testified that while he knew the name Eduardo "Tablas" Ravelo, he had never seen him at any of the meetings.

Gallegos's introduction to the gang was relatively benign: he was tasked with selling small amounts of narcotics in Ciudad Juárez. But by 2008 he was working hand in glove with La Línea smuggling four hundred kilograms of marijuana into the United States every month. Tractor-trailer trucks were the primary conveyance across the border. The next year he was working more on behalf of his original gang, smuggling two hundred seventy pounds of marijuana into the US every week and gaining the attention of the gang's hierarchy for his efforts. In 2009 he was put in charge of BA communications and made responsible for disseminating information throughout the organization.

As part of the interview the agents asked Gallegos why he was limping. He replied that he had injured himself at the time of his arrest when he attempted to escape from the house he was hiding in by jumping out of a second story window to a tree before falling to the ground.

The interview continued in Spanish in a "cordial—nonaccusatory" tone, which is typically used by law enforcement to help a suspect relax. As a career criminal, Gallegos likely recognized the tactic, but still conversed freely, at times speaking for as long as six uninterrupted minutes with the FBI agents, who reciprocated.

"We basically told Mr. Gallegos that we were investigating the consulate murder; that we wanted to speak to him regarding that matter and obtain whatever knowledge he had regarding those murders and, also, his participation and his knowledge of the Barrio Azteca criminal organization—la Voz." The point person Gallegos dealt with was El Diego, the head of La Línea based out of Ciudad Chihuahua.

Gallegos said he was at home that Saturday afternoon monitoring the crews' radios when he heard Camello say he had located the Honda Pilot reportedly belonging to a Ranas by the party store. That particular area was controlled by the BA. Gallegos transmitted the message received from El Diego, who was in la oficina in Chihuahua City, that crews had identified the target vehicle and was occupied by two males, apparently rivals from southern Mexico. That indicated Gallegos had ordered the attacks at El Diego's behest. This gross blunder triggered the sequence of events that ultimately resulted in the ambushes. Camello would "verify" the target and spread the word for the teams to be on alert.

Gallegos said he heard Popeye and Zorro say that they were going to assist Camello in following the vehicle and executing the occupants. He would implicate Popeye and Zorro as the actual triggermen, but did tell the agents there was confusion around Elias Plutarco Street, where the team lost the white Honda Pilot but picked up the white RAV4.

Like the other suspects, Gallegos learned later in the day that the targets were associated with the consulate. A grave error had been made.

"It was a mistake," Gallegos told investigators. Gallegos said that the order for the hits on this particular operation came from El Diego and not from him, giving the impression he was merely the conduit from the gang hierarchy to the streets. He said he had last seen El Diego some thirty days prior to the attack, in Chihuahua City. Although he was answerable to El Diego, Gallegos rarely had face-to-face contact with him.

In an attempt to better implicate El Diego, Hernández patiently worked Gallegos by letting him talk at length, knowing that the veracity of his account was suspect. When asked at trial whether he believed what Gallegos was saying Hernández replied, "Based on the information that we—that we knew at the time, not completely."

The ultimate targets of the investigation would be El Diego, Eduardo "Tablas" Ravelo of the BA, and Luis "Leo" Mendez of La Línea. Throughout the interview Gallegos would lead the agents through a maze of *sicarios*, hideouts, and gang operations—all such revelations anathema to the code they swore to uphold.

During the interview Gallegos served up a multitude of fellow gang members, validating their roles as *sicarios*. Among others he named Lentes; Popeye, who also ran a legitimate bus service; Zorro; Vega, who was assigned to the Aldama colonia in Ciudad Juárez; Rafa Díaz; and Chino, who served as conduit between the BA in Ciudad Juárez and those incarcerated in the United States. Gallegos revealed the existence of *whilas*, the letters Chino used to convey messages across the border and back.

A pivotal element of the interview came when Gallegos disclosed that Mendez, also known as *Leo* or *Luis*, was the second in command of the BA in Ciudad Juárez and served as the close confident of Eduardo "Tablas" Ravelo. Ironically, though his name was toward the top of the FBI's list, Mendez is the only one of the thirty-five indicted in the third RICO case that was never arrested.

Agent Hernandez asked Gallegos if he would cooperate with the investigation into El Diego, Tablas, and Mendez, but he declined. The damage had already been done, however, and their fates sealed.

As his extradition it appeared likely that Gallegos's defense team would fight vigorously against holding the trial in US Federal Court. They hoped to get his confession to Mexican authorities dismissed, claiming it had been obtained during his alleged torture. This last-ditch effort was in vain. On June 28, 2012, he was flown across the border handcuffed and under heavy guard. The next day, facing twelve counts that included racketeering, narcotics distribution and importation, retaliation against persons providing information to US law enforcement, extortion, money laundering, obstruction of justice, and murder, he appeared before US Magistrate Court Judge Robert Castaneda in the El Paso Federal Court.

"We allege that Gallegos Castrellón participated in the US Consulate shootings in March 2010," said Assistant Attorney General Lanny Breuer.

"His extradition to the United States is an important step forward in our pursuit of justice for the victims of those tragic murders in Juárez, Mexico. Innocent men and women on both sides of our border with Mexico should not have to live in fear of Barrio Azteca and other violent criminal gangs" (United States Department of Justice 2012b).

TRIAL

Gallegos's trial began on February 3, 2014, in the downtown El Paso Federal Court building under heavy security. The trial was presided over by Federal District Court Judge Kathleen Cardone. The prosecution team consisted of Brian Skaret from the Human Rights and Special Prosecutions Section of the U.S. Department of Justice; Joseph Cooley, from the USDOJ Criminal Division, Gang Unit; and John Gibson, assistant US attorney from El Paso. (Both Skaret and Cooley came to El Paso from USDOJ headquarters in Washington, DC.) Randolph Joseph Ortega, out of El Paso, was Gallegos's sole attorney in a case that was virtually unwinnable.

The prosecution was not taking any chances with the jury, given the enigmatic nature of the BA and what role Gallegos played in a reign of terror less than a mile from the courthouse. Two dozen witnesses would be called to the stand by the prosecution, the most damaging to the defense likely being Jesús Ernesto Chávez Castillo, who had firsthand knowledge of the attack on Arthur and Lesley because he was directly involved in it. Chávez, who would be Gallegos's Sammy Gravano who testified against his New York Mafia boss John Gotti, gave a detailed account of the attack and described the structure and operations of the gang on both sides of the border in the days leading up it.

Perhaps not surprisingly, Ortega opted not to have any witnesses. His tactic was to poke holes and reveal inconsistencies in the testimony for the prosecution, hoping to establish reasonable doubt among the jury. A key element to his case was attempting to convince the jury that his client's confession in Mexico was extracted through the torture he allegedly endured at the hands of Mexican authorities. The jury didn't bite.

On February 15, 2014, nearly four years to the day Gallegos ordered the ambush on the vehicles of Arthur Redelfs and Lesley Ann Enriquez and Jorge Alberto Salcido Ceniceros, the jury came back with a verdict. About two hours after Judge Cardone sent the jury out to deliberate, she received word that a unanimous decision had been reached. The jury solemnly filed back into the courtroom and took their seats as the spectators in the gallery waited to be seated by the judge.

When everyone was in their respective places, Judge Cardone asked the jury foreman, "Ladies and gentlemen, it is my understanding that you have been able to reach a verdict; is that correct?"

"Yes, ma'am," came the reply.

Each of the eleven counts, which included murder in a foreign nation, racketeering, narcotics trafficking and importation, and money laundering (Fox News 2014), were read and each received the verdict . . . GUILTY! Now all that was left was the sentencing hearing, which Cardone scheduled for April 24, 2014, at 9:30 a.m.

Cardone then provided Gallegos and Ortega the plan for the coming weeks. "Between now and then, a Court—a probation officer has been assigned to your case. That probation officer will be preparing a written presentence investigation report. During that—for that report, it is probable that the probation officer may want to interview you for the report. You are—you may have your attorney present for that interview. So if you would like Mr. Ortega to be there, please let him know, let your probation officer know, so they can coordinate a time for your interview. Once all of the information has been gathered, a written sentencing report is prepared for the Court. Mr. Gallegos-Castrellón, it is important that you go over that report with your attorney. If there is anything in that report that is incorrect information, you need to let Mr. Ortega know that so that he can file the appropriate paperwork with this Court and let me know that. And all of that is important, Mr. Gallegos, because the information in your sentencing report is the information that I look at for purposes of sentencing."

On the preassigned day, Gallegos would return to Cardone's courtroom. After brief courtroom formalities, Cardone addressed Gallegos with her final sentencing decision that not only would he spend the rest of his life in prison, he would also be required to pay $1 million in restitution to the families of his victims associated with the case.

"I cannot overstate the significance of this victory in our ongoing efforts to end the depredations of the cartels operating along our Southern border," said US Attorney for the Western Disitrict of Texas Robert Pitman. "This prosecution has called to account Arturo Gallegos Castrellón for the senseless murders he orchestrated in Ciudad Juárez and elsewhere and demonstrates our commitment to ending the murder and mayhem he and the cartels have fomented" (United States Department of Justice 2014).

OUTCOME

The betrayal of the gang's most fundamental tenet of loyalty would have significant implications on the stability of the gang on both sides of the border. A cadre of more than thirty members would spend decades in prison. Gallegos would spend the rest of his life at the Supermax prison in Florence, Colorado, with no chance of ever communicating with his colleagues. (I made an attempt to interview Gallegos, but he declined.)

For his testimony, Jesús Ernesto Chávez Castillo would plead guilty to the RICO charges that included the murder of the consulate workers. Judge Cardone would sentence him to eleven life sentences plus ten years. In return for his testimony against Gallegos, the government would place him and his immediate family in the Witness Security Program because they faced certain execution. As for protection, the government assured Chávez he would be housed in a protective security unit in prison under an assumed name to mitigate his chances of being killed while behind bars—a credible and likely threat.

His parents, who lived in Ciudad Juárez when Chávez first began cooperating, were moved to the United States, where they received protection and financial support.

"Because they're old. They're over seventy years old and they cannot work. And my mom is real sick, and so my father is taking care of my mom," he would testify at Gallegos's trial.

José Guadalupe Díaz Díaz, known as the notorious Zorro and one of the trigger men of the ambush, would eventually be extradited back to the US on November 14, 2019.

Fernando Carrillo would be the next to turn against Gallegos. Joining the gang in 2000, he was fully aware of his obligation to silence, as well the consequences for violating the code. Painted into a corner because of his pending sentence, however, he too opted to break it. At Gallegos's trial he testified that he worked out a deal with the government prosecution to lighten the five-year sentence he had received for illegally reentering the US. His reward was that he would only have to serve thirty months of the sentence. Many members of this and other gangs come to see the futility of the gang life, as Carrillo did, or realize they just want to settle down to a "normal" life on the outside rather than spend the rest of their lives in prison.

"I just want to get out from the gang. I'm tired of me following something that's not worth it," he said. He was also assured that if he stayed out of trouble he would not be deported back to Mexico, where he faced certain death. His comments are a compelling indictment of gang culture. The author has spoken to many high-raking gang members who feel "the life" and its scarifices were not worth it at the price of freedom, relationships, and lives.

Gualberto "The Bird" Marquez, a career criminal, joined the gang at Coffield in 1996. He was serving a life sentence for a narcotics conviction and started cooperating before he was sentenced. This trial wasn't the first time he testified against a fellow gang member. After his initial foray the presiding judge reduced his sentence to twenty years, with entry into the Witness Security Program.

Manuel Lopez, a US citizen and leader of the El Paso element of the gang, joined in 2008 and, like his fellow witnesses, had also renounced his association with the gang. Lopez was wrapped up in the RICO case and would plead guilty in exchange for leniency. Not only had Lopez ordered violent assaults, he had coordinated the smuggling of thirty kilograms of heroin and 150 kilograms of cocaine into the US from Mexico. He too had testified in a previous trial and would get Judge Cardone to approve a reduction in his sentence from twenty years to twelve, again with admission into the Witness Security Program.

Lopez had no pretentions of civil obligation.

"Well, I have to tell the truth, basically, me, myself," he said in court. "But I'm also hoping for a time cut. That's all."

One of the biggest consequences to the gang that emerged from the trial was the public erosion of its most fundamental tenet. When a member was pushed into a corner, loyalty to self and family quickly supplanted loyalty to the gang. The BA were no longer a criminal enigma to the general public. Extensive national media coverage provided some answers about who was behind the Ciudad Juárez carnage. The whys were still an enigma to many outside the region. Those who knew firsthand of the slaughter occurring on the streets of Ciudad Juárez could at least see, in the faces of the perpetrators, what caused not only the loss of their loved ones, but the loss of of their city. Unfortunately, this would be a mere wave in the steady ebb and flow of violence within and between criminal organizations.

CHAPTER 11

Insurgency

In 2010 US officials, including Secretary of State Hillary Rodham Clinton, referred to the turmoil surrounding the drug war in Mexico as an insurgency—"in some cases, morphing into or making common cause with what we would consider an insurgency in Mexico and in Central America" (BBC 2010). By this time nearly thirty thousand people had been killed across Mexico in Felipe Calderón's two-year war against the cartels.

Ordnance that would support Clinton's assertion included hand grenades (Miller 2014), .50 caliber machine guns, semiautomatic weapons, and rocket-propelled grenade launchers, which were used with great regularity. This insurgency was unique compared to what was then occurring in Iraq and Afghanistan. Mexico's conflict arose not from an ideology but from greed. Both insurgencies presented unique challenges to the government's efforts to maintain public safety and deliver the intended fruits of the North American Free Trade Agreement. They also resulted in extraordinary incidents that resembled conventional battle scenes.

The singular incident that validated the statements made by some American officials that the Mexican drug war had disintegrated into an outright insurgency was the detonation of a vehicle-borne improvised explosive device in downtown Ciudad Juárez, less than a half mile from the border, that killed four and injured six.

July 17, 2010, was a hot day along the El Paso–Ciudad Juárez corridor. Dusk did little to abate the sweltering temperature, which scratched at triple digits. Pedestrian traffic was light on Avenida 16 de Septiembre since the majority of stores along this once-vibrant shopping district had been shuttered, victims of extortion. By now residents had imposed a curfew on themselves, fearful of being out at night due to the violence and the possibility of witnessing things that would put their lives in jeopardy.

At around 8 p.m. an emergency call was made for an ambulance. A policeman appeared to be dead on the street. Such calls had become commonplace events: between January and May there had already been 1,075 homicides (Borderland Beat 2010). Realizing there is no such thing as a routine call in this atmosphere, the crew knew to be vigilant, but they had little warning for what was waiting for them.

The road to this incident was paved when two inmates met in a Texas prison. In 2003 or 2004 Miguel Ángel Nevarez was incarcerated in the prison in Woodville, Texas, where he made the acquaintance of Barrio Azteca member José Duran, also known as *Caballo*. After proving himself there by providing shanks to gang members and spending lengthy periods in segregation as a result, when he was released in 2006 he was deported back to Mexico. He settled in his place of origin, Guadalupe Distrito Bravo in the notorious Juárez Valley, made up of small towns vulnerable to narco rule. Nevarez maintained his gang association and finally became a full-fledged member in 2009. He worked for the gang with his brother-in-law, José Ángel Perez Marrufo, known as *Casitas*. After Casitas's arrest, Nevarez rose to a leadership role.

In July 2010, Nevarez received an unusual order from Arturo Gallegos Castrellón. He was to go to the Ciudad Juárez bus station and pick up a man named *Lince*, who was to manufacture a bomb. The cartels already had abundant experience with military-grade automatic weapons, hand grenades, and even rocket-propelled grenades. Bringing in a specialized bomb maker suggested a real insurgent strategy. The origin of the order lay with José Antonio "El Diego" Acosta Hernández, the Ciudad Juárez leader of La Línea (Covert 2014), with Gallegos as the conduit.

After arriving at a safe house in the city, Lince instructed Nevarez to purchase items specific to the construction of the bomb, which included diesel fuel, screws, marbles, plastic bags, and some paper to tint car windows. Off he went to purchase the deadly ingredients. When he arrived at the safe house, Nevarez found Lince and Fresa, who brought explosives and fertilizer to manufacture the bomb.

"Lince gives me the order that I should start taking parts out of the car, which were the doors, everything in the interior which included the seats, and that I use or install the tinting on the window," according to Nevarez in court testimony.

After completing this task it was on to actually making the bomb.

"Fresa and I mixed the diesel and the fertilizer in plastic bags," he said. The concoction is known as Ammonium Nitrate and Fuel Oil (ANFO), which had been used in such devastating events as the Oklahoma City bombing in the mid-1990s.

Officials would later estimate that the likely trigger for the ANFO mixture was twenty two pounds of Tovex, an industrial explosive used frequently in oil exploration projects, which was probably stolen from a company in the US and was detonated by a mobile phone (Grillo 2010).

"He (Lince) started putting them together so that he could put them in each part of the car," says Nevarez. These locations included the doors, rear seat and trunk, with a generous amount of screws and marbles placed on top for maximum devastation of human tissue. "He connected the detonator, the radio to the detonator, which was—which was going to detonate the explosive in the front headlight."

It wasn't long before Gallegos radioed them with their orders. They were to park the car on the busy downtown street *Dieciséis de Septiembre*, which is located only a few blocks from the border. They were to position themselves in a vehicle about two blocks away.

"After we parked the car, minutes after that, someone else had the order to put a body in it and to fire some shots so that they could divert the attention of the feds."

The ruse was to dress the body up as a policeman, then call authorities to say that an officer had been shot. The body, placed on the side of the street, was not actually that of a police officer. It was the body of thirty-year-old Cesar Gamino, who owned a nearby auto repair shop and was likely kidnapped and murdered for the sole purpose of this operation.

When the ambulance and police arrived at the corner of Avenida 16 de Septiembre and Calle Bolivia, they saw a bound, bloodied uniformed officer on the sidewalk, and did not pay attention to a nearby vehicle. Some reports said it was a Pontiac, others a Ford. Unbeknownst to the first responders, Gallegos had given the code to the detonation team to "go out and buy me some hot dogs."

Rushing to the "wounded officer," three first responders wearing red vests over their dark blue uniforms began feverishly rendering aid. A female responder was near the victim's head while another prepared an intravenous bag a few feet away and the third crouched on the victim's right side, wiping blood away from the victim's head.

The detonation of a vehicle-borne improvised explosive device in downtown Cd. Juárez on July 16, 2010, rang in a new era for the Barrio Azteca.
Courtesy of the *El Diario de Juarez*.

Federal police arrived in two vehicles to start the investigation and cordon off the scene with the ubiquitous yellow crime-scene tape that had become a macabre decoration throughout the city.

Hearing the commotion outside, medical doctor Guillermo Ortiz ran from his office with his son to see if they could help. After taking a few steps outside and seeing what was occurring, the doctor sent his son back into the office to retrieve his medical bag—a directive that saved his life.

A local news crew was taking a video of the incident. At one point the female first responder looks over her right shoulder in the direction behind her. Then a loud explosion and a flash of light.

"We were waiting for feds to arrive. And as soon as we got the call [from Gallegos] that several trucks with *federales* had arrived, Lince pushed the buttons on the radio, and it was detonated," Nevarez said. The killing of others was inconsequenctial as long as the federal officers were targeted.

Fernando Contreras Meraz would make the fateful cell phone call that would detonate the bomb (Borderland Beat 2010d).

The first responders were bloodied and shaken but alive, the blast just out of their range. Two federal police officers and Dr. Ortiz were not as lucky. The fifty-year-old doctor lay dead. Also killed in the blast was a local musician walking on the sidewalk who was at the wrong place at the wrong time.

In the wake of the attack the victims showed no reluctance in disclosing their feelings. Two victims who knew firsthand the extent of the blast were paramedics Nancy Paz Mares, who was struck by fragments from the explosion, and Philip Caldera, who sustained a head wound.

Paz described the perpetrators as heartless, while her partner Caldera likened the attack to 9/11. "They just wanted to kill many people."

Lince nonchalantly left the area, hardly noticed amidst the chaos. After a quick dinner, he was on a bus leaving the city.

The attack coincided with the arrest earlier in the day of Jesús Armando "El 35" Acosta Guerrero, a high-ranking leader of La Línea in Ciudad Juárez, raising the perception that this was a revenge attack. This would have been impossible to coordinate in such a short period of time, but it was an explicit message to both law enforcement and their rivals that the gang was prepared to escalate the war.

Enjoying the success of this attack, about a week later Nevarez and team began constructing a second explosive on Gallegos's orders, but this time they were unsuccessful.

"The reason that it didn't explode is that the person that drove the car there left the keys totally off, and so there was no electrical current running to the radio so that—to enable the explosive to detonate." This saved an unknown number of lives and would have sealed the city's reputation of an insurgency-fraught metropolis in the already failed Mexican state.

In September 2010 the police experienced déjà vu when they received a call that there was a dead man in a car parked at a shopping center. When they arrived they found the corpse, but having learned a valuable lesson from the July attack, they located a bomb in a nearby car. When they dismantled it they retained many major components for analysis, then conducted a controlled detonation of the vehicle. There were no injuries in this incident, but the message was clear (Fox News 2010).

US federal agents noted the level of sophistication of the explosive device, saying it was unlikely it could have been made by someone without formal training. The possibility that the bombers had received training from Los Zetas immediately surfaced, since the first generation Zetas had received training from US special forces while they were serving in the Mexican army.

It was four years later, at the trial of Gallegos, that the picture was made more vivid by a former gang member who admitted the BA were involved in the attempted second bombing. Like the successful bomb before it, the second device employed an explosive to trigger the ANFO mixture and would have been detonated by a cell phone. Tightly wrapped around the explosive were three-inch dry-wall nails to increase the lethality of the detonation.

These incidents rang in a disturbing era of the Mexican drug war. An explosives expert told the *Washington Post* that the device was not unlike the kinds of IEDs seen in Iraq, although not quite as sophisticated. The expert went on to say instructions for making such bombs are not easily gleaned from the internet. The gang's tactics were also similar to those used by Colombian narcos at the height of their power in the 1980s.

The message being sent by the BA on behalf of VCF was clear: they were still in control of Ciudad Juárez, or at least they thought, and meddling by law enforcement would have dire consequences. Following the explosion, a *narco manta* message appeared downtown in black spray paint. It announced that "what happened on September Avenue will keep happening to all the authorities who keep supporting El Chapo. Sincerely—the Juarez Cartel. We still have car bombs."

The car bombing may have been a harbinger of more sinister events. Prior to his arrest, when he realized binational law enforcement was closing in on him, José Antonio "El Diego" Acosta Hernández vowed that his organization would kill DEA agents and intended to bomb the US Consulate in Ciudad Juárez and the international bridges (Borderland Beat 2011c). These threats were taken seriously and accelerated the search for the La Línea leader, who would be arrested in Chihuahua City in July 2011.

Not long after the bombing five suspects were arrested by federal police, none of whom were the high-ranking orchestrators.

In September police arrested José Ivan "El Keiko" Contreras Lumbreras. He was suspected of killing garage owner Cesar Gamino, whose dead body was intended to dupe first responders (Valencia 2010f).

"[He] is the leader, of a group of murderers who implemented the logistics for conducting criminal activities arranged by 'La Línea,' such as drug trafficking, illegal deprivation of liberty, extortion, and homicide, among other things," a police press release said (Valencia 2010f).

In October Fernando "El Dorado" Contreras Meraz and other coconspirators were arrested in Ciudad Juárez.

"Contra Meraz knew the composition of the explosive material that was armed and set to detonate in a car that was carefully positioned to cause the most casualties and was specifically intended to intimidate the Federal Police," Luis Cárdenas Palomino, regional chief of security, told the media at the time (Borderland Beat 2010f).

More suspects would eventually be taken into custody by federal police. Then something went horribly wrong in the pursuit of justice, as so often happens in Mexico. It may have brought into clearer focus why federal police were targeted.

According to published reports in the Mexican media, the unit that was heading the investigation as well as patrolling the Centro Zone of Ciudad Juárez, where the bombing occurred, had a dubious reputation for corruption and for violence against suspects, a scourge the agency would long have to battle against.

In 2014 five suspects in the bombing would be released from prison under a cloud of allegations that they had been tortured by federal police. An attorney with *Centro de Derechos Humanos Paso del Norte* (CDHPN) invoked the Istanbul Protocol, formally referred to as The Manual on the Effective Investigation and Documentation of Torture and Other Cruel, Inhuman or Degrading Treatment or Punishment, a 1999 nonbinding United Nations document that establishes specific criteria for identifying incidents of torture, the recourse victims have against their accusers, and the impact it could have on their allegations. The reckoning for Acosta and Gallegos would wait for another day.

CHAPTER 12

Transitions

Every organization goes through periods of conflict, destabilization, and vulnerability. These can be created internally through poor strategic or financial decisions and personnel issues, or externally through aggressive competition and unexpected factors that can impact market prices, delivery chains, and customer preference.

R. V. Gundur (2020) correlated the prison-gang dynamic to the corporate paradigm described by Donald Lester, John Parnell, and Shawn Carraher (2003), whereby an organization must first be established, then must survive its development as it establishes organizational structure, goals, and competencies. The ultimate goal is success which would ideally be maintained and enhanced through management-level planning and strategy, followed by renewal. Finally, an absence of resiliency results in declination. The authors contend this can occur anywhere in an organization's lifespan.

This brings into question how stable the Barrio Azteca, or for that matter, any criminal organization can actually be. Of course, they can be profitable and ruthless, but when middle- and lower-level actors assume a larger risk in terms of vulnerability to arrest and death, the equity share based on risk and benefit is negligible. This creates an undercurrent of uncertainty for leadership that would adversely impact resiliency. The stability of the Azteca was coming into question. Then there is the conundrum of self-preservation over loyalty when the specter of a long prison term becomes a stark reality, compelling members on all levels to cooperate with law enforcement at the expense of their "brothers."

Jon Katzenbach and Douglas Smith (2001) describe this as an organization "getting stuck," and outlines the consequences this can create. The authors identify the factors that contribute to this phenomenon as unclear goals, mistaken attitudes, missing skills, membership changes, time pressure, and lack of discipline and commitment. "Any erosion or lack of attention to any of the six basics will confuse, if not derail, the team" (185). Katzenbach and Smith go on to say, "When a stuck team cannot work things out among themselves, however, outside intervention can help." If efforts to emerge from the rut fail, it is time to consider restructuring or terminating the team.

This management paradigm can be readily applied to a criminal organization such as the BA. External pressures from law enforcement and competitors, attrition through death and arrest, eroding loyalties, lack of a clear strategy, and costly operational decisions have all contributed to the decline in succeeding generations of BA. An understanding of these business management principles may benefit law enforcement in devising suppression strategies specific to the criminal organization's current state of existence. An understanding of these vulnerabilities can and should be strategically exploited.

By 2007 the BA were beginning to "get stuck." That was when gang member Johnny "Conejo" Michelletti essentially opened the books to the FBI. His cooperation helped launch an effective RICO case against his fellow gang members that resulted in sweeping federal indictments. Ranking members indicted and convicted were gang captains Carlos Perea, Manuel Cardoza, Benjamin Alvarez, Francisco Herrera, Eugene Mona, and Arturo Enriquez.

This betrayal deeply impacted the BA, since Conejo had been working undercover for the FBI for nearly three years. Conejo, who had been a member of the El Paso street gang Los Fatherless, joined the BA when he was incarcerated for assaulting a police officer (Mennem 2013).

Michelletti would be followed by a string of former members who opted to cooperate, primarily to save their own necks, with law enforcement, allowing officials to piece together the gang's structure, operations, and cross-border relationships.

The BA's own behavior would contribute to the disruption of the gang's fundamental organizational structure. Alliances would crumble. Internecine fighting would result in intra-gang casualties. Law enforcement would drop a powerful hammer on the organization. And the betrayal by dozens of members, including high-ranking ones, would call into question the validity of the loyalty oath every member swore to uphold—and therefore the validity of the organization itself.

Upon his arrest in Mexico in July 2010, Jesús Ernesto Chávez Castillo wasted no time in making a deal to mitigate his sentence at the expense of his gang. Many more followed Chávez in turning against the BA, Gallegos in particular. The concept of loyalty to the death in most organized crime groups evaporates when it comes down to an individual's fight for life or the lives of his or her loved ones, or when a convicted gangster faces decades if not a lifetime of slamming steel doors, cinderblock walls, and segregated isolation.

What occurred with the BA was not unique. Turncoats have greatly impacted other more established organized crime groups around the country.

The American Mafia code of Omerta was initially shattered in 1963 by Genovese crime family soldier Joseph Valachi, who was serving a prison sentence with his boss for heroin trafficking. During the McClennan hearings, Valachi would bring to the fore validation of the Mafia, its codes and hierarchy. More recently, under boss Sammy "The Bull" Gravano of the Gambino crime family put his boss John Gotti away for life (Gotti died in prison of throat cancer in 2002).

The federal government has launched legal offensives against criminal organizations such as the Mafia, Bandidos, MS-13, and Syndicato de Nuevo Mexico with the RICO (Racketeering Influenced Corrupt Organizations) statute, which allows for sweeping indictments of members involved in activities that further the enterprise of criminal organizations.

Many of the BA's upper echelon were removed after successful RICO prosecutions, leaving the lower ranks fighting among themselves in violent but ultimately futile power grabs. Sometimes power vacuums resulted in the development of splinter groups. The first set of four RICO indictments against the gang was handed down in 2001 during Operation Penco Negro, a joint federal and local operation that netted sixty-two BA members. This was followed by massive roundups in 2008, 2011, and 2014, with more on the horizon. The most recent task force was called Operation Ome Ce, and netted nineteen members after a three-year investigation. Informants emerged quickly as pressure mounted from American law enforcement.

"We are also seeing that a lot of BAs are leaving the gang," testified El Paso gang Detective Andres Sanchez. "That can be attributed to the disruption because they don't want the problems. They don't want the RICO. They don't want FBI and PD breathing down their necks. They may be the next potential subjects in the next investigation, because there will always be a next investigation when it comes to these guys because it's a revolving door."

A former member told the author that the gang was deeply affected by the hundreds who were killed on the streets of Juárez in the war with the Sinaloans, by the dozens of arrests in the RICO cases, and by all the members who testified against other members.

"I was in custody at the time, but it was floating around that BA members were renouncing in handfulls," said the former member.

He said members fleeing to the US from carnage in Ciudad Juárez were quickly turned into valuable resources by US law enforcement.

"This became a weakness for the BA, because this in turn gave the government an advantage on intel on BA operations in Ciudad Juárez," he said.

The former member said the sweeping arrests of thirty-five members in the wake of the consulate killings took out major players. "Most BA members that were apprehended in that RICO case were major players in hardcore BA organized crimes, from key drug distributors to straight assassins," he said.

Swept up in the RICO case filed in 2011 were extreme executioners from the US, one of whom was a hardcore killer in Ciudad Juárez living in El Paso. A total of thirty-five members were named in the indictment that included charges of drug smuggling, extortion, robbery, trafficking of firearms, money laundering, obstruction of justice, witness retaliation, kidnapping, and murder. Among the murders mentioned in the indictment were those connected to the US Consulate in 2010. A second RICO punch in 2014 netted eight more influential members. Charges in this case included the collection of "quotas" or street taxes from drug dealers, used to purchase money orders mailed through the US Postal Service to imprisoned members as well as for other criminal enterprises.

The author's informant said the two rounds of RICO indictments swept out the old leadership either directly, with their arrests, or by forcing them underground. "This blood line of members is gone but still run the streets from behind prison bars," he said.

At the core of the assault on the BA was the case brought under the RICO statute, the government's best tool for dismantling large criminal organizations.

"RICO is so effective that BA members often think twice about being in leadership positions, although you are not asked but rather ordered to do so," said the informant. "It's tough because you are at these terms guaranteed to lose your life; whether murdered or imprisoned your life is lost. You must be willing to give up everything for the BA."

Internal strife rapidly eroded the stability of the gang. Meting out retribution against their own further weakened their infrastructure. In August 2005, Chato Flores was kidnapped and murdered by fellow gang members for allegedly stealing thousands of dollars from VCF. In 2006, eight Azteca were murdered by their own clique during an internal power struggle. In June 2006, twenty-nine-year-old member David Fonseca Jr. brutally murdered ex-member Raul Esquivel, who was on a gang hit list. On April 17, 2008, former BA leader David "Chicho" Meraz, forty-nine, was murdered by the gang in Ciudad Juárez.

The BA suffered numerous casualties on the streets at the hands of the Sinaloa DTO, but arguably the largest attack was on September 3, 2009, when eighteen Azteca were gunned down in a Ciudad Juárez drug rehab center, many of whom became casualties of their own products.

While it may not be possible to prove how many murders are attributable to the BA or the cartel it worked for, what is certain is that after the arrests of thirty-five members for the 2010 killings, the murder rate in the violent city dropped to 2,086 in 2011 from 3,622 a year earlier. In 2012, it plummeted to 751. Other variables for the drop in murders, not least of which is the presumed victory of the Sinaloa DTO over VCF, included the pull-out of the large military contingent from the city, the appointment of the aggressive Julián Leyzaola to lead the municipal police department, and the destabilization of the BA model.

In 2010 Gaudelto Marquez, who had been a member since 1996, received a life sentence. Most gang members believed that anyone who received a life sentence would be unlikely to cooperate. That wasn't the case with Marquez, however. At Gallegos's trial Marquez provided a vivid account of the gang's reach into small and large Texas towns along the border, validating records presented to him by the federal prosecutor. He confirmed that the gang would move fluidly back and forth across the border and that under increased pressure from US law enforcement, many of the capos fled to Ciudad Juárez.

Becoming an informant is a dangerous proposition for any criminal. Correctional facilities have protective custody units exclusively for those who other inmates suspect have cooperated with law enforcement. "Snitches get stiches" the cell block saying goes, but when involved in a blood-in-blood-out organization, cooperation with authorities can be fatal. The BA refer to their green-lighting a member for death as being X'd.

Jesús Ernest Chávez joined the gang while imprisoned at the Federal Bureau of Prisons facility in Oakdale, Louisiana, in 2006. In August 2010 he was charged in the consulate murders, one of a slew of other federal charges in the RICO indictment. After he was arrested by the Mexican Federal Police in Ciudad Juárez, Chávez, probably aware of the dismal prospects he was facing, wasted no time in cooperating with both Mexican and US officials.

"When I was in Mexico, I find out that the United States, they have something on me, so I waived my—my extradition," he said, voluntarily surrendering to be extradited to the US.

This was a prudent move on his part, since he knew his life would be in greater jeopardy in a Mexican jail. Surrendering to US officials was attractive because of the prospect of applying to the Witness Security Program for his immediate family, who would likely be executed by the gang, in return for his testimony implicating fellow gang members. His other concern was that he would likely be deported after serving his sentence.

His expectation was that if he testified for the prosecution, "They don't send me back to Mexico if my life is in risk." He was also hoping for a reduced sentence.

To his relief Chávez was accepted into the Witness Security Program, but this arrangement isn't as attractive as most think. Chávez would still be incarcerated first, although now he was guaranteed protective custody and a name change. The charges against him would also be obscured. In correctional facilities inmates who "run" a unit may demand to see what charges were brought against a new inmate to ensure they are not a sexual predator or child molester. They also insist on knowing where new prisoners come from and what their alliances are.

"In that unit, it's only witness—somehow witness from the government."

The deal for Chávez didn't end with his safety. As noted earlier, the government also protected and supported his elderly parents.

Whether sincere or not, Chávez also expressed a sense of remorse for what he did as a gang member. "I feel that is the right thing to do, since I did so much things wrong," he said in trial testimony.

Even a member who was in the direct blood line of Vicente Carrillo Fuentes would turn on the organization. Fernando Carrillo, who was born in Mexico but moved to El Paso when he was about five or six years old, first got into trouble with US authorities in 2000 when he was charged with possession with intent to distribute more than a thousand pounds of marijuana and was sentenced to three years in federal prisons in Big Spring and Pecos, Texas. He told investigators he had moved two large loads into the US previously, but had avoided getting caught. He was moving the drugs for one of his uncles and stood to make almost $4,000.

His reasoning to do the work transcended money.

"I want to join the Juárez Drug Cartel."

Even as a family member he would still have to prove his worth. Never having become a US citizen, Carrillo was deported back to Mexico upon his release.

While in Pecos, Carrillo earned his huarchas, but his work would take off at the Big Spring facility. His attraction to the BA was not just because of its regional reputation but because of Alberto Fresa Núñez, whom he knew from the streets.

Fresa wasn't the first gang member he testified against. In a previous case he testified against a member and received a reduced sentence.

"I just want to get out from the gang. I'm tired of me following something that's not worth it."

Carrillo also worked out a deal with federal prosecutors and entered the Witness Security Program, but that arrangement was short-lived.

"It's real hard to be separated from your loved ones, talking about my family," he said, although he was well aware that violating the Sacred Rule was extremely risky.

"Well, they kill—you are a target right after you cooperate with any law enforcement or government."

For Gallardo, Chávez, and even Gallegos, their cooperation made their futures bleak and further eroded the stability and aura of the gang.

EL DIEGO

A single thread appears to tie the party massacre, the US Consulate murders, and the car bomb in downtown Juárez: José Antonio Acosta Hernández, "El Diego." While media reports place Castrellón as the mastermind of these incidents, it is more likely Acosta served as the instigator who trickled the orders down to the street level. Considering the hierarchical nature of La Línea, it's unlikely the BA would have undertaken these attacks without La Línea's direct orders.

Acosta was eventually arrested with information provided by the DEA and CIA on July 31, 2011, after a shootout with police and military officials. He would be paraded before the media by heavily armed federal police, their faces covered with black balaclavas, while their prisoner wore a bulletproof vest and a long-sleeved white T-shirt that had *Rebel Spirit* silk screened on the sleeves. He stood stoically between two much taller officers, scowling at the camera with his hands cuffed in front of him, his black hair cut short, and his face stubbled with whiskers.

He would ultimately admit to his offenses, most striking among them his complicity in ordering the execution of more than fifteen hundred souls in Mexico, mostly in Ciudad Juárez (Justice in Mexico 2011). It would only be a matter of time before he faced extradition to the US. That day would come on March 16, 2012, when he was brought to face multiple federal indictments out of the US Attorneys Western District office in El Paso. Less than a month later, on April 5, he pleaded guilty to four counts of racketeering, narcotics trafficking, and money laundering, and seven counts of murder, including the three US Consulate-related homicides. With his confession Federal District Court Judge Kathleen Cardone sentenced Acosta to seven concurrent life terms, three additional consecutive life terms, and twenty years in federal prison (United States Department of Justice 2012a).

At his sentencing Acosta, the VCF's plaza boss, explicitly laid out the La Línea/BA relationship, confirming that the overall relationship between La Línea and the BA served to further their criminal enterprise (United States Department of Justice 2012a).

"As the leader of La Línea's enforcement wing, Mr. Acosta-Hernández directed a reign of terror," said Assistant Attorney General Breuer. "Today's guilty plea and sentence are a significant step in our effort to bring to justice those responsible for the consulate murders, and it would not have been possible without the extraordinary assistance of our law enforcement partners in Mexico, including Attorney General Marisela Morales Ibáñez. We are determined to hold accountable those individuals who committed the consulate murders, and to dismantle the dangerous criminal enterprise that fueled these and many other tragic and senseless acts of violence. Gangs and other criminal organizations that threaten public safety on both sides of the border are on notice that we are working more closely than ever with our Mexican counterparts to shut them down" (United States Department of Justice 2012a).

FBI TEN MOST WANTED FUGITIVE

EDUARDO RAVELO

Conspiracy to Conduct the Affairs of an Enterprise, Through a Pattern of Racketeering Activity; Conspiracy to Distribute and Possess with the Intent to Distribute Controlled Substances; Conspiracy to Import Controlled Substances; Conspiracy to Launder Monetary Instruments; Conspiracy to Kill Persons in a Foreign Country; Murder Resulting from the Use and Carrying of a Firearm During and in Relation to Crimes of Violence and Drug Trafficking; Murder in Aid of Racketeering Activity

Captured
Photograph taken in 1998

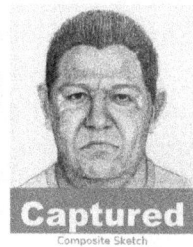
Captured
Composite Sketch

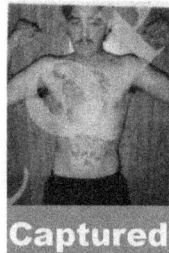
Captured
Photograph taken in 1992

Captured
Photograph taken in 1992

DESCRIPTION

Aliases: "Tablas", Eduardo Rabelo, Eduardo Acevedo, Eddie Rabelo, Eduardo Rodriguez, Eddie Ravelo, Eduardo Rabelo Rodriguez, Eduardo Ruiz, Eduardo Simental Ruiz, Eduardo Saenz, "T-Blas", "2x4", "Blas", "Lumberman", "Boards", "Tablero", "56"

Date(s) of Birth Used: October 13, 1968, December 22, 1965, October 15, 1968, November 13, 1968, October 13, 1969

Place of Birth: Mexico

Hair: Black (possibly bald)

Eyes: Brown

Height: 5'9"

Weight: 150 to 180 pounds

Build: Medium

Complexion: Medium

Sex: Male

Race: White (Hispanic)

Nationality: Mexican

Scars and Marks: Ravelo has a scar on his face. He also has tattoos, shown above, on his chest, abdomen, and back.

REWARD

The FBI is offering a reward of up to $100,000 for information leading directly to the arrest of Eduardo Ravelo.

REMARKS

Ravelo is known to be a Captain (Capo) within the Barrio Azteca criminal enterprise and is allegedly responsible for issuing orders to the Barrio Azteca members residing in Juarez, Mexico. Allegedly, Ravelo and the Barrio Azteca members act as "hitmen" for the Vicente Carrillo Fuentes Drug Trafficking Organization and are responsible for numerous murders. Ravelo has ties to Mexico and El Paso, Texas. He may have had plastic surgery and altered his fingerprints.

CAUTION

Eduardo Ravelo, aka "Tablas", is being sought for his alleged involvement in the Barrio Azteca transnational gang and their money-laundering, racketeering, and drug-related activities in El Paso, Texas. Additionally, he is wanted for numerous murders in Juarez, Mexico. His alleged criminal activities began in 2003. In 2008 and 2011, Ravelo was indicted in the United States District Court, Western District of Texas.

SHOULD BE CONSIDERED ARMED AND EXTREMELY DANGEROUS

If you have any information concerning this person, please contact your local FBI office or the nearest American Embassy or Consulate.

Field Office: El Paso

The FBI Wanted Poster for Eduardo "Tablas" Ravelo.
Courtesy of the Federal Bureau of Investigation.

TABLAS

To understand the impact the arrest of Eduardo "Tablas" Ravelo Rodriguez had on the BA is to understand his life's work and the impact it had on crime in the El Paso-Ciudad Juárez corridor.

Tablas (wooden plank) maintained a strong insular security detail that allowed him to live with his wife and children in relative anonymity and safety. It is said that his nickname derived from his preferred method of using a two-by-four to beat his victims (Midgley 2018). This was in stark contrast to the persona of El Chapo Guzmán Loera who, although evasive when it came to law enforcement, took a flamboyant public turn when he accepted a visit from actors Sean Penn and Kate del Castillo—a miscalculation that may have contributed to his capture.

Ravelo was born October 13, 1968, in Mexico but ultimately received permanent resident status in the United States where he resided in El Paso. In March 2008 he would assume control of the BA in Ciudad Juárez after a brutal takeover where he killed the reigning capo (Borderland Beat 2009b). Now likely on law enforcement's radar, the new capo shaved his head and reportedly had plastic surgery that included changing his fingerprints (CNN 2009). His ascension to power and the anonymity he desperately sought was facilitated by his close relationship with La Línea and VCF. But as time passed, law enforcement diligently collected intelligence and won cooperation from arrested gang members. Ravelo could only be protected for so long.

Tablas remained relatively anonymous north of the border until enough information had been obtained by the FBI to name him to their notorious Most Wanted list on October 20, 2009 (FBI 2009). In addition to leaving a trail of bodies in Mexico, Ravelo was facing a litany of charges in the US that included racketeering, money laundering, and possession with intent to distribute heroin and cocaine.

"If he gets picked up," Special Agent Samantha Mikeska said, "it will put a big dent in the gang's operation" (FBI 2009).

On the morning of June 26, 2018, a raid on a house in Uruapan, Michoacán state, yielded the new most wanted narco since El Chapo's arrest January 8, 2016, in his native Sinaloa. While Tablas's arrest was tactically precise it was somewhat anticlimactic, since he simply surrendered without a shot being fired. With his arrest significant quantities of weapons and methamphetamine were discovered, along with some of his cohorts.

With the arrest of Tablas Ravelo the binational effort to dismantle the Azteca gained momentum, and his successor was arrested just five months later. René Gerardo Santana Garza, alias "N" or "El 300," was caught at the Chihuahua International Airport in 2018 in an SUV that had come under suspicion. This arrest followed a wave of violence against regional law enforcement. El 300 was implicated in the murder of the presumed second in command of the BA, Juan Arturo "El Genio" Padilla Juárez (Borderland Beat 2018). He would also become associated with La Empresa, a new hybrid organization aligned with the old structure of VCF (Resendiz 2020).

El Genio's murder was perhaps the first of several fatal blows to the BA organization. Rampant infighting ensued. Following his death, thirty people were murdered in a span of only twenty hours (Resendiz 2020).

As of this writing, Tablas remains incarcerated in Mexico awaiting his inevitable extradition to the United States and a fate similar to that of his Sinaloan counterpart, El Chapo Guzmán.

REBRANDING

By 2011 the murder rate had dropped more than 60 percent from the previous year. The reasons for the lull in homicides are somewhat nebulous. According to InSight Crime (Pachico 2013), which conducts extensive analyses of the region, the reasons included not just the dwindling military presence, the crime-fighting initiaties of Leyzaola, and the putative Sinaloa DTO victory, which restored a sense of narco-trafficking order, but also such social rejuvenation programs as Todos Somos Juárez (We Are All Juárez).

Jorge Villa, the state medical examiner at the time, took a more cynical position. He knew firsthand why the death rate had plummeted after the recent carnage: "There just isn't anyone else to kill."

The relative calm would be short-lived. In 2017 there would be 773 homicides culminating with the dangling of a dead man from a bridge. In 2018 this number would nearly double to 1,247 (Arce 2019). In the first three and a half months of 2020 there were already 560 homicides (Borunda 2020). Some experts expressed concern that the business shutdowns associated with the COVID-19 crisis from the spring of 2020 would adversely impact the multibillion dollar remittances sent back to Mexico from the United States. That in turn may have propelled some toward criminal enterprises just to survive. Criminal diversity would also increase to include human and sex trafficking as additional streams of revenue. An interesting comparison in homicide rates can be made between Ciudad Juárez and Baltimore, Maryland. Juárez has a population of around 1.2 million while Baltimore has a population half that number, yet in 2016 the latter had 318 homicides (Rector 2017).

Rene Gerardo Santana Garza, "El 300" (Borunda 2018e), who assumed the leadership mantle after the arrest of Tablas, would launch a split with the "Old Guard" (Borunda 2020b).

Cracks began appearing in the organization well before the war with Sinaloa unfolded. Early signs of dissension due to revenue and leadership problems emerged around 2007. The BA were in a chaotic state of transition when David "Chicho" Meraz and Miguel Ángel "Angelillo" Esqueda competed for the leadership of the El Paso faction (Mennem 2013), setting a precedent for questioning the leadership structure of the gang. Another incident occurred that demonstrated lapses in leadership supervision.

Just as the relationship with the VCF was unfolding, trust issues arose and the latter accused the El Paso gang of stealing millions of dollars in products and proceeds. Something needed to be done, and fast, to the extent that the VCF wanted to eliminate the BA entirely. It was their good luck that they failed, since the BA would be needed in the coming conflict few realized was percolating.

VCF dispatched emissaries to El Paso, who ordered the gang's cooperation in identifying the main culprit in the robberies. Not to bite the hand that was feeding them, the gang turned over Chato Flores, who would be abducted from El Paso to Ciudad Juárez. There he underwent a brutal and ultimately fatal interrogation, doubtless to discover where the money was and who else was involved.

In 2013 Borderland Beat ran the headline "Infighting Hurt the Barrio Aztecas Who Worked for Juárez Cartél" over a post by K. Mennem (2013). The core of the early disruption in organizational stability, especially on the El Paso side, was the power struggle between David "Chicho" Meraz and Miguel Ángel "Angelillo" Esqueda. The former would be murdered in 2008.

"It was always all—all this struggling, fighting against each other," testified a former member (Mennem 2013).

Such internal instability, compounded with the external conflicts generated by the Sinaloan rivalry, began to shred alliances. The gang would continue to operate as a criminal organization but would fade to a shadow of their former selves.

Adding to the eroding stability of the Ciudad Juárez narco scene would be the 2014 arrest of the jefe himself, Vicente Carrillo Fuentes. The man who oversaw the actions of La Línea and the BA for the burgeoning wealth of his drug empire would be taken into custody October 9, 2014, in Torreon, Coahuila. Once a suave, striking figure and one of the most powerful drug lords in Mexico, the fifty-one year old *El Viceroy* was seen being led to a white military helicopter by federal police, his hands cuffed in front of his body, his shoulders hunched forward, his gray hair short, and his face covered with a stubble of whiskers. It would be the end of his era. As far back as June 1, 2000, he had been sanctioned by the US Department of Treasury under the Foreign Narcotics Kingpin Designation Act. He would also face US federal charges through the Western District of Texas and Eastern District Court in New York. The US government put a five million dollar bounty on Carrillo's head for information leading to his arrest (InSight Crime 2017b). Carrillo would sit in a maximum security prison waiting to be extradited to the US. The US made a request in 2015 that was suspended by the Mexican government.

The deaths and arrests and members cooperating with US prosecutors shook the Azteca gang to its core. Within their own ranks a fissure had emerged with the rise of the Los Aztecas Vieja Escuela, or "Old School Aztecas." The fissure that had been developing had devolved into a full-blown schism after Tablas Ravelo was arrested. The Vieja Escuela remained loyal to Ravelo and launched a violent dispute with their younger counterparts while also splitting from La Línea, which was by now under the leadership of Carlos Arturo Quintana (Arce 2018). According to Arce (2019c), a new company, La Empresa, would essentially serve as an ancillary structure to an element of the BA. The new group was founded in 2018 by Luis "El Tío," "El 58," "Narizón" Mendez, a lieutenant in the BA in 2010 who was the last suspect arrested in connection with the Consulate murders. He was also implicated in the Villas de Salvarcar massacre. La Empresa—The New Company—was a hybrid organization that included members of La Línea, BA, and their former nemesis, Mexicles (Borunda 2020b). La Empresa would continue a wave of violence in Ciudad Juárez. One seventeen-year-old recruit was arrested and charged with committing six murders, earning $180 per murder (Borunda 2020b).

On the US side, in 2015 the Texas DPS Gang Threat Assessment dropped the BA to second place in Tier 2, behind the Sureños (Texas

Department of Public Safety 2015). According to that document, the reasons for downgrading the BA from a Tier 1 to Tier 2 threat included the dissolution of the exclusive relationship with VCF and a proliferation of debilitating RICO convictions which drastically diminished "operational effectiveness."

Three years later the BA had re-established themselves. Their extensive sphere of operation, their excessive level of violence, their role in exploiting both sides of the border, and the resurgence of those operations has led to an upgrade in 2018 as a Tier 1 threat to the State of Texas (Texas Department of Public Safety 2018).

According to the report, the DPS upgrade was the result of "their expansion of operating areas, propensity for violence, continued and evolving relationships with cartels and gangs, involvement in human, drug, and weapons smuggling, continuous exploitation of the US and Texas border, and the increase of reporting from law enforcement investigations. Barrio Azteca maintains a significant presence on both sides of the border as members continue their transnational criminal activities around the El Paso and Juárez corridor, including working with both the Sinaloa Cartel and Juárez Cartel. Younger and newer Barrio Azteca members are opportunistic and will work with other gangs and cartels, despite traditional gang rivalries or alliances. Regardless of alliances or rivalries, Barrio Azteca's ability to establish and maintain relationships in Mexico and in the United States, as well as their historic presence in Mexico, has aided in their recovery of power and influence in El Paso. Though its power and influence has fluctuated, Barrio Azteca has been able to regain a strong influence in both Ciudad Juárez and El Paso. Relationships with the cartels and gangs in Mexico and the United States, though fluid, are integral to Barrio Azteca's success as a criminal enterprise."

This report was a stark validation that elements of the Azetca were no longer exclusively loyal to La Línea and the VCF DTO and had opted to explore greener pastures with their previous enemies, the Sinaloa DTO and even the Mexicles.

The BA wasn't the only criminal gang going through internal turmoil. The Doble A would split from their alliance with the Sinaloa DTO and Mexicles, creating a level of chaos in Ciudad Juárez that replicated the bloodshed a decade earlier

In 2017, under Mayor Armando Cabada, the Mexican military resumed patrols in Ciudad Juárez as violence returned on an epic scale.

The commanding general of the Fifth Military Zone, General Ricardo Fernandez Acosta, said the difference between this new deployment of forces and the previous deployment is they vowed to cooperate more with civilian law enforcement agencies (Fierro 2017). Cabada told El Universal that the majority of the homicides occurring in the city were being ordered from CERESO prison (Fierro 2017). The 4,500 troops deployed were spread throughout Chihuahua state, but the situation had grown so dire by February 2019 that an additional six hundred soldiers would be placed specifically in Ciudad Juárez, where roving patrols and checkpoints would resume (Borunda 2019b).

In 2018 the arrest of thirty-eight-year-old Bruno Ángel "El Bruno" Rangel by Juárez Municipal Police demonstrated the surgical separation of the BA from La Línea. At one time Rangel was a high-ranking BA, but when the alliance with La Línea evaporated, he decided he would be better served by the latter.

Officials said that Rangel was an "'Azteca radical' who climbed the gang's hierarchy to control several drug-sales cells in various parts of Juárez. . . . He joined the criminal group 'La Línea,' causing a rupture with several commanders of the 'Aztecas,' generating the rise of homicides" (Borunda 2018d).

This apparently traitorous act demonstrates the weakening of the BA structure in the wake of the internal split. Rangel likely recognized where the power lay and exploited an opportunity.

A murder in January 2019 revealed a significant split even between Los Artistas Asesinos, or "Doble A," and Los Mexicles. Thirty-four-year-old Edgar Roberto "El Garfield" Oliver Romo, the leader of Los Artistas Asesinos, was gunned down inside one of the motels that dot Ciudad Juárez. Investigators found thirteen .40-caliber shell casings by Romo's lifeless body, sparking fears of escalating gang violence in the city (Arce 2019a).

The following month the schism between La Línea and Los Aztecas Vieja Esquela widened when Jesús Alfredo "El Freddy" Martinez Mendoza gunned down Adrian Ruiz Felix, twenty-two, at the Las Misiones shopping center in Ciudad Juárez. Martinez had been a high-ranking member of the Old School Aztecas who had been loyal to Tablas Ravelo. Martinez was arrested when he attempted to walk across the border carrying a backpack loaded with eleven pounds of heroin. The arrest likely saved Martinez's life. The previous two leaders of the Old School Aztecas had been murdered in the power struggle. The year 2019 would end with a tally of 1,497 murders in Ciudad Juárez (Borunda 2020).

La Línea, BA, and VCF weren't alone in corporate restructuring. The Mexicles severed their relationship with Sinaloa and allied with La Línea, which caused an eruption of violence, especially in the Valley of Juárez (Borunda 2019). They went to war with their former partner Gente Nueva, causing extensive death and destruction in the Valley of Juárez east of the city (Arce 2019a).

In January 2019 the La Línea-Mexicles alliance made a show of strength when they launched an offensive against law enforcement in Ciudad Juárez. A series of concerted attacks included the ambush of police patrol vehicles, shots fired at a police station, and setting a public bus ablaze. The rampage left eight police officers wounded (Borunda 2019a).

According to Mexican law enforcement officials, as of this writing, La Empresa is allied with one element of the Mexicles and La Línea, while rivals include the BA and another factor of the Mexicles, the latter embroiled in a multiple-faction internal battle.

A NEW PLAYER, A NEW WAVE OF VIOLENCE

Cocaine, heroin, and marijuana will always be mainstays of the narco trafficking across the border, but by 2015 the paradigm had shifted to crystal meth. The establishment of super meth labs, using supplies shipped from China, made the highly addictive drug more lucrative and less risky for American producers, who could now concentrate on larger bulk distribution rather than manufacturing in haphazard and often remote kitchen operations. Lower cost and higher profit margin made meth the gold standard in the drug business.

A 2012 *USA Today* article described the DTOs "quietly" filling the US demand for the meth's highly addictive and rapid high, which now accounted for 80 percent of US sales. "These are sophisticated, high-tech operations in Mexico that are operating with extreme precision," said Jim Shroba, a DEA agent in St. Louis. "They're moving it out the door as fast as they can manufacture it."

The shift accelerated in 2006 with the passing of the Combat Methamphetamine Epidemic Act, which resulted in tighter control over medications with pseudoephedrine, a key component in many cold and allergy medications and an ingredient in "kitchen meth." This limitation, combined with unfettered, abundant shipments of precursors from China, created another perfect storm in Mexico. Capitalizing on this would be the enigmatic El Menchito.

At the end of February 2020 the photo of Jessica Oseguera González appeared in newspapers across the United States (Hsu and Sheridan 2020). She had been arrested in a Washington state courtroom where she was attending a hearing for her brother, Ruben Oseguera González, who was recently extradited to the United States from Mexico. The Osegueras were identified as the son and daughter of a notorious kingpin who was pouring methamphetamine across the border and leaving bodies piled up throughout Mexico, ringing in a new era of violence in Mexico's unstable narco structure.

Both the thirty-three-year-old Jessica, who went by the nom de guerre "La Negra," and her thirty-year old brother, who went by *El Menchito* (The Little Mencho), were fully knowledgeable and complicit in their father's empire, which was quickly becoming the dominant drug trafficking organization in Mexico.

Their father, Nemesio Oseguera Cervantes, founded and led the Cartel Jalisco New Generation (CJNG) and was considered the new "most wanted" man in Mexico after the arrest of Joaquín "El Chapo" Guzmán and Tablas Ravelo. El Menchito, as he was known, started his criminal career in the United States as a heroin dealer. After serving his sentence he was deported back to Mexico, where he briefly served as a municipal police officer in the village of Tomatlan, south of Puerta Vallarta Jalisco.

El Menchito, born in Michoacan state on July 17, 1966, achieved narco kingpin status relatively late, establishing the cartel in 2011. Thrice deported from the US for street sales of heroin and methamphetamine, he rapidly rose to international dominance. Within five years, however, his group had become the dominant trafficker of methamphetamine into the US, and El Menchito had become the most wanted man in Mexico and the number one target of the Drug Enforcement Administration in the US (Díaz 2019).

In the early 2000s, after being forced out of the Arellano Felix organization in Tijuana, El Menchito arrived in Guadalajara, where he began working with the Milenio Cartel as a hit man, *sicario*. Los Zetas were his main targets. Expecting but failing to be appointed to a prominent position in the cartel, an angry El Menchito split from the group and launched the Cartel Jalisco New Generation (Warren 2019).

El Menchito, who bears a striking resemblance to the narco saint Jesús Malverde, is an enigma, rarely seen and virtually never heard from. His reach into the US is broad and deep. By September 2019 he was credited with supplying more than 90 percent of the drugs in Chicago and a third of narcotics in the US (Bigos 2019). His organization is becoming the most dominant in Mexico and is a killing machine, using sophisticated weaponry such as .50-caliber machine guns and rocket-propelled grenades. In one 2015 attack they shot down a Mexican army helicopter.

His rise to the top has left gang and cartel relationships along the border in chaos. In Ciudad Juárez traditional alliances have weakened to the point that allegiance is based mainly upon opportunity. El Menchito saw a weakening of the Sinaloa faction and a resurgence of the Carrillo Fuentes faction and wanted to capitalize on the resulting instability. With methamphetamine now the preferred product to ship north, his operation quickly moved into Ciudad Juárez. Law enforcement on both sides of the border was surprised to discover that the organization had gained a foothold before many realized it was happening (Esquivel 2017).

The DEA saw an uptick of seizures and arrests attributable to the Jalisco organization as well as a teaming with La Línea.

"Nueva Generacion and La Línea, aka the Juárez Cartel, have formed an alliance to finish off a deeply fragmented Sinaloa cartel and take control of one of the most lucrative routes, the Juárez-El Paso distribution route that supplies chains all over the United States, particularly the southwest, where meth's epidemic is high," Alfredo Corchado of the *Dallas Morning News* stated at a panel discussion at the Wilson Center, Washington, DC, in February 2017 (Woody 2017).

Scott Stewart, vice president of Stratfor, an Austin-based geopolitical intelligence organization, concurs with Machado's assessment.

"In the mountains, you still had the remnants of the Carrillo Fuentes organization that were fairly significant and strong, so the conflict persisted. And now CJNG has gotten involved in it . . . with La Línea and some street allies in Juarez itself," Stewart says. (Resendiz 2020). This was a prescient statement. By 2021 the Azteca Vieja Esquela had aligned with CJNG, allowing them to establish a foothold in Ciudad Juárez (El Diario de Juarez 2021).

The dynamic is simple. Drug trafficking organizations will continue to flourish in Mexico. Criminal street gangs will serve as valuable and expendable fodder to supply trafficking and enforcement support.

In the US, a maxim evolved out of the financial crisis of 2008: some organizations are too big to fail. This may be true of the Mexican drug trafficking organizations and those who support their enterprises. The jefes know their twenty billion dollar enterprises, feeding a bottomless market in the US, are unlikely to fail. The many Mexican officials who benefit from the DTO's largesse, from the federal down to the municipal levels, realize it, too. This is why violence will continue with gangs such as the BA on the front lines.

Epilogue

In the thirty years of its existence the Barrio Azteca has gone full circle. From inception in Texas prison cells to dominance through allegiance to a major Mexican drug trafficking organization, they created an organization that appeared strong but wound up being more fragile than many could have realized. As pressure mounted from law enforcement and multiple RICO cases, the fabric of the organization became fully transparent. Loyalty meant little compared to one's own survival. This dynamic was repeated in other criminal organizations ranging from the American Mafia to other prison gangs such as the Syndicato de Nuevo Mexico. Violating the primary rule of noncooperation with law enforcement was an attractive option to a member if it meant his survival and the survival of his family.

The goal of this treatise is to reveal the social dynamic of a major barrio in the United States and its profound impact on the evolution of the street to prison gang culture in the United States, as well as how US deportation policy contributed to making the BA a prolific killing machine in Ciudad Juárez. This criminal subculture is just that—a subculture—and its existence in no way should impugn the honorable reputations of hardworking immigrant families from the El Segundo and Chihuahuita Barrios, many of whom went on to noble endeavors such as law enforcement, the military, civil services, education, and entrepreneurship.

Understanding the roots and proliferation of the BA, however, should serve as a cautionary tale for law enforcement and policy makers on how to effectively eradicate gangs in one area while mitigating their impact on another from displacement. Part of the solution is working closely with not only law enforcement but social service, educational, and religious organizations in the countries that receive deported US criminals. Cooperation with these agencies can create opportunities to quell the desire of prospective young street gang members and ex-convicts to continue their criminal activities, at the same time discouraging their return to the streets of the United States—a scenario that has been played out numerous times by MS-13 and the BA cohorts. The lack of a comprehensive border control strategy aids in the return of these criminals to US streets.

As long as there are criminal opportunities such as narco, human, and sex trafficking there will be waves of organizations attempting to capitalize on virtually unlimited income potential. When annual narcotics sales account for more than $20 billion a year to the cartels and ostensibly to the Mexican economy, which is inextricably tied to that country's officials, there will be warring factions among gangs such as the BA.

There will always be gangs. Suppression effrots are daunting. The gang may cease to exist in its original form yet the criminal elements who comprised the membership will simply shift their allegiances to another "hybrid" gang or create a new gang under a new name.

I have been going to Ciudad Juárez on assignment for more than fifteen years, and I am struck by the resilience of its residents. After more than a decade of violence residents still see hope amid the chaos. It is a hope not fostered by trust in the government or even law enforcement. There is a flame that still burns in the souls of the good people in Ciudad Juárez. In the western *colonia* of Rancho Anapra, a violent ghetto of cinderblock houses with tin and tarp roofs, there is a Catholic church that has held its share of funerals for victims of drug-related violence. At a youth-group concert I interviewed a sixteen-year-old girl and asked whether she would ever want to live in the US. She displayed the spirit of defiant optimism that Juárenses will need in order to stage a real comeback. "If I ever had the chance to go to the US, I would still stay here," she said. "How can I make my city better off if I leave?"

ACKNOWLEDGMENTS

Friend and colleague Mike Tapia, PhD, has been a longtime sounding board and cross-border travel partner. Amanda Rodriguez, public services librarian at the El Paso Public Library Border Heritage Center, opened the archives to the history of El Paso, Texas, my home away from home. The staff of *El Diario* El Paso/Juarez provided many of the photos for the project. I can't ignore their staff members, some of whom have paid the ultimate sacrifice for reporting the truth on the criminal organizations in Ciudad Juárez. I have chosen not to identify by name a number of law enforcement colleagues on both sides of the border, since many are still working cases. We in the US have a cynical attitude toward Mexican law enforcement, but given the constant threats to themselves and their families at the minimal pay they receive, they deserve a little slack.

Thanks to TCU Press staff Rebecca Allen, production manager; Molly Spain, assistant editor; Kathy Walton, editor; and Dan Williams, director, who approved this project and saw it through to a quality product.

And most importantly, thanks to my family. Many of my exploits on both sides of the border and in El Salvador caused moments of great anxiety, yet they always supported the mission, albeit begrudgingly. I love you all and hope you never fear telling the truth.

REFERENCES

Alamogordo Daily News. 2018. "Barrio Azteca member sentenced to 19 years for drug trafficking." August 10, 2018. https://www.alamogordonews.com/story/news/local/community/2018/08/10/ybarra-barrio-azteca-member-sentence-19-years-drug-trafficking/929709002/.

Albuquerque Journal. 2011a. "Juarez's New Top Cop Vows to Clean Up Force, Fire 400." June 9, 2011. https://www.abqjournal.com/35380.

———. 2011b. "UPDATED: Mexican Authorities Arrest Juarez Prison Chief." August 3, 2011. https://www.abqjournal.com/47237/updated-mexican-authorities-arrest-chief-of-juarez-prison.html.

Arce, Robert. 2018. "14 Cartel Assassins Captured in El Paso-Juárez Metro Border Area." Breitbart News, July 9, 2018. https://www.breitbart.com/border/2018/07/09/14-cartel-assassins-captured-in-el-paso-juarez-metro-border-area/.

———. 2019a. "Gang Leader's Murder Sparks Fears of More Violence in Juárez." Breitbart News, January 4, 2019. https://www.breitbart.com/border/2019/01/04/gang-leaders-murder-sparks-fears-of-more-violence-in-juarez/.

———. 2019b. "Juárez Registers 889 Homicides So Far in 2019." Breitbart News, August 5, 2019. https://www.breitbart.com/border/2019/08/05/juarez-registers-889-homicides-so-far-in-2019/.

———. 2019c. "Cartel Hitman Captured in Mexican Border City." Breitbart News, September 15, 2019. https://www.breitbart.com/border/2019/09/15/cartel-hitman-captured-in-mexican-border-city/.

Associated Press. 2019. "National Geographic journalist shot in leg working in Mexico." October 5, 2019. https://apnews.com/article/212dd6e639dc4b889a882ad2bd54e8c2.

Attkisson, Sharyl. 2013. "Family of second murdered federal agent files lawsuit against U.S. government over 'Fast and Furious.'" CBS News, February 13, 2013. https://www.cbsnews.com/news/family-of-second-murdered-federal-agent-files-lawsuit-against-us-government-over-fast-and-furious/.

Barger, Jennifer. 2019. "The 28 friendliest neighborhoods in U.S. cities: Where are the most welcoming urban enclaves?" *National Geographic*, June 3, 2019. https://www.nationalgeographic.com/travel/destinations/north-america/united-states/best-american-neighborhoods/.

BBC. 2010. "Clinton says Mexican drug crime like an insurgency." September 9, 2010. https://www.bbc.com/news/world-us-cahttps://www.bbc.com/news/world-us-canada-11234058nada-11234058.

Beaubien, Jason. 2010. "Grief, Rage Fuel Juarez Mothers' Search For Justice." NPR, March 15, 2010. https://www.npr.org/templates/story/story.php?storyId=124572344.

REFERENCES

Bigos, Audrina. 2019. "Mexican Drug Lord 'El Mencho' Supplies Nearly 90% of the Illegal Drugs in Chicago." CBS Chicago, September 27, 2019. https://chicago.cbslocal.com/2019/09/27/mexican-drug-lord-el-mencho-supplies-nearly-90-of-the-illegal-drugs-in-chicago/.

Borderland Beat. 2009a. "Los Linces." October 16, 2009. http://www.borderlandbeat.com/2009/10/los-linces.html.

———. 2009b. "FBI most Wanted Ruthless Killer." October 23, 2009. http://www.borderlandbeat.com/2009/10/fbi-most-wanted-ruthless-killer.html.

———. 2009c. "More Gangs in El Paso than Juarez?" November 14, 2009. http://www.borderlandbeat.com/2009/11/more-gangs-in-el-paso-than-juarez.html.

———. 2009d. "Barrio Azteca." November 15, 2009. http://www.borderlandbeat.com/2009/11/barrio-azteca.html.

———. 2010a. "Alleged Cartel Ties to Massacre in Juarez." February 3, 2010. http://www.borderlandbeat.com/2010/02/alleged-cartel-ties-to-massacre-in.html.

———. 2010b. "President Felipe Calderón in Juarez." February 12, 2010. http://www.borderlandbeat.com/2010/02/police-disperse-protest-against.html.

———. 2010c. "Barrio Azteca: Slain Was Retaliation." April 1, 2010. http://www.borderlandbeat.com/2010/04/barrio-azteca-slain-was-retaliation.html.

———. 2010d. "Ciudad Juarez: 242 murders in May." June 1, 2010. http://www.borderlandbeat.com/2010/06/ciudad-juarez-242-murders-in-may.html.

———. 2010e. "Operation Chihuahua." July 13, 2010. http://www.borderlandbeat.com/2010/07/operation-chihuahua.html.

———. 2010f. "More Juarez car bombing suspects apprehended." October 21, 2010. http://www.borderlandbeat.com/2010/10/mastermind-of-juarez-car-bombing.html.

———. 2010g. "Murders in Ciudad Juarez Top 2009 Total." November 10, 2010. http://www.borderlandbeat.com/2010/11/murders-in-ciudad-juarez-top-2009-total.html.

———. 2011a. "Business Owners Look for Way Out of Violent Ciudad Juarez." March 5, 2011. http://www.borderlandbeat.com/2011/03/business-owners-look-for-way-out-of.html).

———. 2011b. "Police captain gunned down in Juárez." May 26, 2011. http://www.borderlandbeat.com/2011/05/police-captain-gunned-down-in-juarez.html.

———. 2011c. "'El Diego' arrested in Chihuahua." July 30, 2011. http://www.borderlandbeat.com/2011/07/el-diego-arrested-in-chihuahua.html.

———. 2018. "'El 300' Los Aztecas leader arrested." November 8, 2018. http://www.borderlandbeat.com/2018/11/el-300-los-aztecas-leader-arrested.html.

Borunda, Daniel. 2014. "Texas DPS report: Sureños street gang has grown in El Paso." *El Paso Times*, April 22, 2014. https://www.elpasotimes.com/story/archives/2016/07/13/texas-dps-report-sureo-street-gang-has-grown-el-paso/87033028/.

———. 2015. "Former Juarez police chief Julián Leyzaola says shooting was 'message' from current police chief." *El Paso Times*, May 15, 2015. https://www.elpasotimes.com/story/news/world/juarez/2015/05/15/former-juarez-police-chief-julia-leyzaola-says-shooting/31255129/.

REFERENCES

———. 2016. "Birthday party attack directed by cartel, gang." *El Paso Times*, February 10, 2016. https://www.elpasotimes.com/story/archives/2016/02/10/birthday-party-attack-directed-cartel-gang/80207464/.

———. 2017. "Gang member gets 430 years in killing of 11 women forced into prostitution at Juarez hotel." *El Paso Times*, October 11, 2017. https://www.elpasotimes.com/story/news/local/juarez/2017/10/11/gang-member-gets-430-years-killing-11-women-forced-into-prostitution-juarez-hotel/752535001/.

———. 2018a. "Juárez police arrest alleged gang leader accused of double-cross fueling Mexico violence." *El Paso Times*, May 25, 2018. https://www.elpasotimes.com/story/news/local/juarez/2018/05/25/barrio-azteca-gang-leader-double-cross-juarez-mexico-homicides-violence/641927002/.

———. 2018b. "Juárez police make arrests in murders of 11. A day later, AMLO promises to combat violence." *El Paso Times*, August 7, 2018. https://www.elpasotimes.com/story/news/local/juarez/2018/08/06/juarez-police-arrests-murders-11-bodies-home-barrio-azteca-gang-revenge/917815002/.

———. 2018c. "Juárez gang brawl: Suspect in slayings of 11 people dies in Mexico state prison." *El Paso Times*, August 22, 2018. https://www.elpasotimes.com/story/news/local/juarez/2018/08/22/juarez-mexico-prison-gang-brawl-suspect-dies-murders-11-people/1064056002/.

———. 2018d. "Gang videos: Artistas Asesinos threaten Mexicles amid violence in Juárez, Mexico." *El Paso Times*, August 28, 2018. https://www.elpasotimes.com/story/news/local/juarez/2018/08/28/gang-videos-artistas-asesinos-threaten-rival-mexicles-juarez-mexico/1114328002/.

———. 2018e. "Mexico federal police arrest reputed Barrio Azteca gang leader 'El 300' in Chihuahua City." *El Paso Times*, November 9, 2018. https://www.elpasotimes.com/story/news/crime/2018/11/09/mexico-federal-police-arrest-barrio-azteca-gang-leader-el-300-juarez-chihuahua/1932483002/.

———. 2019a. "U.S. issues security alert for Juárez after wave of drug cartel, gang attacks on police." *El Paso Times*, January 20, 2019. https://www.elpasotimes.com/story/news/local/juarez/2019/01/20/u-s-issues-security-alert-after-attacks-police-juarez-mexico-violence/2634280002/.

———. 2019b. "Mexico deploys 600 soldiers, federal police to quell violence in Juárez, 16 other cities." *El Paso Times*, February 20, 2019. https://www.elpasotimes.com/story/news/local/juarez/2019/02/20/mexico-deploys-600-soldiers-police-quell-border-violence-juarez/2920659002/.

———. 2019c. "Mexico drug cartel violence flares as Mexicles, Gente Nueva war rattles Valley of Juárez." *El Paso Times*, June 19, 2019. https://www.elpasotimes.com/story/news/local/juarez/2019/06/19/mexico-violence-mexicles-gente-nueva-gang-war-rattles-valley-juarez/1489874001/.

———. 2020a. "Juárez police arrest reputed Azteca 'Old Guard' gang leader on binational wanted list." *El Paso Times*, January 7, 2020. https://www.elpasotimes.com/story/news/local/juarez/2020/01/07/reputed-barrio-azteca-old-guard-el-ferro-gang-leader-binational-se-busca-wanted-list-arrest/2820348001/.

———. 2020b. "La Nueva Empresa crime group founder is final FBI fugitive sought in US Consulate slayings." *El Paso Times*, March 11, 2020. https://www.elpasotimes.com/story/news/crime/2020/03/11/us-consulate-murders-final-fugitive-luis-mendez-founder-la-empresa-cartel-juarez/4945438002/.

———. 2020c. "Violence in Mexico: New York man, girlfriend fatally shot as murders continue in Juarez." *El Paso Times*, April 23, 2020. https://www.elpasotimes.com/story/news/local/juarez/2020/04/23/violence-mexico-new-york-man-patrick-landers-girlfriend-karla-baca-killed-juarez/3011030001/.

Braddy, Haldeen. 1960. "The Pachucos and Their Argot." *Southern Folklore Quarterly* 24, no. 4 (December).

Burton, Fred and Ben West. 2008. "The Barrio Azteca Trial and the Prison Gang-Cartel Interface." Stratfor, November 19, 2008. https://worldview.stratfor.com/article/barrio-azteca-trial-and-prison-gang-cartel-interface.

Campbell, Howard. 2009. *Drug War Zone: Frontline Dispatches from the Streets of El Paso and Juárez*. Austin: University of Texas Press.

Cárdenas, Lourdes. 2012. "Juarez police chief: 'No safe place in Mexico for me.'" *El Paso Times*, December 17, 2012. https://warpony2310.blogspot.com/2012/12/mexico-juarez-police-chief-ready-to.html.

Cardona, Julián. 2010. "Families slam Mexico's Calderon over massacre." Reuters, February 2, 2010. https://www.reuters.com/article/us-mexico-drugs-idUSTRE6115IJ20100202.

Carey, Elaine and José Carlos Cisneros Guzmán. 2011. "The Daughters of La Nacha: Profiles of Women Traffickers." *North American Congress on Latin America Report on the Americas* 44, no. 3: 23-24. https://nacla.org/article/daughters-la-nacha-profiles-women-traffickers.

Castillo, Mariano. 2009. "Mayor of violence-torn Juarez: 'We're at a turning point.'" CNN, August 9, 2009. http://www.cnn.com/2009/WORLD/americas/08/31/mexico.juarez.mayor/index.html.

CBS News. 2010a. "FBI: No proof hitmen targeted Americans." March 17, 2010. https://www.cbsnews.com/news/fbi-no-proof-hit-men-targeted-americans/.

———. 2010b. "Mexico Nabs Suspect in U.S. Consulate Murders." July 2, 2010. https://www.cbsnews.com/news/mexico-nabs-suspect-in-us-consulate-murders/.

Center on Hemispheric Affairs. 2011. "The Rise of Femicide and Women in Drug Trafficking." October 28, 2011. https://www.coha.org/the-rise-of-femicide-and-women-in-drug-trafficking/.

Chávez, Julio-Cesar. 2019. "National Geographic reporter shot in Juarez while interviewing drug trafficker." KVIA, October 5, 2019. https://www.kvia.com/news/border/national-geographic-reporter-shot-in-juarez-while-interviewing-drug-trafficker/1129256562.

City-data.com. n.d. "Segundo Barrio neighborhood." http://www.city-data.com/neighborhood/Segundo-Barrio-El-Paso-TX.html. Accessed August 19, 2019.

———. n.d."Chihuahuita neighborhood." http://www.city-data.com/neighborhood/Chihuahuita-El-Paso-TX.html. Accessed August 19, 2019.

REFERENCES

City of El Paso. 1970. Department of Planning R & D. January 1970. https://www.elpasotexas.gov/planning-and-inspections/applications.

Corchado, Alfredo. 2016. "Why El Paso prospers while Juarez struggles." *Dallas Morning News*, September 23, 2016. https://www.dallasnews.com/opinion/commentary/2016/09/23/why-el-paso-prospers-as-juarez-struggles/.

Corchado, Alfredo and Angela Kohcerga. 2011. "American says he witnessed corruption in Mexican prison." *Deseret News*, December 10, 2011. https://www.deseret.com/2011/12/11/20237469/american-says-he-witnessed-corruption-in-mexican-prison.

Corcoran, Patrick. 2011. "Juarez prison riot points to lawlessness in Mexican system." *Christian Science Monitor*, July 29, 2011. https://www.csmonitor.com/World/Americas/Latin-America-Monitor/2011/0729/Juarez-prison-riot-points-to-lawlessness-in-Mexican-system.

Covert, Chris. 2014. "5 suspects in Juarez car bomb released." Borderland Beat, March 11, 2014. http://www.borderlandbeat.com/2014/03/5-suspects-in-2010-juarez-car-bomb.html.

CNN. 2009. "Alleged Hit man Changes Appearance, FBI Says." WIBW.com, October 21, 2009. https://web.archive.org/web/20120226001958/http://www.wibw.com/nationalnews/headlines/65270052.html.

CNN. 2019. "Operation fast and Furious fast facts." September 13, 2019. https://www.cnn.com/2013/08/27/world/americas/operation-fast-and-furious-fast-facts/index.html.

Daily Mail. 2014. "Mexican drug cartel hitman tells how he committed 800 murders before he stopped keeping track." February 11, 2014. https://www.dailymail.co.uk/news/article-2557171/Mexican-drug-cartel-hitman-says-committed-800-murders-stopped-keeping-track.html.

del Bosque, Melissa. 2011. "In Juarez the Prison Inmates Run the Asylum." *Texas Observer*, July 28, 2011. https://www.texasobserver.org/in-juarez-the-inmates-run-the-asylum/.

Díaz, Adriana. 2019. "Who is El Mencho? Mexican cartel boss behind one-third of drugs in the U.S." CBS News, September 26, 2019. https://www.cbsnews.com/news/el-mencho-mexican-cartel-boss-behind-one-third-of-drugs-in-the-us-2019-09-26/.

Dodson, John. 2013. *The Unarmed Truth: My Fight to Blow the Whistle and Expose Fast and Furious*. New York: Threshold Editions.

Dowd, Vincent. 2013. "Operation Hold the Line." National Border, National Park: A History of Organ Pipe Cactus National Monument. https://organpipehistory.com/orpi-a-z/operation-hold-the-line-2/.

Dudley, Steven. 2013. "Barrio Azteca Gang Poised for Leap into International Drug Trade." InSight Crime, February 13, 2013. https://www.insightcrime.org/investigations/barrio-azteca-gang-poised-leap/.

Dudley, Steven and Juan José Martínez D'Aubuisson. 2017. "El Salvador Prisons and the Battle for the MS13's Soul." InSight Crime, February 16, 2017. https://insightcrime.org/investigations/el-salvador-prisons-battle-ms13-soul/.

REFERENCES

Durán, Robert. 2018. *The Gang Paradox: Inequalities and Miracles on the U.S.-Mexico Border.* New York: Columbia University Press.

Eaton, Tracey. 2006a. "Prisoners' kin slam Mexican officials." Chron.com, March 13, 2006. https://www.chron.com/news/nation-world/article/Prisoners-kin-slam-Mexican-officials-1892711.php.

———. 2006b. "Prisoners moved, gang broken up." Chron.com, March 21, 2006. https://blog.chron.com/americas/2006/03/prisoners-moved-gang-broken-up/.

EIDEARD. 2011. "NM Town Swamped in Corruption Abolishes Police Department." July 12, 2011. https://eideard.com/2011/07/12/nm-town-swamped-in-corruption-abolishes-police-department/.

El Diario de Juárez. 2014. "Zetas entrenan a miembros del 'Barrio Azteca' en Juárez y Torreón: testigo." February 4, 2014. https://diario.mx/Local/2014-02-04_563948f4/zetas-entrenan-a-miembros-del-barrio-azteca-en-juarez-y-torreon-testigo/.

———. 2019. "Eran 'Aztecas' los ejecutados durante entrevista de National Geographic." October 5, 2019. https://diario.mx/juarez/eran-aztecas-los-ejecutados-durante-entrevista-de-national-geographic-20191005-1570582.html.

———. 2021. "Aceptan presencia del CJNG en Juárez: Cártel Jalisco Nueva Generación está activo con secuestros: Seguridad Pública." June 15, 2021. https://diario.mx/juarez/aceptan-presencia-del-cjng-enjuarez-20210615-1807577.html.

El Parece. 2020. "The Shadow War." narco.news, October 28, 2020. https://narco.news/the-shadow-war.

El Paso Herald

Esquivel, Jesús J. 2017. "El Cártel de Jalisco se cierne sobre Ciudad Juárez." Proceso, February 11, 2017. https://www.proceso.com.mx/474104/cartel-jalisco-se-cierne-ciudad-juarez.

Estrada, Ismael, Michael Ware, and Rey Rodriguez. 2009. "Death threats force Juarez police chief to resign, mayor says." CNN, February 20, 2009. https://www.cnn.com/2009/WORLD/americas/02/20/juarez.police/.

Federal Bureau of Investigation (FBI). 2009. "New Top Ten Fugitive: Leader of Violent Barrio Azteca Gang." October 20, 2009. https://archives.fbi.gov/archives/news/stories/2009/october/ravelo_102009.

———. 2011. "Thirty-Five Members and Associates of Barrio Azteca Gang Charged with Racketeering and Other Offenses, Including 10 Charged in U.S. Consulate Murders in Juarez, Mexico." March 9, 2011. https://archives.fbi.gov/archives/news/pressrel/press-releases/thirty-five-members-and-associates-of-barrio-azteca-gang-charged-with-racketeering-and-other-offenses-including-10-charged-in-u.s.-consulate-murders-in-juarez-mexico.

———. n.d. "Gangs." What We Investigate. Accessed August 12, 2019. https://www.fbi.gov/investigate/violent-crime/gangs.

Felson, Marcus. 2006. "The Ecosystem for Organized Crime." The European Institute for Crime Prevention and Control, affiliated with the United Nations, Helsinki, no. 26. http://www.heuni.fi.

Fierro, Luis. 2017. "Military returns to Ciudad Juárez due to outbreak of violence."

REFERENCES

El Universal, April 7, 2017. https://www.eluniversal.com.mx/articulo/english/2017/07/4/military-returns-ciudad-juarez-due-outbreak-violence.

Figueroa, Lorena. 2017. "Juárez among the most dangerous cities in the world." *El Paso Times*, April 13, 2017. https://www.elpasotimes.com/story/news/2017/04/13/jurez-among-most-dangerous-cities-world/100425962/.

Fleisher, Mark S., and Scott H. Decker. 2001. "An Overview of the Challenge of Prison Gangs, *Corrections Management Quarterly* 5, no. 1: 1-9. https://pdfs.semanticscholar.org/6d93/c0192ff35a2e3ee04e954a692de8f3b3de08.pdf.

Fox News. 2010. "Mexican police find car bomb in border city of Juarez; no one hurt in controlled detonation." September 10, 2010. https://www.foxnews.com/world/mexican-police-find-car-bomb-in-border-city-of-juarez-no-one-hurt-in-controlled-detonation.

———. 2012a. "2,500 Cops in Mexico Abandon Their Homes Thanks to Cartels." February 2, 2012. https://www.foxnews.com/world/2500-cops-in-mexico-abandon-their-homes-thanks-to-cartels.

———. 2012b. "'Furious' guns tied to 2010 Juarez massacre, other murders in Mexico." October 1, 2012. https://www.foxnews.com/politics/furious-guns-tied-to-2010-juarez-massacre-other-murders-in-mexico.

———. 2014. "Guilty: Texas Jury Convicts Cross-Border Gang Leader of Slaying U.S. Consulate Workers." February 19, 2014. https://www.foxnews.com/world/guilty-texas-jury-convicts-cross-border-gang-leader-of-slaying-u-s-consulate-workers.

Fregoso, Juliana. 2018. "'La Nacha' y 'La Chata', las 'madres fundadoras' que inventaron todo en el narcotrafico mexicano." Infobae, June 2, 2018. https://www.infobae.com/america/mexico/2018/06/02/la-nacha-y-la-chata-las-madres-fundadoras-que-inventaron-todo-en-el-narcotrafico-mexicano/.

Gallagher, Mike. 2018. "Federal indictment details smuggling operation in southern New Mexico." *Las Cruces Sun News*, June 10, 2018. https://www.lcsun-news.com/story/news/local/2018/06/10/federal-indictment-details-smuggling-operation-southern-new-mexico/689402002/.

Garcia, José Z. 2009. "Mayor of Juarez Moving to Las Cruces." *La Politica New Mexico* (blog), December 28, 2009. https://lapoliticanewmexico.blogspot.com/2009/12/mayor-of-juarez-moving-to-las-cruces.html.

———. 2010. "Police Kidnap Youths Who Survived Massacre: Is This Normal Police Procedure?" *La Politica New Mexico* (blog), February 5, 2010. http://lapoliticanewmexico.blogspot.com/2010/02/police-kidnap-youths-who-survived.html.

Gaytan, Samuel. 2019. "National Geographic journalist shot while interviewing purported drug dealer in Mexico." *El Paso Times*, October 5, 2019. https://www.usatoday.com/story/news/world/2019/10/05/national-geographic-journalist-shot-mexico/3881369002/.

Gibson, Josh. 2012. "Juarez Cartel threatens to kill 'One officer daily.'" Borderland Beat, January 28, 2012. http://www.borderlandbeat.com/2012/01/juarez-cartel-threatens-to-kill-one.html.

REFERENCES

Gill, Julian. 2018. "Barrio Azteca makes resurgence as top gang threat in Texas." *Chron*, December 17, 2018. https://www.chron.com/news/houston-texas/houston/article/Barrio-Azteca-makes-resurgence-as-top-gang-threat-13471487.php.

Grillo, Ioan. 2010. "In Juarez car bomb, a ruthless trap for police." *The World*, July 26, 2010. https://www.pri.org/stories/2010-07-26/juarez-car-bomb-ruthless-trap-police.

Grissom, Brandi. 2010. "Blood Lines: Prosperity Amid Peril." *Texas Tribune*, July 14, 2010. https://www.texastribune.org/2010/07/14/tragedy-in-jurez-spurs-economy-in-el-paso/.

Gundur, R. V. 2019a. "Finding the Sweet Spot: Optimizing Criminal Careers within the Context of Illicit Enterprise." *Deviant Behavior* 41, no. 3 (January): 378-97. https://doi.org/10.1080/01639625.2019.1565851.

———. 2019b. "Settings matter: Examining Protection's influence on illicit drug trade in convergence settings in the *Paso del Norte* metropolitan area." *Contemporary Crises* 72, no. 3 (October): 339-60. https://doi.org/10.1007/s10611-019-09810-3.

———. 2020. "Negotiating Violence and Protection in Prison and on the Outside: The Organizational Evolution of the Transnational Prison Gang Barrio Azteca." *International Criminal Justice Review* 30, no. 1 (March): 30-60. https://doi.org/10.1177/1057567719836466.

Haussaman, Heath. 2011. "Columbus mayor, police chief charged with firearms trafficking." NMPolitics.net, March 10, 2011. https://nmpolitics.net/index/2011/03/columbus-mayor-police-chief-charged-with-drug-trafficking/comment-page-1/.

Hernandez, Anabel. 2013. *Narcoland: The Mexican Drug Lords and Their Godfathers*. London: Verso. 5.

Howell, James C., and John P. Moore. 2010. "History of Street Gangs in the United States." *National Gang Center Bulletin*, no. 4 (May). https://www.nationalgangcenter.gov/Content/Documents/History-of-Street-Gangs.pdf.

Hsu, Spencer and Mary Beth Sheridan. 2020. "Daughter of alleged drug kingpin 'El Mencho' arrested trying to see brother in U.S. court in Washington." *Washington Post*, February 27, 2020. https://www.washingtonpost.com/local/legal-issues/daughter-of-alleged-mexico-drug-kingpin-el-mencho-arrested-trying-to-see-brother-in-us-court-in-washington/2020/02/27/8c822914-5987-11ea-9000-f3cffee23036_story.html.

Ibarra, Porfirio. 2011. "UPDATED: Smuggled females, guns marked Juarez prison riot." *Albuquerque Journal*, July 27, 2011. https://www.abqjournal.com/45994/updated-2-u-s-citizens-among-17-dead-at-juarez-prison.html.

InSight Crime. 2011. "Ciudad Juarez Registers Record Murder Rate." January 5, 2011. https://www.insightcrime.org/news/analysis/ciudad-juarez-records-record-murders/.

———. 2016. "Heriberto Lazcano, alias 'Z3.'" October 20, 2016. https://www.insightcrime.org/mexico-organized-crime-news/heriberto-lazcano-z3/.

———. 2017a. "Barrio Azteca." February 8, 2017. https://es.insightcrime.org/mexico-crimen-organizado/barrio-azteca/.

REFERENCES

———. 2017b. "Vicente Carrillo Fuentes, alias 'El Viceroy.'" March 10, 2017. https://www.insightcrime.org/mexico-organized-crime-news/vicente-carrillo-fuentes-el-viceroy/.

———. 2018. "Barrio Azteca." July 9, 2018. https://www.insightcrime.org/mexico-organized-crime-news/barrio-azteca-profile/.

Jimenez, Marina. 2010. "Felipe Calderon: The man who took on the drug cartels." *The Globe and Mail*, May 28, 2010. https://www.theglobeandmail.com/news/world/felipe-calderon-the-man-who-took-on-the-drug-cartels/article4353244/.

Justice in Mexico. 2011. "Juárez Cartel's 'El Diego' Arrested." August 1, 2011. https://justiceinmexico.org/juarez-cartels-el-diego-arrested/.

Katzenbach, Jon R. and Douglas K. Smith. 2001. *The Discipline of Teams: A Mindbook-Workbook for Delivering Small Group Performance*. New York: John Wiley & Sons Inc., 180-86.

Knox, George. 2019. National Gang Research Center. Email correspondence.

Kolb, Joseph. 2012a. "Under pressure in Ciudad Juarez, cartel killer 're-brand' themselves." Fox News, June 4, 2012. https://www.foxnews.com/world/under-pressure-in-ciudad-juarez-cartel-killers-re-brand-themselves.

———. 2012b. "Violence Against Women Worse Than Ever in Juarez, Experts Say." Fox News, July 5, 2012. https://www.foxnews.com/world/violence-against-women-worse-than-ever-in-juarez-experts-say.

Lacey, Marc. 2009a. "With force, Mexican drug cartels get their way." *New York Times*, February 28, 2009. https://www.nytimes.com/2009/03/01/world/americas/01juarez.html.

———. 2009b. "17 killed in Mexican rehab center." *New York Times*, September 3, 2009. https://www.nytimes.com/2009/09/04/world/americas/04mexico.html.

Lee, Morgan. 2010. "Mexican murder suspect: U.S. consulate infiltrated." *Washington Times*, July 2, 2010. https://www.washingtontimes.com/news/2010/jul/2/mexican-murder-suspect-us-consulate-infiltrated/.

Lester, Donald, John A. Parnell, and Shawn Carraher. 2003. "Organizational Life Cycle: A Five-Stage Empirical Scale." *The International Journal of Organizational Analysis* 11, no. 4 (April): 339-54.

Levario, Miguel. n.d. "El Paso Race Riot of 1916." Texas State Historical Association, *Handbook of Texas Online*. Accessed November 25, 2019. https://tshaonline.org/handbook/online/articles/jce01.

Logan, Samuel. 2012. "A Profile of Los Zetas: Mexico's Second Most Powerful Drug Cartel." *CTC Sentinel* 5, no. 2 (February). https://ctc.usma.edu/a-profile-of-los-zetas-mexicos-second-most-powerful-drug-cartel/.

Macrotrends. 2019. "El Salvador Murder/Homicide rate 1995-2019." https://www.macrotrends.net/countries/SLV/el-salvador/murder-homicide-rate.

Madrid, Salina. 2019. "El Paso ranks as one of the Top 10 Safest Cities in America for 2019." KFOX14, April 26, 2019. https://kfoxtv.com/news/local/el-paso-ranks-as-one-of-the-top-10-safest-cities-in-america-for-2019.

Malkin, Elisabeth. 2010. "Mexican Drug Gang Leader Confesses to Killings." *New*

York Times, November 28, 2010. https://www.nytimes.com/2010/11/29/world/americas/29mexico.html.

McCormack, David. 2013. "Cartel hit man accused of killing two U.S. citizens claim he should walk free because Mexican police 'shocked his testicles and raped his wife' to get a confession." *Daily Mail*, November 27, 2013. https://www.dailymail.co.uk/news/article-2514737/Cartel-hit-man-Arturo-Gallegos-Castrellon-claims-Mexican-police-raped-wife-confession.html.

McGahan, Jason. 2017. "Juarez's Missing Girls Were Sex Slaves—And Everyone Knew It." *Daily Beast*, April 14, 2017. https://www.thedailybeast.com/juarezs-missing-girls-were-sex-slavesand-everyone-knew-it.

McKinley Jr., James C. 2010. "Suspect says Juarez killers had pursued jail guard." *New York Times*, March 31, 2010. https://www.nytimes.com/2010/04/01/world/americas/01mexico.html.

Mennem, K. 2013. "Infighting Hurt the Barrio Aztecas Who Worked for Juarez Cartél." Borderland Beat, August 27, 2013. http://www.borderlandbeat.com/2013/08/infighting-hurt-barrio-aztecas-who.html.

Mexico Daily News. 2015. "Former police chief is victim of shooting." May 9, 2015. https://mexiconewsdaily.com/news/former-police-chief-is-victim-of-shooting/.

Midgley, Justin. 2018. "FBI's Ten Most Wanted…Captured! Eduardo Ravelo Wiki." Crimeola, August 24, 2018. https://crimeola.com/fbi-ten-wanted-eduardo-ravelo-wiki/.

Milenio. 2019. "'Barrio Azteca,' el socio en EU de 'La Línea,' grupo ligado a ataque a familia LeBarón." March 12, 2019. https://www.milenio.com/policia/linea-grupo-ligado-caso-lebaron-socio-barrio-azteca-eu.

Miller, Joshua Rhett. 2014. "Hand grenades becoming key weapon in Mexican cartels' arsenals, say authorities." Fox News, August 16, 2014. https://www.foxnews.com/us/hand-grenades-becoming-key-weapon-in-mexican-cartels-arsenals-say-authorities.

Morales, Fred. 1991. "Chihuahita: A Neglected Corner of El Paso." *Password* 36, no. 2 (Spring).

National Institute on Drug Abuse. 2021. "Overdose Death Rates." Last modified January 29, 2021. https://www.drugabuse.gov/related-topics/trends-statistics/overdose-death-rates.

Ortiz, Jennifer M. 2018. "Gangs and environment: A comparative analysis of prison and street gangs." *American Journal of Qualitative Research* 2, no. 1 (June), 97-117. https://doi.org/10.29333/ajqr/5796.

Pachico, Elyssa. 2013. "Juarez Murder Rate Reaches 5-Year Low." InSight Crime, January 4, 2013. https://www.insightcrime.org/news/analysis/juarez-murder-rate-reaches-5-year-low/.

Pacilla, Matthew. 2012. "Los Mexicles Profile." http://research.ridgway.pitt.edu/wp-content/uploads/2012/05/LosMexiclesPROFILEFINAL.pdf.

Payan, Tony. 2016. "How a Forgotten Border Dispute Tormented U.S.-Mexico Relations for 100 Years. *Americas Quarterly*, February 8, 2016. https://www.americasquarterly.org/content/how-forgotten-border-dispute-tormented-us-mexico-relations-100-years.

REFERENCES

Perez Jr., Maclovio. n.d. "El Paso Bath House Riots." Texas State Historical Association, *Handbook of Texas Online*. Accessed November 24, 2019. https://tshaonline.org/handbook/online/articles/jce02.

Prison Insider. 2017. "The penitentiary system." https://www.prison-insider.com/countryprofile/prisonsofmexico?s=le-systeme-penitentiaire#le-systeme-penitentiaire.

Public Intelligence. 2010. "El Paso Intelligence Center: Mexican U.S. Consulate Murderers Gang Warning." March 22, 2010. https://publicintelligence.net/el-paso-intelligence-center-mexican-u-s-consulate-murderers-gang-warning/.

Ramirez, Marc. 2019. "National Geographic reporter shot while interviewing drug supplier in Juarez." *Dallas Morning News*, October 5, 2019. https://www.dallasnews.com/news/mexico/2019/10/05/national-geographic-reporter-shot-interviewing-drug-supplier-juarez/.

Ramsey, Geoffrey. 2011. "Cable Suggests Mexican Army May Have Worked with Juarez Paramilitary Group." InSight Crime, March 28, 2011. https://www.insightcrime.org/news/analysis/cable-suggests-mexican-army-worked-with-juarez-paramilitary-group/.

Rector, Kevin. 2017. "In 2016, Baltimore's second-deadliest year on record, bullets claimed targets and bystanders alike." *Baltimore Sun*, January 2, 2017. http://www.baltimoresun.com/news/crime/bs-md-ci-homicides-2016-20170102-story.html.

Resendiz, Julian. 2019. "National Geographic reporter was shot during ambush on Aztecas gang in Juarez, authorities say." BorderReport, October 7, 2019. https://www.borderreport.com/hot-topics/national-geographic-reporter-was-shot-during-ambush-on-azteca-gang-in-juarez-authorities-say/.

———. 2020a. "Jalisco cartel continues bloody march to border despite extradition of leader's son, experts say." BorderReport, February 21, 2020. https://www.borderreport.com/news/jalisco-cartel-continues-bloody-march-to-border-despite-extradition-of-leaders-son-experts-say/.

———. 2020b. "Three more killed in Juarez as police say gangs now targeting victims at home." KVEO-TV, October 7, 2020. https://www.valleycentral.com/border-report/three-more-killed-in-juarez-as-police-say-gangs-now-targeting-victims-at-home/.

Reuters. 2010. "TIMELINE-Events in Mexico's drug war city Ciudad Juarez." June 16, 2010. https://www.reuters.com/article/idUSN16449.

Reyes, Gerardo and Santiago Wills. 2012. "Cartel Leader Behind Mexican Massacres Linked to Operation Fast and Furious." ABC News, September 30, 2012. https://abcnews.go.com/ABC_Univision/News/cartel-leader-mexican-massacres-linked-operation-fast-furious/story?id=17362442\.

Robillard, Kevin. 2012. "Report: 'Furious' guns in massacres." *Politico*, October 1, 2012. https://www.politico.com/story/2012/10/report-furious-guns-in-massacres-081852.

Romo, Rene. 2011. "Former Columbus, N.M., Police Chief Pleads Guilty in Gun-Smuggling Case." *Albuquerque Journal*, August 25, 2011. https://www.abqjournal.com/52446/updated-former-columbus-n-m-police-chief-pleads-guilty-in-gun-smuggling-case.html.

Roth, Garrett M. and David Skarbek. 2014. "Prison Gangs and the Community Responsibility System." *Review of Behavioral Economics* 1, no. 3 (May): 223-43.

Salazar, Paris Alejandro. 2016. "Artistas Asesinos, de pandilleros a sicarios." *La Silla Rota*, February 2, 2016. https://lasillarota.com/artistas-asesinos-de-pandilleros-a-sicarios/1-3329.

Sanchez, Sara. 2016. "Segundo Barrio, Chihuahuita on endangered list." *El Paso Times*, October 5, 2016. https://www.elpasotimes.com/story/news/local/el-paso/2016/10/05/segundo-barrio-chihuahuita-endangered-list/91548474/.

———. 2017. "Your complete guide to shopping in Downtown El Paso." *El Paso Times*, December 27, 2017. https://www.elpasotimes.com/story/news/local/el-paso/2017/12/27/find-bargains-culture-el-centro-downtown-el-paso/982501001/.

Santiago, Diego. 2019. "'Artistas Asesinos,' el brazo armado del Cártel de Sinaloa que secuestra y mata en Juárez." GrupoFórmula, August 27, 2019. https://www.radioformula.com.mx/noticias/mexico/20190827/artistas-asesinos-brazo-armado-cartel-de-sinaloa-secuestra-mata-ciudad-juarez/.

Saviano, Roberto. 2015. "El Chapo's Rise to Power And His First Prison Break." *Time* magazine, July 21, 2015. https://time.com/3966611/roberto-saviano-el-chapo-prison-escape/.

Schapiro, Rich. 2009. "Gunmen kill 17 execution style at El Aliviane drug rehab center in Ciudad Juarez, Mexico." *New York Daily News*, September 3, 2009. https://www.nydailynews.com/news/national/gunmen-kill-17-execution-style-el-aliviane-drug-rehab-center-ciudad-juarez-mexico-article-1.401982.

Shoichet, Catherine E., Ed Payne, and Don Melvin. 2015. "Mexican drug lord Joaquín 'El Chapo' Guzmán escapes." CNN, July 12, 2015. https://www.cnn.com/2015/07/12/world/mexico-el-chapo-escape/index.html.

Tapia, Mike. 2017. *The Barrio Gangs of San Antonio, 1915-2015*. Fort Worth, Texas: TCU Press.

———. 2019. *Gangs of the El Paso-Juárez Borderland: A History*. Albuquerque: University of New Mexico Press.

Texas Department of Public Safety. 2011. "Texas Gang Threat Assessment 2011." Texas Fusion Center Intelligence & Counterterrorism Division, November 2011. https://wikileaks.org/gifiles/attach/138/138146_Texas%20Gang%20Threat%20Assessment%202011%20Final.pdf.

———. 2015. "Texas Gang Threat Assessment." Texas Joint Crime Information Center Intelligence & Counterterrorism Division, August 2015. https://www.dps.texas.gov/director_staff/media_and_communications/2015/txGangThreatAssessment.pdf.

———. 2018. "Texas Gang Threat Assessment." Texas Joint Crime Information Center Intelligence & Counterterrorism Division, November 2018. https://www.dps.texas.gov/director_staff/media_and_communications/2018/txGangThreatAssessment201811.pdf.

The Cartel War (blog). 2011. "Calderon Admits He Has No Clue As to the Power of the Cartels." August 21, 2011. https://thecartelwar.blogspot.com/2011/08/calderon-admits-he-has-no-clue-as-to.html.

REFERENCES

Trulson, Chad R., James W. Marquart, and Soraya K. Kawucha. 2008. "Gang suppression and institutional control." Corrections1, April 5, 2008. https://www.correctionsone.com/prison-gangs/articles/gang-suppression-and-institutional-control-zrwUPhjCTc7DObFU/.

Tuckman, Jo. 2009. "At least 20 dead in Mexican prison riot." *The Guardian*, March 4, 2009. https://www.theguardian.com/world/2009/mar/05/ciudad-juarez-mexico-prison-riot-deaths.

U.S. Customs and Border Protection. 2019a. "Brian A. Terry." In Memoriam. Last modified June 17, 2019. https://www.cbp.gov/about/in-memoriam/brian-terry.

———. 2019b. Data obtained from public record request. September 1, 2019.

———. 2019c. "CBP Enforcement Statistics Fiscal Year 2019." Newsroom Stats. https://www.cbp.gov/newsroom/stats/cbp-enforcement-statistics.

United States Department of Justice. 2012a. "Juarez Drug Cartel Leader Pleads Guilty to Charges Related to U.S. Consulate Murders and Is Sentenced to Life in Prison." Department of Justice Office of Public Affairs, April 5, 2012. https://www.justice.gov/opa/pr/juarez-drug-cartel-leader-pleads-guilty-charges-related-us-consulate-murders-and-sentenced.

———. 2012b. "Barrio Azteca Leader Extradited from Mexico to United States to Face Charges Related to U.S. Consulate Murders in Juarez, Mexico." Department of Justice Office of Public Affairs, June 29, 2012. https://www.justice.gov/opa/pr/barrio-azteca-leader-extradited-mexico-united-states-face-charges-related-us-consulate.

———. 2014. "Barrio Azteca Lieutenant Who Ordered the Consulate Murders in Ciudad Juarez Sentenced to Life in Prison." Department of Justice Office of Public Affairs, April 24, 2014. https://www.justice.gov/opa/pr/barrio-azteca-lieutenant-who-ordered-consulate-murders-ciudad-juarez-sentenced-life-prison.

U.S. Department of the Treasury. 2012. "Treasury Sanctions Latin American Criminal Organization." Press Center, October 11, 2012. https://www.treasury.gov/press-center/press-releases/Pages/tg1733.aspx.

———. 2015. Office of Foreign Assets Control: Transnational Criminal Organizations Sanctions Program. April 14, 2015. https://www.treasury.gov/resource-center/sanctions/Programs/Documents/tco.pdf.

———. 2020. "Sanctions pursuant to the Foreign Drug Kingpin designation act." Transnational Criminal Organizations Sanctions Program. March 19, 2020. https://www.treasury.gov/resourcecenter/sanctions/Programs/Documents/narco_sanctions_kingpin.pdf.

USA Today. 2012. "Mexican cartels fill demand for meth in USA." October 11, 2012. https://www.usatoday.com/story/news/nation/2012/10/11/mexico-cartels-meth/1626383/.

Utley, Robert M. 1996. *Changing Course: The International Boundary, United States and Mexico, 1848-1963*. Tucson, Arizona: Southwest Parks and Monuments Association.

Valdemar, Richard. 2011. "Knocking Down Barrio Azteca." *Police* magazine, December 27, 2011. https://www.policemag.com/373990/knocking-down-barrio-azteca.

Valdez, Diana Washington. 2009. "After threats, Juárez mayor in El Paso." *El Paso Times*, February 24, 2009. https://www.city-data.com/forum/politics-other-controversies/576023-mayor-mexican-city-moves-u-s.html.

Valencia, Nick. 2010a. "Second arrest made in connection with Juarez party massacre." CNN, February 7, 2010. https://www.cnn.com/2010/WORLD/americas/02/06/mexico.juarez.drugs/index.html.

———. 2010b. "Third suspect arrested in Juarez party killings." CNN, February 28, 2010. https://www.cnn.com/2010/WORLD/americas/02/28/mexico.juarez.arrest/index.html.

———. 2010c. "Four more arrested in Juarez house party massacre." CNN, March 21, 2010. https://www.cnn.com/2010/CRIME/03/21/mexico.juarez.arrests/index.html.

———. 2010d. "Arrest made in deaths of 3 linked to U.S. Consulate in Ciudad Juarez." CNN, March 29, 2010. https://www.cnn.com/2010/WORLD/americas/03/29/mexico.juarez.arrest/index.html.

———. 2010e. "Groups of Mexican federal police clash over allegations." CNN, August 8, 2010. http://www.cnn.com/2010/WORLD/americas/08/08/mexico.federal.police/index.html.

———. 2010f. "Suspect in Juarez car bombing arrested, Mexican police say." CNN, September 27, 2010. https://www.cnn.com/2010/WORLD/americas/09/27/mexico.car.bomb.suspect/index.html.

Warren, Beth. 2019. "Who is El Mencho? He's the most powerful drug kingpin you've never heard of." *Courier Journal*, November 24, 2019. https://www.courier-journal.com/in-depth/news/crime/2019/11/24/el-mencho-what-know-powerful-cjng-mexican-drug-cartel-leader/4086498002/.

Winter, Russ. 2020. "The Juárez Organized Crime Sex Trafficking and Murder Cartel." *Winter Watch*, February 3, 2020. https://www.winterwatch.net/2020/02/the-juarez-organized-crime-sex-trafficking-and-murder-cartel/.

WOLA. 2010. "Human Rights Violations Commited by the Military in Ciudad Juarez Documented in New Report." Washington Office on Latin America, October 5, 2010. https://www.wola.org/2010/10/human-rights-violations-committed-by-the-military-in-ciudad-juarez-documented-in-new-report/.

Woody, Christopher. 2017. "Mexico's ascendant cartel is making a deadly addition to a trafficking hub on the US border." *Business Insider*, March 7, 2017. https://www.businessinsider.com/jalisco-cjng-sinaloa-cartel-violence-in-ciudad-juarez-mexico-2017-3.

INDEX

BA = Barrio Azteca

"18, El." *See* Hernandez Lozano, Aldo Favio ("El 18")
18th Street (gang), 1; in El Salvador prisons, 50; US deportations and, 58
"24, El." *See* Arzate Meléndez, Israel ("El 24," "El Country")
"35, El." *See* Acosta Guerrero, Jesús Armado ("El 35")
"51." *See* Gallegos Castrellón, Arturo ("51," "Benny," "Farmero," "Guero," "Manon," "Tury")
"58, El." *See* Mendez, Luis ("El Tío," "El 58," "Narizón")
"97." *See* Núñez Payan, Alberto ("Fresa," "Fresca," "97")
"300, El." *See* Santana Garza, René Gerardo ("N," "El 300")

Abraham Gonzalez International Airport (Ciudad Juárez): in Joint Operation Chihuahua, 92
Acosta, Benito ("Benny"), 29
Acosta Guerrero, Jesús Armado ("El 35"): arrest of, 137
Acosta Hernández, José Antonio ("El Diego"): arrest of, 112, 147; attack on US Consulate workers (2010) and, 127; Avenida 16 de Septiembre bombing (2010) and, 134; El Aliviane rehabilitation center massacre (2009) and, 113; conviction of, 146–47; extradition of, 125, 147; as La Línea leader, 77, 108; sentencing of, 114, 147; threat to US authorities by, 138; Villas de Salvarcar massacre (2010) and, 108, 110; on Villas de Salvarcar massacre (2010), 111
Aguilar, Rafael: killing of, 75
Almaraz, David, 119

Altiplano federal maximum security prison: Joaquín Guzmán's escape from, 48
Alvarez, Benjamin: cooperation with US authorities of, 141
American Mafia: BA compared to, 129, 142, 159; decline of, 142; RICO statute used against, 142
Ammonium Nitrate and Fuel Oil (ANFO), 135
"Angelillo." *See* Esqueda, Miguel Ángel ("Angelillo")
Antillon, Hilda, 122–23
Arellano Félix, Enedina, 17
Arias, Juan Alfredo Soto ("Arnold"), 112
"Arnold." *See* Arias, Juan Alfredo Soto ("Arnold")
Arroyo Chavarría, José Dolores: arrest of, 111; prison sentence of, 112; Villas de Salvarcar massacre (2010) blamed on, 110
Artistas Asesinos (gang). *See* Doble A (gang)
Aryan Brotherhood (gang), 1; as Texas Syndicate rival, 27, 28
Arzate Meléndez, Israel ("El 24," "El Country"): arrest of, 112; confession of, 112; on Villas de Salvarcar massacre (2010), 110; Villas de Salvarcar massacre (2010) blamed on, 110
Avenida 16 de Septiembre (Ciudad Juárez): bombing on (2010), 133–37
Ávila Beltrán, Sandra, 17
Avilla, Victor: attack on, 95–96
Aztec (Native American civilization) culture: BA imagery and, 2, 37, 39
Aztecas Vieja Escuela, Las. *See* Old School Aztecas

Baltimore, Maryland: Ciudad Juárez's homicide rate compared to homicide rate of, 151
Banco, El (BA treasurer), 37

INDEX

Bandidos (gang): RICO statute used against, 142

Barrio Azteca (BA): Arturo Gallegos Castrellón's conviction and, 131–32; bombings by, 133–39; "church" meetings of, 64, 126; codes of, 40–41; Coffield Unit (Texas prison system) and, 23; communication methods and network of, 31, 34, 73–74, 80; decline of, 114, 140–58; geographic expansion of, 44; hand signs of, 40; human trafficking by, 85–87; income of, 33–34; independence of, 153; internal strife in, 144–55; as La Empresa member, 152, 155; maquiladoras created by 81–82; membership numbers of, 43–44; mesa mayor (leadership board) of, 45; in Mexican prisons, 25–26; MS-13 compared with, 2–3, 5–6, 32, 46–47; origins of, 29–30; prostitution and, 66–67, 84–85, 85–88; public perception of, 2–3, 47, 77–78, 117–18; recent revival of, 153; rules of, 30, 31, 32–33; in Sinaloa DTO-Juárez Cartel conflict, 93, 123–24; structure of, 30, 31–32, 33, 34; tattoos of, 37–40; threat assessment of, 45, 152–53; US deportations and, 58; vetting of potential members of, 31; violence and, 36–37, 43, 49, 50–52, 72, 77, 83–84, 87–88, 114–15; X list of, 33, 145

barrio gangs: in El Paso, 18–22. *See also* street gangs

Bath Riots (1917), 3, 14–15, 19

"Benny." *See* Acosta, Benito ("Benny"); Gallegos Castrellón, Arturo ("51," "Benny," "Farmero," "Guero," "Manon," "Tury")

Big Spring, Texas: Fernando Carrillo incarcerated at, 146

"Bird, The." *See* Marquez, Gualberto ("The Bird")

bombings, 133–39

"Boots," 64

Border Brothers (gang): BA and, 43

"Borrego," 63, 64, 66

Bracero Program, 57

Breuer, Lanny, 128–29, 147

"Bruno, El." *See* Rangel, Bruno Ángel ("El Bruno")

Building Tender program, 27–28; abolition of, 28

Bureau of Alcohol, Tobacco, Firearms, and Explosives (ATF): Operation Fast and Furious of, 95, 112, 113

Burquenos (gang), 25

Cabada, Armando, 153–54

"Caballo." *See* Duran, José ("Caballo")

"Cabezón, El." *See* Serenil Luna, Hugo Alonso ("El Cabezón")

Caldera, Philip: Avenida 16 de Septiembre bombing (2010) and, 137

Calderón, Felipe: drug policy of, 70, 72, 76, 82, 89, 92, 99, 100, 103, 133; on Villas de Salvarcar massacre (2010), 110–11

Calo (slang), 20

Camacho Ramos, Luis Alberto ("El Shoker," "El Flaco"): Villas de Salvarcar massacre (2010) blamed on, 112

Camarena, Enrique ("Kiki"): torture and murder of (1985), 115, 118, 123

"Camello Joroado." *See* Chávez Castillo, Jesús Ernesto ("Camello Joroado")

"Cantinflas" (BA gang member), 61–62, 64

Cantinflas (comedian), 61

capo (BA rank), 32, 34, 36; insignia of, 40

Cárdenas Guillén, Osiel, 78

Cárdenas Palomino, Luis, 139; on Arturo Gallegos Castrellón, 125

Cardone, Kathleen, 129–30, 131, 132, 147

Cardoza, Manuel ("Tolon"), 29, 72; cooperation with US authorities of, 141

carjacking: in Ciudad Juárez, 106

carnal (BA rank), 34

Carranza, Venustiano, 13

Carrillo, Carlos: on potential for cross-border violence during drug war, 103

Carrillo, Fernando, 71–74; as Arturo Gallegos Castrellón trial witness, 131–32; on BA's role in Sinaloa DTO-Juárez Cartel conflict, 93; cooperation with US authorities of, 145–46

Carrillo Fuentes, Amado, 17, 75

Carrillo Fuentes, Vicente ("El Viceroy"), 71, 75–76; arrest of, 152; cartel run by (*see* Juárez Cartel); designated as kingpin, 47

INDEX

Cartel Jalisco New Generation (CJNG), 156–57
Casas, Irma: on feminicide in Ciudad Juárez, 98
"Casitas." *See* Perez Marrufo, José Ángel ("Casitas")
Castaneda, Robert, 128
Castañeda Alvarez, Jesús Antonio ("El Güero"), 91
Catholicism: *pachuco* culture and, 21; Sacred Heart Roman Catholic Church (El Paso), 11
"Caudillo," 79
Central Intelligence Agency (CIA): José Antonio Acosta Hernández's arrest and, 112, 147
CERESO 3 (Ciudad Juárez), 43, 48–54, 154; drug smuggling into, 61, 62; homicides in, 66; Jesús Ernesto Chávez Castillo incarcerated in, 62–63, 65, 68, 82
"Chabez": as hit team leader, 84
Chamizal Dispute (1963), 3, 15–16, 19
Chamizal Park (El Paso): Perla Cristal Garcia Ponte's body found in (2012), 97–98
Chaparral, New Mexico: weapons smuggling in, 94
"Chapo, El." *See* Guzmán Loera, Joaquín Archivaldo ("El Chapo")
Chavez, Eduardo, 95
Chávez Castillo, Jesús Ernesto ("Camello Joroado"), 30–31; arrest of, 124, 142; as Arturo Gallegos Castrellón trial witness, 58, 77, 118, 122, 123, 129, 131; in attack on US Consulate workers (2010), 118, 119, 122, 127, 129; on BA communication methods, 31; BA history of, 59–71, 145; on BA homicides, 5, 77–78; BA initiation of, 62; as BA leader at CERESO 3 (Ciudad Juárez), 52–54; on BA rules, 31; commercial extortion by, 105–6; cooperation with US authorities of, 141–42, 145, 146; as crack producer, 81–82; as drug dealer, 68–69; on feminicide, 85; guilty plea and sentencing of, 131; as hit team leader, 73, 83–85, 87; murders by, 77, 87; as surveillance supervisor, 82–83; torture and dismemberment used by, 79–80, 87–88; wife ordered murdered, 124
"Chepe," 82
Chicano Park (El Paso): *pachuco* culture and, 20
Chicas, Jacson: stabbing of (2019), 26
"Chicho." *See* Meraz, David ("Chicho")
Chihuahuita (El Paso): Bath Riots (1917), 14–15; described, 9–10, 11; Ignacia Jasso Gonzales in, 17; Mexican immigration to, 2; during Mexican Revolution, 13–14; *pachucos* in, 21; "Us versus Them" attitude in, 12
Chinese: in Ciudad Juárez, 16, 17; exclusion of, 56; impact on El Paso, of, 16–17
Chinese Exclusion Act (1882), 56
"Chino, El." *See* Valles de la Rosa, Ricardo ("El Chino")
Chuco Tangos (gang), 19
Ciudad Juárez, Chihuahua: Chinese in, 16, 17; crime in, US immigration policy and, 57–58; drug war's effect on, 97–107; El Paso, and, 2; homicides in, 5–6; reputation of, 110; Sinaloa DTO insertion into, 70, 89. *See also* CERESO 3 (Ciudad Juárez)
Clinton, Hillary Rodham: on Mexico's drug war, 133
Club Verde (Ciudad Juárez), 85; pictured, 86
cocaine, 155; American demand for, gang explosion and, 35; BA as traffickers of, 34–35, 80; in Ciudad Juárez, 67; codes for, 41; Colombian cartel routes of, 75; Eduardo Ravelo Rodriguez charged with possession of, 149; processing of, 77, 80, 81; smuggled into CERESO 3 (Ciudad Juárez), 53; smuggled into US, 132; sold by Fernando Carrillo, 71; sold by Gualberto Marquez, 58–59; sold by Jesús Ernesto Chávez Castillo, 52, 53–54, 63, 69; sold by La Línea, 76, 77. *See also* crack cocaine
codes: of American Mafia, 142; of BA, 40–41
Coffield Unit (Texas prison system), 9, 23, 58, 132; as BA headquarters, 33, 36, 45; BA-Mexicle rivalry in, 43; BA's origins in, 29–30; Mexicle origins at, 41–42
Cohen, David S.: on MS-13, 46

179

INDEX

Colombian cartels: BA as traffickers for, 34–35; Mexican cartels compared to, 76; routes of, 75
Columbus, New Mexico: Pancho Villa's raid against (1916), 14; weapons smuggled from, 94–95
Combat Methamphetamine Epidemic Act (2006), 155–56
commercial extortion: by BA, 47, 74, 86; in Ciudad Juárez, 33, 100–101, 105–6, 133; José Marquez's opposition to, 41
"Conejo." *See* Michelletti, Johnny ("Conejo")
Contreras Lumbreras, José Ivan ("El Keiko"): arrest of, 138
Contreras Meraz, Fernando ("El Dorado"): arrest of, 138–39; Avenida 16 de Septiembre bombing (2010) and, 136
Cooley, Joseph, 129
Corchado, Alfredo: on methamphetamine epidemic in the United States, 157
Cordova Island, 15–16
Corrales, Arturo: death of, 22
corridos, 20
Council on Hemispheric Affairs: on feminicide in Ciudad Juárez, 100
"Country, El." *See* Arzate Meléndez, Israel ("El 24," "El Country")
COVID-19: effect on Ciudad Juárez gangs of, 150–51
crack cocaine, 18; in Ciudad Juárez, 67; production of, 81; sold by Jesús Ernesto Chávez Castillo, 63, 69; sold by La Línea, 77
Cuevas Sanchez, Lucio: arrest of, 51

Dávila, José Luis: killing of, 109
Dávila, Luz María, 109; on Villas de Salvarcar massacre (2010), 111
Dávila, Marcos: killing of, 109
del Castillo, Kate, 149
Deming, New Mexico: weapons smuggling in, 94
Díaz, Porfirio, 2, 13
Díaz, Rafa, 52–53, 66, 68, 69, 77, 83; implicated to US authorities, 128; turned into kidnappers, 87
Díaz Díaz, José Guadalupe ("Zorro"), 87; in attack on US Consulate workers (2010),

120–21, 127; commercial extortion by, 106; extradition of, 131; as hit team leader, 84; human trafficking by, 69–70; implicated to US authorities, 128
"Diego, El." *See* Acosta Hernández, José Antonio ("El Diego")
dismemberment: of Gilberto Ontiveros Lucero, 88; used by BA and La Línea, 79–80
Doble A (gang): art of, 93–94; BAs and, 50–51, 52, 61, 66, 84, 96, 114–15; at CERESO 3 (Ciudad Juárez), 49; drug trafficking by, 94; Gente Nueva and, 94; Mexicles and, 94, 153, 154; origins of, 93; Sinaloa DTO and, 153; Villas de Salvarcar massacre (2010) and, 108, 109, 110, 113–14
"Doce, El": death of, 111
Dodson, John: on Operation Fast and Furious, 95
"Dorado, El." *See* Contreras Meraz, Fernando ("El Dorado")
Downtown Management District (El Paso), 9
"Dream, El." *See* Sáenz, Jorge Ernesto ("El Dream")
Drug Enforcement Administration (DEA), 157; agents of, threatened with murder, 112, 138; El Menchito targeted by, 156; José Antonio Acosta Hernández's arrest and, 147; US Consulate worker attack (2010) investigation by, 124. *See also* Camarena, Enrique ("Kiki")
drug trafficking: by BA, 2–3, 34–35, 37, 46, 55–74, 76–79; by Doble A, 94; by MS-13, 2–3, 46; origins of, in El Paso, 16–18; in prisons, 60–61, 62; proxies used in, 75. *See also specific drugs*
Duran, José ("Caballo"), 134

educational organizations: need for, to eradicate gangs, 81, 159–60
El Aliviane rehabilitation center (Ciudad Juárez): massacre at (2009), 89, 113
El Centro District (El Paso), 9
El Paso, Texas: barrio gangs in, 18–22; Chinese immigrants to 16; Ciudad Juárez and, 2; gang violence in, 36–37; Mexican immigration to, 2, 10, 101; poverty in,

11; prosperity in, as a result of drug war in Ciudad Juárez, 101; turf wars in, 19; violent crime in, 19, 21
El Paso Race Riot (1916), 3, 13–14, 19
El Salvador: murder rate in, 6; gang member segregation in prisons of, 50; as recipient of deported aliens from the United States, 57
Ele, Jota, 73; crew murdered, 93
Empresa, La, 150, 152; current status of, 155
End, Tanisha, 116–17
Enriquez, Arturo: cooperation with US authorities of, 141
Enríquez, Jesús: eighteenth birthday party of, 108
Enriquez, Lesley Ann, 119; murder of, 121, 122, 129
Escobar, Pablo: death of, 76
Espinosa, Cecilia: on feminicide in Ciudad Juárez, 98
Esqueda, Miguel Ángel ("Angelillo"), 151
esquina (BA rank), 34, 37
Esquivel, Raul: murder of (2006), 144
Estelle, William J., 27
Estévez Zuleta, María Dolores ("Lola la Chata"), 17
Estrada, Alberto ("Indio"), 29
Estupiñan Ibarra, Amador: body found, 115
"Executioner, The." *See* Lazcano, Heriberto ("The Executioner," "Z3")
extortion. *See* commercial extortion

"Farmero." *See* Gallegos Castrellón, Arturo ("51," "Benny," "Farmero," "Guero," "Manon," "Tury")
Fast and Furious. *See* Operation Fast and Furious
Fatherless, Los (gang), 21, 119, 141
Federal Bureau of Investigation (FBI): Arturo Gallegos Castrellón interrogated by, 92, 93, 114, 125–29; Eduardo Ravelo Rodriguez wanted poster of, pictured, 148; on gang numbers in the United States, 1; Johnny Michelletti and, 141; Ten Most Wanted List of, 64, 125, 149; US Consulate worker attack (2010) investigation by, 124
feminicide: BA and, 87; in Ciudad Juárez, 85, 97–100

Fernandez, Enrique, 16
Fernandez, Manuel ("El Grande"), 29, 58
Fernandez Acosta, Ricardo: on deployment of military in Chihuahua, 154
Fernández Ordóñez, Juan: on violence in Mexican prisons, 49–50
Ferrer Perez, Alejandro ("El Veneno"): murder of, 49
"Ferro, El." *See* Martinez Mendoza, Jesús Alfredo ("El Freddy," "El Ferro")
"Flaco, El." *See* Camacho Ramos, Luis Alberto ("El Shoker," "El Flaco")
Florence, Colorado: Arturo Gallegos Castrellón incarcerated at, 131
Flores, Chato: kidnapping and murder of (2005), 144, 151
Folsom Prison (California): Texas Syndicate's emergence at, 28
Fonseca, David, Jr.: murder by, 144
Foreign Narcotics Kingpin Designation Act (1999), 45, 47, 152
Fort Bliss, 13, 14; drug trafficking in, 17
"Freddy, El." *See* Martinez Mendoza, Jesús Alfredo ("El Freddy," "El Ferro")
"Fresa." *See* Núñez Payan, Alberto ("Fresa," "Fresca," "97")
"Fresca." *See* Núñez Payan, Alberto ("Fresa," "Fresca," "97")
Frías Salas, Nicolás ("El Nico"): death of, 51

Gallardo, Miguel Ángel Félix ("El Padrino"), 17, 35, 75, 146
Gallegos Castrellón, Arturo ("51," "Benny," "Farmero," "Guero," "Manon," "Tury"), 17, 64, 65, 69, 73; on alignment with La Línea, 77; arrest and torture of, 124–25; in attack on US Consulate workers, 120–21, 122; on attack on US Consulate workers, 127–29; Avenida 16 de Septiembre bombing (2010) and, 134, 135; BA history of, 126; extradition of, 125, 128–29; Federal Bureau of Investigation (FBI) interrogation of, 125–29; Gilberto Ontiveros-Lucero (son of "Greñas") ordered killed by, 88; hit teams established by, 83, 84; as hit team leader, 84, 85; on homicides, 5, 78, 100; Jesús Ernesto Chávez Castillo's wife

ordered murdered by, 124; maquilladoras and, 81–82; pictured, 117; on Sinaloa DTO-Juárez Cartel conflict, 92–93; torture and dismemberment used by, 79–80; trial of (2014), 31, 32–33, 58, 74, 118, 123, 129–30, 131–32, 138; on Villas de Salvarcar massacre (2010), 114; on weaponry, 94

Gamino, Cesar: body of, used as decoy in Avenida 16 de Septiembre bombing (2010), 135, 138

gang membership: causes of, 3, 4, 9, 18–19

Garcia, Josias, 95

Garcia Ponte, Perla Cristal: murder of, 97–98

"Garfield, El." *See* Oliver Romo, Edgar Roberto ("El Garfield")

"Genio, El." *See* Padilla Juárez, Juan Arturo ("El Genio")

Gente Nueva (gang): Doble As and, 94; El Aliviane rehabilitation center massacre (2009) by, 89; La Línea and, 155; Mexicles and, 42, 155; as proxy for Sinaloa DTO, 42, 75, 76–77

Gibson, John, 129

"Gitano." *See* Ledesma, José ("Gitano")

Golden Horseshoe (El Paso). *See* El Centro District (El Paso)

Gotti, John, 142; Arturo Gallegos Castrellón compared to, 129

graffiti, 4; by Doble A members, 93–94

"Grande, El." *See* Fernandez, Manuel ("El Grande")

Gravano, Sammy ("The Bull"): cooperation with US authorities of, 129, 142

"Greñas." *See* Ontiveros-Lucero, Gilberto ("Greñas")

Guadalajara Cartel, 76, 115

"Guero." *See* Gallegos Castrellón, Arturo ("51," "Benny," "Farmero," "Guero," "Manon," "Tury")

"Güero, El." *See* Castañeda Alvarez, Jesús Antonio ("El Güero")

Gulf Cartel, 78–79

Gutierrez, David Galvez, 42

Guzmán Decena, Arturo, 78

Guzmán Loera, Joaquín Archivaldo ("El Chapo"), 17, 48, 138; arrest, 149, 156; cartel run by (*see* Sinaloa DTO); Eduardo Ravelo Rodriguez compared to, 149, 150; expansion into Ciudad Juárez, by, 67, 72, 76, 89, 92

Gypsy Jokers, 1

hand signs: BA use of, 40

Hernandez, Carlos: Arturo Gallegos Castrellón interrogated by, 125–29

Hernandez Lozano, Aldo Favio ("El 18"), 111–12

Hernandez Perez, Jonathan Rene: murder of, 114–15

heroin, 155; American demand for, gang explosion and, 35; in Ciudad Juárez, 67; code for, 41; in El Paso in the 1920s and 1930s, 16–17; Jesús Alfredo Martinez Mendoza arrested for possession of, 154; mural about use of, pictured, 12; Ruben Oseguera González and, 156; in Sinaloa, 17, 118; smuggled into CERESO 3 (Ciudad Juárez), 53, 61; sold by BA, 76, 77; sold by Rafa Díaz, 69, 83; trafficked by Joseph Valachi, 142; trafficked by Manuel Lopez, 132

Herrera, Francisco: cooperation with US authorities of, 141

Holder, Eric, 95

homicides: in Ciudad Juárez, 110, 150–51. *See also specific murders*

Hotel Verde (Ciudad Juárez): as BA prostitution headquarters, 85

huaraches, 32; earned by Jesús Ernesto Chávez Castillo, 62

human trafficking, 69–70, 151; by BA, 85–87

Immigration and Naturalization Act (1952), 56, 57

Immigration Control and Reform Act (1986), 56–57

immigration restriction in the United States: history of, 56–57

"Indio." *See* Estrada, Alberto ("Indio")

initiation: of Jesús Ernesto Chávez Castillo, 62; in prison gangs, 24, 32

institutional racism: as explanation for public's ignorance of BA, 2

Irish: street gangs of, 1

INDEX

jail art: by Doble A members, 93–94
Jasso Gonzales, Ignacia ("La Nacha"): as genesis of border narcos, 16–17
Jasso Gonzales, Pablo ("El Pablote"): as genesis of border narcos, 16–17
"JL." *See* Ledesma, José Luis ("JL")
Joint Operation Chihuahua, 92
Juárez Cartel, 75–76; BA as drug traffickers for, 35, 56, 75, 77, 123–24, 153; designated a transnational criminal organization, 47; Sinaloa DTO and, 67, 72, 89–96

"Keiko, El." *See* Contreras Lumbreras, José Ivan ("El Keiko")
kidnapping: in Ciudad Juárez, 106; by MS-13, 3, 47; prostitution and, 99
kites. *See whilas*

La Tuna Federal Correctional Institution (Anthony, Texas): Arturo Gallegos Castrellón at, 126; José Ángel Perez Marrufo at, 126; Ricardo Valles de la Rosa at, 119
Lam, Manny, 63
Las Cruces, New Mexico: BA expansion to, 44; José Reyes Ferriz's move to, 103; weapons smuggling in, 95
Lazcano, Heriberto ("The Executioner," "Z3"), 79
Lea, Tom, Jr.: in Bath Riots (1917), 14
Ledesma, José ("Gitano"), 29
Ledezma, Juan Pablo ("JL"), 76, 108
"Lentes," 88; implicated to US authorities, 128
"Leo." *See* Mendez, Luis ("Leo")
Leyzaola, Julián, 90–91, 100, 107, 144, 150
"Lince" (bomb maker): Avenida 16 de Septiembre bombing (2010) and, 134–35, 136, 137
Linces, Los (gang), 96; Villas de Salvarcar massacre (2010) blamed on, 110, 112
Lincoln Park (El Paso): *pachuco* culture and, 20
Línea, La (gang): BA and, 42, 72, 75, 77, 79, 80, 93, 96, 123, 147, 152, 153, 154; cocaine market cornered by, 77; Fernando Carrillo and, 71; Foreign Narcotics Kingpin Designation Act's ignorance of, 47; hierarchical structure of, 146; Juárez Cartel and, 75, 76, 77, 149; as La Empresa, member, 152, 155; maquiladoras created by 81–82; marijuana smuggled by, 126; origins of, 76; restructuring of, 155, 157; targeted by US government, 128, 138; torture and dismemberment used by, 79; Villas de Salvarcar massacre (2010) and, 108–15; weapons smuggling by, 94
"Lola la Chata." *See* Estévez Zuleta, María Dolores ("Lola la Chata")
Lopez, Manuel: cooperation with US authorities of, 132
Lopez, Pablo: in Mexican Revolution, 13
López Valles, Roberto, 90
loyalty: of BA members after government crackdown, 131, 132, 140, 141, 159; in prison gangs, 24, 26, 31, 37
Lynx, The (gang). *See* Linces, Los (gang)

"Maestro, El." *See* Marquez, José ("El Maestro")
"Maguro": as hit team leader, 84
"Manon." *See* Gallegos Castrellón, Arturo ("51," "Benny," "Farmero," "Guero," "Manon," "Tury")
Mara Salvatrucha. *See* MS-13
Marcos B. Armijo Community Center (El Paso), 22–23
"Margarito," 63–64, 66, 82
maquiladoras, 80–82; effect on Ciudad Juárez, 97
marijuana, 155; American demand for, gang explosion and, 35; in Ciudad Juárez, 67; *pachuco* culture and, 21; in Sinaloa, 17; smuggled by La Línea, 126; smuggled into CERESO 3 (Ciudad Juárez), 53; sold by BA, 77; sold by Fernando Carrillo, 71, 146; sold by Gualberto Marquez, 58–59; sold by Jesús Ernesto Chávez Castillo, 59, 69, 83; traded for weapons, 93
Marquez, Gualberto ("The Bird"), 58–59; on BA's rules, 33, 34; cooperation with US authorities of, 132, 144
Marquez, José ("El Maestro"), 41
Martínez, Éder Ángel ("El Saik"), 93

Martínez, Heriberto, 112
Martinez Mendoza, Jesús Alfredo ("El Freddy," "El Ferro"), 67, 68, 69, 70, 82–83, 84, 154
Massachusetts: BA expansion to, 44
membership control: in prison gangs, 26. *See also* loyalty
"Menchito, El." *See* Oseguera González, Ruben ("El Menchito")
Mendez, Luis ("Leo"), 64, 69, 125; Arturo Gallegos Castrellón on, 128; in attack on US Consulate workers (2010), 119, 128
Mendez, Luis ("El Tío," "El 58," "Narizón"), 152
Meraz, David ("Chicho"), 151; murder of (2008), 144, 151
Merida Initiative, 104–5
methamphetamine, 52, 149; American demand for, gang explosion and, 35; trafficking of, 155–58
Mexican Farm Labor Agreement, 57
Mexican Mafia, 1, 27; *pachuco* origins of, 2; as Texas Syndicate rival, 28
Mexican Revolution: El Paso in, 13–15; immigration to El Paso and, 2, 10, 12, 20
Mexicles (gang): BA and, 50–51, 52, 66, 96, 114–15; Coffield Unit (Texas prison system) and, 23, 41; Doble As and, 94, 153, 154; Gente Nueve and, 42, 155; internal strife in, 155; as La Empresa member, 152, 155; in Mexican prisons, 49; origins of, 41–42; restructuring of, 155; US deportations and growth of, 58
Mexico: BA members in prisons of, 25–26; prison culture in, 49; as recipient of deported aliens from the United States, 57. *See also* Ciudad Juárez, Chihuahua
Mexikanemi (gang). *See* Texas Mexican Mafia-Mexikanemi (gang)
Michelletti, Johnny ("Conejo"): cooperation with US authorities of, 141
Midland, Texas: BA expansion to, 44; weapons purchased in, 93
Mikeska, Samantha: on Eduardo Ravelo Rodriguez's arrest, 149
Milenio Cartel, 156
Mona, Eugene: cooperation with US authorities of, 141

Morales Ibáñez, Marisela, 147
Morton, John: on MS-13's designation as a transnational criminal organization, 47
MS-13 (gang), 1; apprehensions of, 4; BA compared to, 2–3, 5–6, 32, 46–47; border crossings by, 4; Coffield Unit (Texas prison system) and, 23; danger posed by, 5–6; in El Salvador prisons, 50; initiation rituals of, 32; membership control of, 26; murder rate of, 5–6; public perception of, 2–3, 46–47; RICO statute used against, 142; transnational criminal organization designation of, 1, 2, 46–47; US deportations and, 58, 160
murals: in El Paso, 4, 11–12, 14, 20
Murguía, Héctor: on crime in Ciudad Juárez, 106–7; drug war and, 104–5; on gang threats, 90; on maquiladoras, 81

"N." *See* Santana Garza, René Gerardo ("N," "El 300")
"Nacha, La." *See* Jasso Gonzales, Ignacia ("La Nacha")
Nahuatl language: spoken by BA members, 37, 40
Najera, Silvia: on feminicide in Ciudad Juárez, 99
"Narizón." *See* Mendez, Luis ("El Tío," "El 58," "Narizón")
National Strategy to Combat Transnational Organized Crime, 47
nativism: street gangs and, 1
Naturalization Act (1790), 56
"Negra, La." *See* Oseguera González, Jessica ("La Negra")
Nevarez, Miguel Ángel, 137; in attack on US Consulate workers (2010), 119–20; on attack on US Consulate workers (2010), 124; Avenida 16 de Septiembre bombing (2010) and, 134, 135, 136; BA history of, 134
"Nico, El." *See* Frías Salas, Nicolás ("El Nico")
Norte, Rafa, 73
Norteños (gang): *pachuco* origins of, 2
North American Free Trade Agreement (NAFTA), 113; maquiladoras and, 80, 97

Northern Triangle (gang): deportation of members of, 6
Nuestra Familia (gang): as Texas Syndicate rival, 28
Núñez, Magda, 49
Núñez Payan, Alberto ("Fresa," "Fresca," "97"), 65–66, 82–83, 146; in attack on US Consulate workers (2010), 119; Avenida 16 de Septiembre bombing (2010) and, 134–35; on BA's role in Sinaloa DTO-Juárez Cartel conflict, 93; Fernando Carrillo and, 71, 72, 74

Oakdale, Louisiana: Jesús Ernesto Chávez Castillo incarcerated at, 30, 59–60, 61, 145
Obama, Barack: on transnational criminal organizations, 45–46, 47
Odessa, Texas: BA expansion to, 44
Old School Aztecas, 152, 154–55
Oliver Romo, Edgar Roberto ("El Garfield"): murder of, 154
Oliverez, Benjamin ("T-Top"), 29
Omerta, 142
Ontiveros-Lucero, Gilberto ("Greñas"), 87–88
Ontiveros-Lucero, Gilberto (son of "Greñas"): torture and dismemberment of, 87–88
Operation Blockade, 55, 105
Operation Fast and Furious, 95–96; weapons from, used in Villas de Salvarcar massacre (2010), 112–13
Operation Hold the Line, 55, 116
Operation Ome Ce, 142
Operation Penco Negro, 142
Operation Wetback, 57
opium, 16–17, 55, 56
Orduna, Robert: resignation of, 101
O'Rourke, Beto: on Merida Initiative, 105
Ortega, Randolph Joseph, 129, 130
Ortega, Rodolfo: Arturo Gallegos Castrellón interrogated by, 125–29
Ortiz, Guillermo: killing of, 136
Oseguera Cervantes, Nemesio, 156
Oseguera González, Jessica ("La Negra"): arrest of, 156
Oseguera González, Ruben ("El Menchito"), 156
Oyuki, Meibi: body found, 114–15

"Pablote, El." *See* Jasso Gonzales, Pablo ("El Pablote")
"Pac": as hit team leader, 84
pachucos: criminal activities of, 21; gang culture's origins and, 2, 20–21
Padilla, Ernesto, 66, 81–82
Padilla Juárez, Juan Arturo ("El Genio"): murder of, 150
padrino (BA rank), 32
"Padrino, El." *See* Gallardo, Miguel Ángel Félix ("El Padrino")
"Pájaro." *See* Solis-Vela, Juan ("Pájaro").
Palacios, Shorty, 88
Partido Revolucionario Mexicano: BA and, 43. *See also* Mexicles (gang)
Paseo del Norte Bridge. *See* Santa Fe Bridge
"Patachu, El." *See* Perez, Jesús Damian ("El Patachu")
Payan Gloria, Pedro ("El Pifas"): as leader of BA's prositution ring, 86–87
Paz Mares, Nancy: Avenida 16 de Septiembre bombing (2010) and, 137
Pecos, Texas: Fernando Carrillo in, 71, 146
"Pelon, El." *See* Queen Calderón, Daniel ("El Pelon")
Penn, Sean, 149
Pennsylvania: BA expansion to, 44
Perea, Carlos: cooperation with US authorities of, 141
Perez, Jesús Damian ("El Patachu"): as leader of BA's prositution ring, 86
Perez, Lorenzo: Arturo Gallegos Castrellón interrogated by, 125–29
Perez Marrufo, José Ángel ("Casitas"), 88, 126, 134
Perez Marrufo, Martin ("Popeye"), 88; in attack on US Consulate workers (2010), 119, 121, 127; implicated to US authorities, 128
Pérez Serrano, Sacramento, 101
Pershing, John ("Black Jack"), in El Paso Race Riot (1916), 13–14; in Punitive Expedition (1916–17), 14
"Pifas, El." *See* Payan Gloria, Pedro ("El Pifas")
Pitman, Robert: on Arturo Gallegos Castrellón's conviction, 130
Plato o Plomo philosophy, 103

INDEX

Playa Hotel (Ciudad Juárez): demonstration in front of (2008), 204
Poire, Alejandro: on Mexican prison violence, 51
police: attacks against, 90, 101; BA's relationship with, 84; corruption of, 90, 102, 103, 105, 139; feminicide and, 98, 99
"Popeye." *See* Perez Marrufo, Martin ("Popeye")
poverty: in El Paso, 4, 11
Pradera de los Oasis neighborhood (Ciudad Juárez): homicide in, 114
Primer Barrio (El Paso). *See* Chihuahuita (El Paso)
prison gangs: causes for, 23–24; codes of, 24; dynamics of, 23–27; early history of, 1; initiation procedures of, 24; loyalty in, 24; membership control in, 26; reasons for, 24–25; street gangs and, 24–25, 26, 27; violence by, 24, 26, 43
Procuraduría General de la República (PGR), 52, 125; US Consulate worker attack (2010) investigation by, 124
prospecto (BA rank), 31–32, 34
prostitution: BA and, 66–67, 84–85, 85–88; commercial extortion and, 100. *See also* sex trafficking
proxies: used in drug trafficking, 75
Puente Grande prison: Joaquín Guzmán's escape from, 48
Punitive Expedition (1916–17), 14

Queen Calderón, Daniel ("El Pelon"): murder of, 52
"Quintan": as hit team leader, 84
Quintana, Carlos Arturo, 152
quotas, 33–34, 37, 86, 143

Racketeering Influenced Corrupt Organizations (RICO) statue: used against organized crime organizations, 117, 125, 128, 131, 132, 141, 142–44, 153, 159
Rahm, Harold Joseph: mural of (El Paso), 4
"Rama, El." *See* Ramirez, Adrian ("El Rama")
Ramirez, Adrian ("El Rama"): Villas de Salvarcar massacre (2010) blamed on, 110

Ramirez, "Sleepy," 59, 61
Rancho Anapra, Chihuahua, 70, 120, 160; Jesús Ernesto Chávez Castillo's *tienda* in, 68–69, 83
Rangel, Bruno Ángel ("El Bruno"): arrest of, 154
"Raulio." *See* Rivera Fierro, José ("Raulio")
Ravelo Rodriguez, Eduardo ("Tablas"), 64–65, 73, 126, 149–50; arrest of, 125, 149, 151, 152, 156; in attack on US Consulate workers (2010), 128; on attack on US Consulate workers (2010), 124; BA history of, 149; Old School Aztecas' loyalty to, 154; Villas de Salvarcar massacre (2010) and, 110; wanted poster for, pictured, 148
Raza, la, 13
Redelfs, Arthur, 119, 120, 122; murder of, 121, 129
Refugee Act (1980), 56
religious organizations: need for, to eradicate gangs, 159–60
Renteria, Ramon ("Spooky"): suicide of, 125
Reyes, Jesús Antonio, 91
Reyes, Silvestre: on Merida Initiative, 105; Operation Blockade of, 55
Reyes Estrada, José, 102
Reyes Ferriz, José, 57–58; on drug war, 101; move to El Paso by, 101, 102–3
Rivas López, José Manuel: murder of, 90
Rivera Fierro, José ("Raulio"), 29
Roosevelt, Franklin D.: Bracero Program and, 57
Rosales, Luis, 63, 65
Ruiz, David, 27
Ruiz Felix, Adrian: murder of (2019), 154
Ruiz v. Estelle (1980): prison gangs' emergence and, 27–28, 29

Sacred Heart Roman Catholic Church (El Paso), 11
Sacred Heart Tortilleria (El Paso), 4
Sáenz, Jorge Ernesto ("El Dream"), 93
Sanchez, Andres: on BA decline, 142–43; on BA rules, 32–33; on BA structure, 35–37; on BA vetting processes, 31
"Saik, El." *See* Martínez, Éder Ángel ("El Saik")

INDEX

Salcido Ceniceros, Jorge Alberto: murder of, 122–23, 129
Santa Fe Bridge, 9, 85; delousing ordered on, 14; in Mexican Revolution, 13
Santana Garza, René Gerardo ("N," "El 300"): arrest of, 150; BA split launched by, 151
sargen (BA rank), 34
segregation: of gangs in penal institutions, 50, 60
Segundo Barrio (El Paso): described, 3, 4, 10, 11; gangs in and gangs from, 28, 29–30; Mexican immigration to, 2; "Us versus Them" attitude in, 12
Serenil Luna, Hugo Alonso ("El Cabezón"), 91
sex trafficking, 151, 160; BA and, 85–86, 99; in El Paso-Ciudad Juárez corridor, 55; MS-13 and, 3, 47. *See also* prostitution
"Shoker, El." *See* Camacho Ramos, Luis Alberto ("El Shoker," "El Flaco")
Sinaloa DTO: Doble A and, 153; insertion into Ciudad Juárez of, 70, 89; Juárez Cartel and, 67, 72, 89–96
Sinaloa Federation: BA and, 46, 76
Skaret, Brian, 129
Smith Unit (Texas prison system), 59
social service organizations: need for, to eradicate gangs, 104, 105, 159–60
Solis-Vela, Juan ("Pájaro"), 28
"Spooky." *See* Renteria, Ramon ("Spooky")
Stewart, Scott: on US methamphetamine epidemic, 157
street gangs: prison gangs and, 24–25, 26, 27. *See also* barrio gangs
Sunland Park, New Mexico, 68, 83, 120; human trafficking into, 70
Sureños (gang): *pachuco* origins of, 2; threat assessment of, 152–53
Syndicato de Nuevo Mexico (gang), 25; BA compared to, 159; RICO statute used against, 142

"Tablas." *See* Ravelo Rodriguez, Eduardo ("Tablas")
"Tablero," 68, 77, 85
Tango Blast (gang): BA and, 43, 44–45; as Texas Syndicate rival, 27; threat assessment of, 45

Tangos (gang), 21; *pachuco* origins of, 2. *See also* Chuco Tangos (gang)
tattoos, 2, 18, 72; of BAs, 37–40; of Doble As, 94; of Jesús Ernesto Chávez Castillo, 63; of Mexicles, 41; *pachuco* culture and, 20; of Ricardo Valles de la Rosa, 122
T-Birds (gang). *See* Thunderbirds (gang)
tenilon (BA rank), 34
Terry, Brian: murder of, 95
Texas Department of Public Safety: Gang Threat Assessments of, 45, 152–53
Texas Mexican Mafia-Mexikanemi (gang): BA and, 43; BA's emergence and, 29; as Texas Syndicate rival, 27, 29; threat assessment of, 45
Texas Syndicate (gang): BA and, 43; BA's emergence and, 25, 29; drug trafficking by, 35; growth of, 28–29; Mexicles' emergence and, 41; *pachuco* origins of, 2; Texas prison system controlled by, 27; threat assessment of, 45
Thunderbirds (gang), 21–22; origins of, 28
tiendas (drug trafficking stores), 37, 63–64; of Jesús Ernesto Chávez Castillo, 68–69
"Tío, El." *See* Mendez, Luis ("El Tío," "El 58," "Narizón")
Todos Somos Juárez program, 150
"Tolon." *See* Cardoza, Manuel ("Tolon")
Torres, Carmelita: Bath Riots (1917) and, 15
Torres, Enrique: on prison gang violence, 51
Torres Larios, Abelardo, 41–42
Torres state prison (Hondo, Texas), 44
torture, 139; alleged, of Israel Arzate Meléndez, 112; alleged, of Jesús Ernesto Chavez Castillo, 52, 124–25, 128, 129; of Enrique Camarena, 115, 118, 123; used by BA and La Línea, 79–80, 87, 88, 105, 115
Tovex, 135
transnational criminal organization designation, 1; BA avoidance of, 2–3, 45–47; of MS-13, 2–3, 46
Transnational Criminal Organizations Sanctions Program, 45–46
Treaty of Guadalupe Hidalgo (1848): US-Mexico border defined by, 15
"T-Top." *See* Oliverez, Benjamin ("T-Top")
turf wars: in El Paso, 19

"Tury." *See* Gallegos Castrellón, Arturo ("51," "Benny," "Farmero," "Guero," "Manon," "Tury")
"Tyson," 62–63, 64–65

US Consulate (Ciudad Juárez): murder of employees of (2010), 118–29, 143, 152

Valachi, Joseph: cooperation with US authorities of, 142
Valenzuela Rivera, Martin Hugo: on Los Linces, 96
Valles de la Rosa, Ricardo ("El Chino"), 58, 72, 73, 105; arrest of, 124; in attack on US Consulate workers (2010), 119, 122; credibility of questioned, 122; gang history of, 119; implicated to US authorities, 128
Vega, Angelo, 94; on attack on US Consulate workers (2010), 124; implicated to US authorities, 128
"Veneno, El." *See* Ferrer Perez, Alejandro ("El Veneno")
Vicente Carrillo Fuentes Drug Trafficking Organization. *See* Juárez DTO
"Viceroy, El." *See* Carrillo Fuentes, Vicente ("El Viceroy")
Villa, Jorge: on Ciudad Juárez homicides, 150
Villa, Pancho, 13; Columbus, New Mexico, raid (1916) of, 14; reputation of, 14
Villas de Salvarcar massacre (2010), 96, 108–15, 118, 152
violence: BA use of, 36–37, 43, 49, 50–52, 72, 77, 83–84, 87–88, 114–15; in CERESO 3 (Ciudad Juárez), 48–53; in Ciudad Juárez, 153–54 prison gangs and, 24, 26, 43, 49
violent crime: in El Paso, 19, 21

weapons: BA need for, 93, 94; smuggling of, 93, 94–96; types, used in Mexican drug war, 133
whilas (secret prison letters), 32, 36, 128
Wiles, Richard, 122
Wilson, Woodrow: Mexican Revolution and, 13
Witness Security Program: Fernando Carrillo in, 146; Gualberto Marquez in, 132; Jesús Ernesto Chávez Castillo in, 131, 145; Manuel Lopez in, 132
Woodville Unit (Texas prison system), 134
World War II: Bracero Program established during, 57; drug trafficking in El Paso during, 17; employment opportunities for Mexicans in the United States during, 2

X14 (gang), 21, 28; BA's emergence and, 29
X list, 33, 145

"Z3." *See* Lazcano, Heriberto ("The Executioner," "Z3")
Zapata, Jaime: attack on, 95–96
Zedillo, Ernesto: drug policy of, 78
Zeta DTO, 78–79, 156; BA and, 78, 123; bombs used by, 137; US Immigration and Customs Enforcements agents attacked by (2011), 95–96
Zoot suits, 20. See also *pachucos*
"Zorro." *See* Díaz Díaz, José Guadalupe ("Zorro")

ABOUT THE AUTHOR

Joseph J. Kolb, MA, is the training coordinator and founding member of the New Mexico Gang Investigators Association; he is a corrections officer in New Mexico; a member of the New Mexico Attorney General's Human Trafficking Task Force; and an instructor in the criminal justice programs at the University of New Mexico Gallup and Valencia campuses.

Kolb has reported on and in Ciudad Juárez for over fifteen years for various news outlets including FoxNews.com, the *Albuquerque Journal*, and *Americas Quarterly*. He has also written for Reuters News Service and the *New York Times*. *Teen Violence in America: How Do We Save Our Children?* was his first book.

www.ingramcontent.com/pod-product-compliance
Lightning Source LLC
Chambersburg PA
CBHW031437160426
43195CB00010BB/768